Detroit Studies in Music Bibliography

Detroit Studies in Music Bibliography

. . . . Bruno Nettl, General Editor

A series devoted to the publication of bibliographical contributions - monographs, essays, and special indexes, lists, and directories - prepared on all aspects of music and its performance by recognized scholars. Its scope is broad and limited only by bibliographical interests.

Number 1   REFERENCE MATERIALS IN ETHNOMUSICOLOGY, by
Bruno Nettl
1961   46p $1.50
A bibliographic essay on primitive, oriental, and folk music which organizes, describes and evaluates books and articles on the subjects.

Number 2   SIR ARTHUR SULLIVAN: AN INDEX TO THE TEXTS OF
HIS VOCAL WORKS, compiled by Sirvart Poladian
1961   91p $2.75
The first comprehensive index to first lines, titles, and refrains of Sir Arthur Sullivan's vocal works, sacred and secular.

Number 3   AN INDEX TO BEETHOVEN'S CONVERSATION BOOKS,
by Donald W. MacArdle
1962   46p $2.00
A complete index of the persons and places named in Georg Schünemann's 'Ludwig van Beethovens Konversationshefte' (3 vols., Berlin, 1941-1943) and in portions of Jacques-Gabriel Prod'homme's 'Les cahiers de conversation de Beethoven' (Paris, 1946)

Number 4   GENERAL BIBLIOGRAPHY FOR MUSIC RESEARCH, by
Keith E. Mixter
1962   38p $2.00
This study of references to general bibliographic tools describes material that would be of direct interest to musicians, as well as pertinent material in related fields such as history, the fine arts, or the social sciences.

A HANDBOOK
OF AMERICAN
OPERATIC PREMIERES
1731-1962

by Julius Mattfeld

1963

Detroit Studies in Music Bibliography

Number 5

Published by
INFORMATION SERVICE, INCORPORATED
10 West Warren   Detroit 1, Michigan

Inscribed to the memory of

Lewis H. deBaun

PREFACE

This guide to operatic performances in the United States attempts to present a record of the premieres of nearly 2,000 operas and related works from 1731 to the end of 1962, or, in the absence of definite information, the earliest dates of performance known to the compiler. Included are operas by native and naturalized composers, which have been performed outside the country; a selection of light operas and musical comedies of European and American origin; dramatic stage pieces with incidental music by important composers; and oratorios and cantatas given in scenic presentations.

The operas are listed alphabetically by title, followed in parenthesis by the name of the composer, the number of acts, the original language, and in the case of European works by the place and the year of first performances. The world premieres of American operas and those of foreign authorship performed in the United States are indicated with an asterisk. All operas are entered under their original title; Russian works are given in English equivalents, except Le Coq d'Or. A composer index is appended.

The information presented is an abridgment of a projected Dictionary of Opera in the United States. The data have been gathered from newspapers, musical journals, specialized essays in serial publications, operatic and theatrical annals, and city histories.

The following symbols and abbreviations are used:

* (asterisk), world premiere
-- (dash), earliest date known to the compiler
Op. H., opera house
orch., orchestra
perf., performance
Th., theatre
TV, television
Univ., university

J.M.

- A -

A BASSO PORTO (N. Spinelli; 3 acts, Italian, Cologne 1894 in
German). St. Louis, Exposition Music Hall, Jan. 8, 1900, in
English, as "At the lower harbor. "

L'ABANDON D'ARIANE (D. Milhaud; 1 act, French, Wiesbaden
1928 in German). Urbana, Ill., Smith Music Hall (Univ. of Illinois),
Mar. 6, 1955, in French (repeated in English).

The Abduction from the seraglio. See Die ENTFUEH-
RUNG AUS DEM SERAIL.

The Abduction of Europa. See L'ENLEVEMENT D'EUROPE.

Ein ABENTEUER HAENDELS (C. Reinecke; 1 act, German,
Schwerin 1874). New York, Terrace Garden, Sept. 5, 1874.

Abou Hassan. See ABU HASSAN.

ABROAD AND AT HOME (W. Shield; English, London 1796). New
York, John Street Th., Nov. 10, 1797.

ABSTRAKTE OPER NO. 1 (B. Blacher; 1 act, German, Frankfurt
1953, in a radio perf.; Mannheim 1953, in a stage perf.). Boston,
Boston Univ., Apr. 19, 1956.

ABU HASSAN (C. M. von Weber; 1 act, German, Munich 1811).
Philadelphia, Chestnut Street Th., Nov. 21, 1827. in English; New
York, Terrace Garden, Sept. 8, 1877, in German.

The ACCUSED (J. L. Strauss; 1 act [monodrama], American). *New
York, Columbia Broadcasting System (CBS-TV), May 7, 1961 (TV
perf.).

ACIS AND GALATEA (G. F. Handel; 2 acts, English, Cannons,
England, 1720-21, in concert form; London 1732, in operatic form).
New York, Lyceum Building, Feb. 14, 1839 (concert form); New
York, Park Th., Nov. 21, 1842 (stage perf.).

ACRES OF SKY (A. Kreutz; 2 acts, American). *Fayetteville, Ark.,
Fine Arts Center (Univ. of Arkansas), Nov. 16, 1950.

ACTEON (D. Auber; 1 act, French, Paris 1836). --Philadelphia, Chestnut Street Th., Oct. 16, 1843 [New Orleans earlier (?)].

ADAM AND EVE AND THE DEVIL (K. Magnuson; 1 act, opera-
ballet, American). *Cincinnati, Odeon, Apr. 1, 1953 (College of
Music of Cincinnati).

ADAM UND EVA (E. Helm; 1 act, American). * Wiesbaden,
Hessisches Staatstheater, Oct. 28, 1951, in German.

Adlers Horst. See DES ADLERS HORST.

ADOLPHE ET CLARA (N. Dalayrac; 1 act, French, Paris 1799).
--New York, Park Th., Aug. 23, 1827 [New Orleans earlier (?)].

The ADOPTED CHILD (T. Attwood; 2 acts, English, London 1795).
New York, John Street Th., May 23, 1796.

ADRIANA LECOUVREUR (F. Cilèa; 4 acts, Italian, Milan 1902).
New Orleans, French Op. H., Jan. 5, 1907, in Italian.

Die AEGYPTISCHE HELENA (R. Strauss; 2 acts, German, Dresden
1928). New York, Metropolitan Op. H., Nov. 6, 1928.

L'AFRICAINE (G. Meyerbeer; 5 acts, French, Paris 1865). New York,
Academy of Music, Dec. 1, 1865, in Italian; New Orleans, French
Op. H., Dec. 18, 1869, in French.

AFRICAN HEARTBEAT (J. Marais; 2 acts, American). *Idyllwild,
Cal., Bowman Art Center Th. (Idyllwild School of Music and the
Arts), Aug. 28, 1953.

Los AFRICANISTAS (M. Fernández Caballero; 1 act, Spanish,
zarzuela, Madrid 1894). --New York, Teatro Apolo, Feb. 23, 1930.

The AGREEABLE SURPRISE (S. Arnold; 2 acts, English, London
1781). Philadelphia, Southwark Th., Jan. 27, 1787.

AHMED AL KAMEL, or The Pilgrim of love (C. E. Horn;
American). *New York, New National Th., Oct. 12, 1840.

AIDA (G. Verdi; 4 acts, Italian, Cairo 1871). New York, Academy of
Music, Nov. 26, 1873.

ALBERT HERRING (B. Britten; 3 acts, English, Glyndebourne 1947).
Tanglewood, Lenox, Mass., Theatre-Concert Hall (Berkshire Music
Center), Aug. 8, 1949.

ALCESTE (C. W. von Gluck; 3 acts, Vienna 1767 in Italian; Paris 1776
in French). Cincinnati, Music Hall, May 14, 1878, in English
(excerpts; concert form); Wellesley, Mass., Alumnae Hall (Wellesley
College), Mar. 11, 1838, in French; New York, Metropolitan Op. H.,
Jan. 24, 1941, in French.

The ALCESTIAD (L. Talma; 3 acts, American). *Frankfurt a/M.,
Schauspielhaus, Mar. 1, 1962, in German.

ALCINA (G. F. Handel; 3 acts, Italian, London 1735). Dallas, State
Fair Music Hall, Nov. 16, 1960.

ALDA (W. F. Harling; 2 acts, American). *Boston, Jordan Hall, Dec.
7, 1908.

ALEKO (S. Rachmaninov; 1 act, Russian, Moscow 1893). New York,
Jolson's Th., Jan. 11, 1926.

ALESSANDRO STRADELLA (F. von Flotow; 3 acts, German, Hamburg 1844). Hoboken, N.J., Vauxhall Garden, Nov. 1853; New York
Niblo's Garden, Apr. 12, 1855.

ALEXIS ET JUSTINE (N. Dèzede; 2 acts, French, Versailles 1785).
Charleston, S.C., Théâtre Français, July 10, 1795.

ALFRED   (T. A. Arne; masque, English, Cliveden, England, 1740).
Philadelphia, College Hall (College of Philadelphia [Univ. of Penn-
sylvania]). Jan. 1757, in concert form, as "The Redemption of the
Danish invasion by Alfred the Great."

ALFRED THE GREAT   (F. Bechtel; American). *New York, (Brooklyn) Athenaeum, Nov. 16, 1880 (excerpts; concert form).

ALGLALA   (F. B. DeLeone; prolog and 2 acts, American). *Akron, O.,
Armory, May 23, 1924.

ALINE, REINE DE GOLCONDE   (H. M. Berton; 3 acts, French,
Paris 1803). --New Orleans, Théâtre d'Orléans, Jan. 8, 1820.

ALMA LATINA   (G. Miceli; 2 acts, Spanish-American). *Los Angeles,
Philharmonic Auditorium, Mar. 27, 1922, in Spanish.

ALONE I STAND   (R. Martinelli; 2 acts, American). *New York,
(Brooklyn) Academy of Music, May 18, 1951.

Der ALPENKOENIG UND DER MENSCHEN FEIND   (F. Raimund;
3 acts, German, Vienna 1828). --Louisville, Ky., Apollo Hall, May
7, 1854.

AMADIS   (J. B. Lully; prolog and 5 acts, French, Paris 1684). Cambridge, Mass., Lowell House, Mar. 15, 1951.

AMAHL AND THE NIGHT VISITORS   (G. C. Menotti; 1 act,
American). *New York, National Broadcasting Company, Dec. 24,
1951 (TV perf.); Bloomington, Ind., East Hall (Indiana Univ.), Feb.
21, 1952 (stage premiere).

L'Amant jaloux. See LES FAUSSES APPARENCES.

L'AMANT STATUE   (N. Dalayrac; 1 act, French, Paris 1785).
Charleston, S.C., Théâtre Français, Aug. 11, 1794.

L'AMANTE ASTUTO   (M. Garcia; 2 acts, Italian). *New York, Park
Th., Dec. 17, 1825.

L'AMBASSADRICE   (D. Auber; 3 acts, French, Paris 1836). New
Orleans, Théâtre d'Orléans, Jan. 8, 1841.

AMELIA AL BALLO   (G. C. Menotti; 1 act, Italian). *Philadelphia,
Academy of Music, Apr. 1, 1937, in English, as "Amelia goes to
the ball."

The AMERICAN IN LONDON   (B. Carr; "musical entertainment,"
American). *Philadelphia, New [Chestnut Street] Th., Mar. 28,
1798.

L'AMFIPARNASSO   (O. Vecchi; prolog and 3 acts, Italian, Modena
1594). New York, French Institute, Mar. 13, 1933 (concert form).

The AMIABLE BEAST   (G. Wehner; 1 act, American). *New York,
Central Park Mall, July 25, 1961.

AMICA   (P. Mascagni; 2 acts, French, Monte Carlo 1905). New Orleans,
French Op. H., Feb. 24, 1906.

L'AMICO FRITZ (P. Mascagni; 3 acts, Italian, Rome 1891). Philadelphia, Grand Op. H., June 8, 1892.

AMILIE, or The Love test (W. M. Rooke; 3 acts, English, London
1837). New York, National Th., Oct. 15, 1838.

L'AMORE DEI TRE RE (I. Montemezzi; 3 acts, Italian, Milan 1913).
New York, Metropolitan Op. H., Jan. 2, 1914.

L'AMORE MEDICO (E. Wolf-Ferrari; 2 acts, Italian, Dresden 1913
in German). New York, Metropolitan Op. H., Mar. 25, 1914, in
Italian (first perf. in that language).

L'AMOUR FILIAL (P. Gaveaux; 1 act, French, Paris 1792). New
Orleans, Théâtre de la Rue St. Pierre, Dec. 31, 1809.

Les AMOURS DU DIABLE (A. Grisar; 4 acts, French, Paris 1853).
New Orleans, Théâtre d'Orléans, 1858.

The ANACHRONISM (Arnold Franchetti; 1 act, American). *Hartford, Conn., Hartt College of Music, Mar. 4, 1956 (concert form).

The ANADALUSIAN, or The Young guard (E. J. Loder;
English, London 1848). --New York, Brougham's Lyceum Th., Jan.
15, 1851.

ANDON (W. Leps; 1 act, American). *Philadelphia, Academy of Music,
Dec. 22, 1905 (concert form); Philadelphia, Broad Street Th., May
28, 1908 (stage premiere).

ANDREA CHENIER (U. Giordano; 4 acts, Milan 1896). New York,
Academy of Music, Nov. 13, 1896.

ANGELIQUE (J. Ibert; 1 act, French, Paris 1927). New York, Forty-
fourth Street Th., Nov. 8, 1937.

ANIMA ALLEGRA (F. Vittadini; 3 acts, Italian, Rome 1921). New
York, Metropolitan Op. H., Feb. 14, 1923.

ANNA BOLENA (G. Donizetti; 2 acts, Italian, Milan 1830). New
Orleans, Théâtre d'Orléans, Nov. 1839, in French; New York, Astor
Place Op. H., Jan. 7, 1850, in Italian.

ANNE OF AUSTRIA (L. LaGrassa; American). *Philadelphia, Musical Fund Hall, May 1856.

ANNETTE ET LUBIN (B. Blaise; 1 act, French, Paris 1762). Charleston, S.C., Théâtre Français, July 16, 1794.

ANNIE GET YOUR GUN (I. Berlin; 2 acts, American). *New
Haven, Conn., Shubert Th., Mar. 28, 1946 (New York, Imperial Th.,
May 16, 1946; 1,147 perf.).

ANTIGONE (F. Mendelssohn-Bartholdy; Potsdam 1841). New York,
Palmo's Op. H., Apr. 7, 1845, in English.

Antonio. See LUCILLE.

APHRODITE (C. Erlanger; 5 acts, French, Paris 1906). New York,
Lexington Th., Feb. 27, 1920.

APOLLO AND PERSEPHONE (G. Cockshott; 1 act, English,
Cheltenham, England, 1955). New York, Finch College Auditorium,
Feb. 22, 1956 (After Dinner Opera Theatre).

The Apothecary (Haydn). See Lo SPEZIALE.

APPLE BLOSSOMS (F. Kreisler and V. Jacobi; 3 acts, American).
*Baltimore, Ford's Th., Sept. 29, 1919 (New York, Globe Th., Oct.
7, 1919).

ARABELLA (R. Strauss; 3 acts, German, Dresden 1933). New York,
Metropolitan Op. H., Feb. 1955, in English.

Gli ARABI NELLE GALLIE (G. Pacini; 4[2] acts, Milan 1827).
New York, Italian Op. H., Jan. 20, 1834.

The ARCHERS, or Mountaineers of Switzerland (B. Carr;
3 acts, American). *New York, John Street Th., Apr. 18, 1796.

archy and mehitabel (G. Kleinsinger; 2 acts, American). *New
York, Town Hall, Dec. 6, 1954 (concert form); New York, Broadway
Th., Apr. 13, 1957, as "Shinebone Alley" (stage premiere).

ARIA DA CAPO (C. V. Burnham; 1 act, American). *New Orleans,
Dixon Hall (Newcomb College, Tulane Univ.), Apr. 17, 1955.

ARIA DA CAPO (B. Fore; 1 act, American). *Stockton, Cal.,
Pacific Auditorium (College of the Pacific), May 19, 1951.

ARIADNE AUF NAXOS (R. Strauss; prolog and 1 act, German,
Stuttgart 1912). Philadelphia, Academy of Music, Nov. 1, 1928.

ARIANE DANS L'ILE DE NAXOS (J. F. Edelmann; 1 act, French,
Paris 1782). New York, Corre's Hotel, Mar. 28, 1791.

ARIANE ET BARBE-BLEUE (P. Dukas; 3 acts, French, Paris 1907).
New York, Metropolitan Op. H., Mar. 23, 1911.

ARLECCHINO (F. Busoni; 1 act, German, Zurich 1917). New York,
Carnegie Hall, Oct. 11, 1951, in English (semi-staged).

L'ARLESIANA (F. Cilea; 3 acts, Italian, Milan 1897 in four acts;
1898 in three acts). Philadelphia, Society Hill Playhouse, Jan. 11,
1962.

L'ARLESIENNE (G. Bizet; 3 acts, French, Paris 1872). New York,
Broadway Th., Mar. 22, 1897, in English; Boston, Boston Op. H.,
Mar. 6, 1913, in French.

ARMIDE (C. W. von Gluck; 5 acts, French, Paris 1777). New York,
Metropolitan Op. H., Nov. 14, 1910.

ARMIDE (J. B. Lully; prolog and 5 acts, French, Paris 1686). New York,
Theresa Kaufmann Auditorium (Y. M. & Y. W. H. A.), Feb. 2,
1953 (concert form).

The ARMOR OF LIFE (K. Newbern; 1 act, American). *New York,
Carl Fischer Concert Hall, Feb. 26, 1957.

AROLDO (G. Verdi; 4 acts, Italian, Rimini 1857). New York, Academy
of Music, May 4, 1863.

ARTAXERXES (T. A. Arne; 3 acts, English, London 1762). Philadelphia, New [Chestnut Street] Th., Dec. 28, 1827.

ASCOLD'S TOMB (A. N. Verstovsky; 3 acts, Russian, Moscow 1835). New York, Theatre Francais, Dec. 15, 1869, in Russian (first Russian opera in the United States).

The ASRA (J. C. Breil; 1 act, American). *Los Angeles, Gamut Club Th., Nov. 24, 1925.

ASRAEL (A. Franchetti; 4 acts, Italian, Reggio Emilia, 1888). New York, Metropolitan Op. H., Nov. 26, 1890, in German.

ASSASSINO NELLA CATTEDRALE (I. Pizzetti; 2 acts, Italian, Milan 1958). New York, Carnegie Hall, Sept. 17, 1958.

L'assedio di Corinto. See Le SIEGE DE CORINTHE.

AT THE BOAR'S HEAD (G. Holst; 1 act, English, Manchester 1925). New York, MacDowell Club, Feb. 16, 1935.

At the lower harbor. See A BASSO PORTO.

ATHALIA (F. Mendelssohn-Bartholdy; 5 acts, German, Charlottenburg 1845). New York, (Brooklyn) Academy of Music, Jan. 26, 1871, in English (concert form).

ATSUMORI (C. W. Lawrence; 1 act, American). *Seattle, Meany Hall (Univ. of Washington), Dec. 11, 1929 (concert form); Tokyo, Japan, Hibiya Public Hall, July 19, 1950, in Japanese (concert form); Dec. 9, 1950, in Japanese (stage premiere); Seattle University Playhouse (Univ. of Washington), Feb. 26, 1954, in English (American stage premiere).

L'ATTAQUE DU MOULIN (A. Bruneau; 4 acts, French, Paris 1893). New York, New Theatre, Feb. 8, 1910.

ATTILA (G. Verdi; prolog and 3 acts, Italian, Venice 1846). New York, Niblo's Garden, Apr. 15, 1850.

L'AUBERGE DE BAGNIERES (C. S. Catel; 3 acts, French, Paris 1807). --New York, Park Th., Aug. 25, 1830 [New Orleans earlier (?)].

The AUDITION (A. G. Goodman; 1 act, American). *Athens, O., Ewing Auditorium (Ohio Univ.), July 27, 1954.

AUFSTIEG UND FALL DER STADT MAHAGONNY (K. Weill; 3 acts, German, Baden-Baden 1927 as "singspiel"; Leipzig 1930, in 3 acts). New York, Town Hall, Feb. 23, 1952 (excerpts; concert form).

AULD ROBIN GRAY (S. Arnold; 2 acts, English, London 1794). Philadelphia, New [Chestnut Street] Th., May 4, 1795, with "new music" by Alexander Reinagle.

Aunt Caroline's will. See Le TESTAMENT DE LA TANTE CAROLINE.

Aunt Simona. See TANTE SIMONA.

AVE MARIA (S. Allegra; 2 acts, Italian, Milan 1936). New York,
    Carnegie Recital Hall, Oct. 24, 1955.
AZARA (J. K. Paine; 3 acts, American). * Boston, Symphony Hall, Apr.
    9, 1907 (concert form).
AZEMIA (N. Dalayrac; 3 acts, French, Fontainebleau 1786). -New
    Orleans, Jan. 2, 1806.
AZORA (H. K. Hadley; 3 acts, American). * Chicago, Auditorium,
    Dec. 26, 1917.

- B -

BABAR, THE ELEPHANT (N. Berezowsky; 1 act, American). * New
    York, Hunter College Assembly Hall, Feb. 21, 1953.
BABES IN TOYLAND (V. Herbert; 3 acts, American). * Chicago,
    Grand Op. H., June 17, 1903 (New York, Majestic Th., Oct. 13,
    1903).
BABY DOE (M. DiJulio; 2 acts, American). * Loretto, Colo., Loretto
    Little Th. (Loretto Heights College), May 24, 1956.
The BALD SOPRANO (R. Gross; 1 act, American). * Los Angeles,
    Thorne Hall (Occidental College), May 13, 1962.
The BALLAD OF BABY DOE (D. Moore; 2 acts, American).
    * Central City, Op. H., July 7, 1956.
Il BALLO DELLE INGRATE (C. Monteverdi; masque, Italian,
    Mantua 1608). Chicago, Civic Op. H., Nov. 16, 1955.
Un BALLO IN MASCHERA (G. Verdi; 3 acts, Italian, Rome 1859).
    New York, Academy of Music, Feb. 11, 1861.
BARBARA ALLEN (D. Broekman; 1 act, American). * New York,
    Theresa Kaufmann Auditorium (Y.M. & Y.W.H.A.), Dec. 26, 1954
    (semi-staged).
BARBE-BLEUE (J. Offenbach; 3 acts, French, Paris 1866). New York,
    Niblo's Garden, July 13, 1868.
The BARBER OF NEW YORK (A. Vernon; 1 act, American). * New
    York, Hunter College Playhouse, May 26, 1953.
The BARBER OF SEVILLE (H. R. Bishop; 2 acts, English, London
    1818). New York, Park Th., May 3, 1819.
El BARBERILLO DE LAVAPIES (F. A. Barbieri; 3 acts, zarzuela,
    Spanish, Madrid 1874). --San Francisco, Orpheum Th., Feb. 1889.
Der BARBIER VON BAGDAD (P. Cornelius; 2 acts, German, Wei-
    mar 1858). New York, Metropolitan Op. H., Jan. 3, 1890.
Il BARBIERE DI SIVIGLIA (G. Paisiello; 4 acts, Italian, St. Peters-
    burg 1782). New Orleans, Théâtre Français, July 12, 1810, in French.

Il BARBIERE DI SIVIGLIA   (G. Rossini; 2 acts, Italian, Rome 1816).
New York, Park Th., Nov. 29, 1825 (first Italian-language opera in
the United States).

The BARGAIN   (P. M. Slates; 1 act, American). *Athens, O., Ewing
Auditorium (Ohio Univ.), July 26, 1956.

The BARREN PINES   (R. Bradley; 1 act, American). *New York,
West Side Branch (Young Men's Christian Association), Feb. 12, 1961.

The BARRIER   (J. Meyerowitz; prolog and 2 acts, American). *New
York, Brander Matthews Hall (Columbia Univ.), Jan. 18, 1950.

The Bartered bride.   See PRODANA NEVESTA.

BARTLEBY   (W. Flanagan; 1 act, American). *New York, York Playhouse, Jan. 24, 1961.

The Basket maker's wife.   See The DEVIL'S IN IT.

Die BASKISCHE VENUS   (H. H. Wetzler; 5 scenes, German-American). *Leipzig, Stadttheater, Nov. 18, 1928, in German.

La BASOCHE   (A. Messager; 3 acts, French, Paris 1890). Chicago,
Auditorium, Jan. 2, 1893, in English.

BASTIEN UND BASTIENNE   (W. A. Mozart; 1 act, German, Vienna
1768). --New York, Theodore Habelmann's Opera School, early 1905,
in German; New York, Empire Th., Oct. 26, 1916, in English; New
York, Cohan Th., Nov. 9, 1932, in German (Wiener Sängerknaben).

The BATTLE OF HEXHAM [or Days of old]   (S. Arnold; 3 acts,
English, London 1789). New York, John Street Th., Mar. 20, 1794.

Les BAVARDS   (J. Offenbach; 2 acts, French, Ems 1862). New York,
Stadt Theater, Oct. 28, 1867, in German, as "Die Schwätzerin von
Saragossa"; New York, Pike's Op. H., Dec. 9, 1868, in French.

BEATRICE   (L. Hoiby; 3 acts, American). *Louisville, Station WAVE,
Oct. 23, 1959 (radio perf.); Louisville, Auditorium, Oct. 30, 1959
(stage premiere).

BEATRICE DI TENDA   (V. Bellini; 3 acts, Italian, Venice 1833).
New Orleans, St. Charles Th., Mar. 5, 1842.

BEATRICE ET BENEDICT   (H. Berlioz; 2 acts, French, Baden-Baden
1862). New York, Carnegie Hall, Mar. 21, 1960, in French.

The Beautiful Galatea.   See Die SCHOENE GALATEA.

BEAUTY AND THE BEAST   (V. Giannini; 1 act, American). *New
York, Columbia Broadcasting System, Nov. 24, 1938 (radio perf.);
Hartford, Conn., Julius Hartt School of Music, Feb. 14, 1946 (stage
premiere).

The BECKONING FAIR ONE   (G. Kechley; 2 acts, American).
*Seattle, University Playhouse (Univ. of Washington), Nov. 30, 1954.

The BEE-HIVE, or A soldier's love   (C. E. Horn; 2 acts,
English, London 1811). New York, Park Th., Oct. 23, 1811.

The Beggar student. See Der BETTELSTUDENT.

BEGGAR'S LOVE (F. Patterson; 1 act, American). --New York, Ambassador Hotel, Dec. 8, 1929.

The BEGGAR'S OPERA (J. C. Pepusch; 3 acts, English, London 1728). New York, Nassau Street Th., Dec. 3, 1750.

BEI SEDAN (H. Zöllner; 2 acts, German, Leipzig 1895). New York, Carnegie Music Hall, Jan. 19, 1896 (concert form).

Die BEIDEN SCHUETZEN (A. Lortzing; 3 acts, German, Leipzig 1837). --New York, Stadt Theater, Dec. 13, 1859.

Die BELAGERUNG VON TOTTENBURG (E. B. Helm; 3 acts, American). *Stuttgart, Süddeutscher Rundfunk, Nov. 1956 (radio perf.).

BELISARIO (G. Donizetti; 3 acts, Italian, Venice 1836). Philadelphia, Chestnut Street Th., July 29, 1843.

The BELL TOWER (E. Krenek; 1 act, American). *Urbana, Ill., Lincoln Hall (Univ. of Illinois), Mar. 17, 1957.

La BELLA ADDORMENTATA NEL BOSCO (O. Respighi; 3 acts, marionette opera, Italian, Rome 1922). New York, George M. Cohan Th., Feb. 8, 1933.

Le BELLE, or Andre goes commercial (L. Kroll; 1 act, American). *New York, Pleasant Little Th., Sept. 30, 1935.

La BELLE ARSENE (P. A. Monsigny; 4 acts, French, Fontainebleau 1773). New Orleans, Le Spectacle de la Rue St. Pierre, Oct. 29, 1806.

La BELLE HELENE (J. Offenbach; 3 acts, French, Paris 1864). --Chicago, Crosby's Op. H., Sept. 14, 1867, in English; New York, Théâtre Français, Mar. 26, 1868, in French.

BELLE LURETTE (J. Offenbach; 3 acts, French, Paris 1880). Boston, Gaiety Th., Oct. 24, 1881, in English.

The BELLE OF NEW YORK (G. Kerker; 2 acts, American). *New York, Casino Th., Sept. 28, 1897.

BELSHAZZAR (G. F. Handel; 3 acts, English, London 1745). Boston, Symphony Hall, Mar. 31, 1907 (concert form); Bloomington, Ind., Auditorium (Indian Univ.), Nov. 22, 1959 (stage perf.).

BELSHAZZAR (N. Perelli; 4 acts, American). *Philadelphia, Musical Fund Hall, Jan. 3, 1850 (Acts III and IV; concert form).

BENVENUTO (E. Diaz; 4 acts, French, Paris 1890). New Orleans, French Op. H., Feb. 16, 1897.

BETLY (G. Donizetti; 2 acts, Italian, Naples 1836). Philadelphia, Academy of Music, Oct. 25, 1861.

BETROTHAL AT A MONASTERY (S. Prokofiev; 3 acts, Russian, Leningrad 1946). New York, Greenwich Mews Playhouse, June 1,

1948, in English, as "The Duenna."

Der BETTELSTUDENT (K. Millöcker; 3 acts, German, Vienna 1882). New York, Thalia Theater, Oct. 19, 1883, in German; Philadelphia, Chestnut Street Th., Oct. 22, 1883, in English, as "The Beggar student."

BEYOND BELIEF (T. Canning; 1 act, American). *Rochester, N. Y., Eastman Th., May 14, 1956.

BIANCA (H. K. Hadley; 1 act, American). *New York, Park Th., Oct. 18, 1918.

Le BIJOU PERDU (A. Adam; 3 acts, French, Paris 1853). New Orleans, French Op. H., Jan. 1861.

BILLEE TAYLOR (E. Solomon; 2 acts, English, London 1880). New York, Standard Th., Feb. 19, 1881.

Le BILLET DE LOTERIE (N. Isouard; 1 act, French, Paris 1811). New Orleans, Théâtre St. Philippe, 1816.

BILLY BUDD (B. Britten; prolog, 4 acts and epilog, English, London 1951). New York, National Broadcasting Company, Oct. 19, 1952 (TV perf.); Bloomington, Ind., East Hall (Indiana Univ.), Dec. 5, 1952 (stage perf.).

BION (E. N. Méhul; 1 act, French, Paris 1800). New Orleans, Théâtre Français, 1815.

The BIRTHDAY OF THE INFANTA (R. Nelson; 1 act, American). *Rochester, N. Y., Eastman Th., May 14, 1956.

BLACK BLOOD (E. Pirani; American). *New York, Powell Institute Little Th., June 3, 1906 (privately).

The Black hen. See La POULE NOIRE.

BLACK ROSES (E. Chisholm; 1 act, English). *New York, Cherry Lane Th., July 6, 1954.

The Blacksmith. See Le MARECHAL FERRANT.

BLAISE ET BABET (N. Dezède; 2 acts, French, Versailles 1783). Charleston, S. C., Théâtre Français, July 23, 1794.

BLANC ET NOIR (P. A. Tirindelli; 1 act, American). *Cincinnati, Auditorium, Dec. 22, 1897.

BLANCHE ET RENE (E. P. Prévost; French). *New Orleans, French Op. H., --? (the composer was conductor here 1838-62).

The BLEEDING HEART OF TIMPANOGAS (W. F. Hanson; 3 acts, American). *Provo, U., College Hall (Brigham Young Univ.), Apr. 7, 1937.

BLENNERHASSET (V. Giannini; 1 act, American). *New York, Columbia Broadcasting System, Nov. 2, 1939 (radio perf.); New York, Institute of Musical Art, Apr. 12, 1940 (stage premiere).

The BLESSED WILDERNESS (J. F. Kilpatrick; 3 acts, American).
* Dallas, Southern Methodist Univ., Apr. 18, 1959.

The BLIND GIRL OF CASTEL-CUILLE (E. R. Drake; 3 acts,
American). * Chicago, Globe Th., Feb. 19, 1914.

The BLOND DONNA (E. T. Carter; 3 acts, American). * New York,
Heckscher Th., Dec. 14, 1931.

BLOOD MOON (N. Dello Joio; 3 acts, American). * San Francisco,
War Memorial Op. H., Sept. 18, 1961.

Blossom time. See Das DREIMAEDERLHAUS.

BLUE FLAME (A. Hovhaness; 4 scenes, American). * San Antonio,
Municipal Auditorium, Dec. 15, 1959.

Blue Monday blues. See 135th STREET.

BLUE WING (G. Tonning; 3 acts, American). * Seattle, Moore Th.,
May 18, 1917.

Bluebeard's castle. See (A) KEKSZAKALLU HERCEG
VARA.

BLUES IN THE SUBWAY. (A. Levister; 1 act, "jazz" opera, American). * New York, Loew's Sheridan Th., Sept. 27, 1958.

BOABDIL (M. Moszkowski; 3 acts, German, Berlin 1892). New York,
Manhattan Op. H., Jan. 24, 1893, in English.

BOCCACCIO (F. von Suppé; 3 acts, German, Vienna 1879). Philadelphia, Chestnut Street Th., Apr. 5, 1880, in English; New York,
Thalia Theater, Apr. 23, 1880, in German.

La BOHEME (R. Leoncavallo; 4 acts, Italian, Venice 1897). New
York, McMillin Th. (Columbia Univ.), Jan. 31, 1960.

La BOHEME (G. Puccini; 4 acts, Italian, Turin 1896). Los Angeles,
Los Angeles Th., Oct. 14, 1897.

The BOHEMIAN GIRL (M. W. Balfe; 3 acts, English, London 1843).
New York, Park Th., Nov. 25, 1844.

BOHEMIOS (A. Vives; 1 act, zarzuela, Spanish, Madrid 1904). New
York, Teatro Español [Park Th.], Apr. 28, 1919.

BOMBASTES FURIOSO (P. Alderman; 1 act, American). * Los
Angeles, Bovard Auditorium (Univ. of Southern California), Apr. 30,
1938.

BONEY QUILLEN (H. Haufrecht; 3 scenes, American). * Chichester,
N.Y., American Legion Hall, Aug. 18, 1951.

The BOOR (D. Argento; 1 act, American). * Rochester, N.Y.,
Kilbourn Hall (Eastman School of Music), May 6, 1957.

The BOOR (M. Bucci; 1 act, American). * New York, Finch College,
Dec. 29, 1949.

The BOOR (M. Fink; 1 act, American). * St. Louis, Jefferson Hotel
Ivory Room, Feb. 14, 1955.

BORIS GODOUNOV (M. Moussorgsky; prolog and 4 acts, Russian, St. Petersburg 1874). New York, Metropolitan Op. H., Mar. 19, 1913, in Italian; San Francisco, Columbia Th., Jan. 15, 1922, in Russian.

BOSTON BAKED BEANS (G. Kubik; 1 act, American). *New York, Museum of Modern Art, Mar. 9, 1952.

The BOTTLE IMP (P. Whiton; 3 acts, American). *Wilton, Conn., Wilton Playhouse, Apr. 10, 1958.

Le BOUFFE ET LE TAILLEUR (P. Gaveaux; 1 act, French, Paris 1804). --New York, Park Th., Aug. 20, 1827 [New Orleans earlier (?)].

La BOULANGERE A DES ECUS (J. Offenbach; 3 acts, French, Paris 1875). New York, New Eagle Th., Feb. 26, 1877.

BOURVILLE CASTLE, or The Gallic orphans (B. Carr; American). *New York, John Street Th., Jan. 16, 1797.

BOW SING (M. Klein; 1 act, American). *New York, Winter Garden, Mar. 20, 1911.

The BOX (C. Hamm; 1 act, American). *New Orleans, Dixon Hall (Tulane Univ.), Feb. 4, 1961.

Les BRACONNIERS (J. Offenbach; 3 acts, French, Paris 1873). --Portland, Me., City Hall, Oct. 14, 1887, in English, as "The Poachers" (Chicago, Grand Op. H., Nov. 29, 1887).

BRANDY IS MY TRUE LOVE'S NAME (M. Kalmanoff; 1 act, American). *New York, Blackfriars Th., June 17, 1953.

Le BRASSEUR DE PRESTON (A. Adam; 3 acts, French, Paris 1838). New Orleans, Théâtre d'Orléans, Nov. 1842.

Il BRAVO (G. S. Mercadante; 3 acts, Italian, Milan 1839). Philadelphia, Walnut Street Th., Oct. 2, 1849, in English, as "The Bravo."

Breaking the spell. See Les VIOLONEUX.

The BRIDE OF BAGDAD (J. Ozier; American). *Kansas City, Mo. Young Men's Hebrew Association Auditorium, Mar. 1928 (excerpts; concert form).

The BRIDE OF MESSINA (J. H. Bonawitz; American). *Philadelphia, Academy of Music, Apr. 22, 1874.

The BRIDE OF SONG (J. Benedict; 1 act, English, London 1864). --Philadelphia, Dec. (?), 1871 (Durang Opera).

The Bridge of sighs. See Le PONT DES SOUPIRS.

BRIGADOON (F. Loewe; 2 acts, American). *New Haven, Shubert Th., Feb. 6, 1947 (New York, Ziegfeld Th., Mar. 13, 1947).

Les BRIGANDS (J. Offenbach; 3 acts, French, Paris 1869). New York, Grand Op. H., Nov. 14, 1870.

Brigham Young. See DESERET.

Die BRILLENINSEL (F. Riemann; German). Philadelphia, Arch Street Th., Feb. 10, 1840.

BRISEIS (A. E. Chabrier; 3 acts, French, Paris 1897). New York, Carnegie Hall, Mar. 3, 1911 (concert form).

The Bronze horse. See Le CHEVAL DE BRONZE.

BROTHER AND SISTER (H. R. Bishop and W. Reeve; 2 acts, English, London 1815). New York, Park Th., Jan. 5, 1816.

BROTHER JOE (L. Engel; 2 acts, American). *Cleveland, Karamu Th., May 28, 1953.

The BROTHERS (G. Antheil; 1 act, American). *Denver, Little Th. (Univ. of Denver), July 28, 1954.

The BROWNINGS GO TO ITALY (E. E. Freer; 1 act, American). *Chicago, Arts Club, May 11, 1938.

BRUEDERLEIN FEIN (L. Fall; 1 act, German, Vienna 1909). *New York, Irving Place Th., Feb. 15, 1915.

The BRUTE (L. Moss; 1 act, American). *Norfolk, Conn., Music Shed (Yale Summer School of Music and Art), July 15, 1961.

BUFFO AND HIS TALKING DOG (L. Gesensway; 1 act, American). *Philadelphia, South Philadelphia High School Auditorium, Feb. 7, 1961 (Academy of Vocal Arts).

BUXOM JOAN (R. Taylor; 1 act, American). *Philadelphia, New [Chestnut Street] Th., Jan. 30, 1801.

BY GEMIMI (M. Baylor; prolog and 2 acts, American). *Galesburg, Ill., Knox College Th., Mar. 2, 1949.

- C -

The CABINET (J. Moorehead, J. Braham, J. Davy, and others; 3 acts, English, London 1802). --Charleston, S.C., Charleston Th., Mar. 27, 1809.

Le CADI DUPE (C. W. von Gluck; 1 act, French, Vienna 1761). Rochester, N.Y., Kilbourn Hall (Eastman School of Music), May 16, 1932, in English, as "The Deceived Kadi."

The CAGE (G. T. Jones; 1 act, American). *New York, National Broadcasting Company, May 10, 1959 (TV tape; Catholic Univ. of America).

Le CAID (A. Thomas; 2 acts, French, Paris 1849). New Orleans, Théâtre d'Orléans, Apr. 18, 1850.

La CALANDRIA (R. Chapi; 1 act, zarzuela, Spanish). --New York, 63rd Street Music Hall, Feb. 20, 1921.

Le CALIFE DE BAGDAD (F. A. Boieldieu; 1 act, French, Paris 1800). --New Orleans, [Théâtre St. Pierre?] Mar. 2, 1806.

CALL ME MADAM (I. Berlin; 2 acts, American). *New Haven, Conn., Shubert Th., Sept. 11, 1950 (New York, Imperial Th., Oct. 12, 1950).

La CAMBIALE DI MATRIMONIO (G. Rossini; 1 act, Italian, Venice 1810). New York, Forty-fourth Street Th., Nov. 8, 1937.

CAMILLE (H. Forrest; prolog and 3 acts, American). *Chicago, Civic Op. H., Dec. 10, 1930.

CAMILLE, ou Le Souterrain (N. Dalayrac; 3 acts, French, Paris 1791). --New York, Park Th., Sept. 8, 1827 [New Orleans earlier (?)].

La CAMPANA SOMMERSA (O. Respighi; 4 acts, Italian, Hamburg 1927 in German). New York, Metropolitan Op. H., Nov. 24, 1928, in Italian (first time in that language).

Il CAMPANELIO DI NOTTE (G. Donizetti; 1 act, Italian, Naples 1836). New York, Lyceum Th., May 7, 1917, in English, as "The Night bell;" New York, Cherry Lane Th., Jan. 12, 1941, in Italian.

Il CANCELLETO D'ORO (A. Bimboni; 1 act, Italian-American). *New York, National Arts Club, Mar. 11, 1936, in English (concert form), as "There was a little gate."

Il CANCELLETO D'ORO (S. Virzi; 1 act, Italian-American). *New York, Henry Hudson Hotel Auditorium, May 18, 1945 (concert form); New York, (Brooklyn) Academy of Music, Apr. 26, 1947 (stage premiere).

CANDIDE (L. Bernstein; 2 acts, American). *Boston, Colonial Th., Oct. 29, 1956 (New York, Martin Beck Th., Dec. 1, 1956).

The CANDLE (P. M. Slates; 1 act, American). *Athens, O., Ewing Hall (Ohio Univ.), July 26, 1956.

The CANTERBURY PILGRIMS (R. DeKoven; 4 acts, American). *New York, Metropolitan Op. H., Mar. 8, 1917.

La CANTERINA (F. J. Haydn; 2 acts, Italian, Esterhaz 1767). Cleveland, Hotel Statler, Dec. 30, 1940, in English, as "The Songstress" (Cleveland Institute of Music).

CAPOCCHIO AND DORINNA (R. Taylor; 1 act, American). *Annapolis, Md., Assembly Room, Jan. 28, 1793.

CAPONSACCHI (R. Hageman; prolog, 3 acts and epilog, American, Freiburg 1932 in German). New York, Metropolitan Op. H., Feb. 4, 1937, in English.

CAPRICCIO (R. Strauss; 1 act, German, Munich 1942). New York, Juilliard School of Music, Apr. 4 (preview Apr. 2), 1954, in English; Dallas, Fair Park Auditorium, Nov. 23, 1954, in German (final scene only).

CAPRICCIO DI MILIARDARIO (F. B. DeLeone; 3 acts, American). *Naples, Teatro Eldorado, July 26, 1910, in Italian.

14

CAPTAIN LOVELOCK   (J. Duke; 1 act, American).   *Hudson Falls, N.Y., Hudson Falls High School, Aug. 18, 1953.

The CAPTIVE OF SPILBERG   (J. L. Dussek and M. Kelly; 2 acts, English, London 1798). New York, Park Th., Mar. 25, 1801.

I CAPULETI E MONTECCHI   (V. Bellini; 2 acts, Italian, Venice 1830). New Orleans, St. Charles Th., Apr. 4 (not 1), 1837.

The Caravan to Mecca.   See La RECONTRE IMPREVUE.

La CARAVANE DU CAIRE   (M. Grétry; 3 acts, French, Fontaine-bleau 1783). Charleston, S.C., Charleston Th., Aug. 3, 1795.

CARMEN   (G. Bizet; 4 acts, French, Paris 1875). New York, Academy of Music, Oct. 23, 1878, in Italian; New Orleans, French Op. H., Jan. 13, 1881, in French.

CARMINA BURANA   (C. Orff; Latin and German, Frankfurt a. M. 1937, in operatic form). San Francisco, War Memorial Op. H., Jan. 10, 1954 (concert form); San Francisco, War Memorial Op. H., Oct. 3, 1958 (stage perf.).

Der CARNEVAL IN ROM   (J. Strauss; 3 acts, German, Vienna 1873). --Milwaukee, Stadttheater, Apr. 1878; New York, Thalia Th., Apr. 1, 1881.

Il CARNEVALE DI VENEZIA   (E. Petrella; 3 acts, Italian, Naples 1851). New York, Academy of Music, Apr. 3, 1867.

CAROUSEL   (R. Rodgers; prelude and 2 acts, American).   *New Haven, Shubert Th., Mar. 22, 1945 (New York, Majestic Th., Apr. 19, 1945).

La CASA DA VENDERE   (C. Salvioni; [1 act?] Italian).   *New York, Italian Op. H., Mar. 22, 1834.

The CASK OF AMONTILLADO   (C. Hamm; 1 act, American).   *Cincinnati, Cincinnati Conservatory of Music, Mar. 1, 1953.

The CASK OF AMONTILLADO   (J. Perry; 1 act, American).   *New York, McMillin Academic Th. (Columbia Univ.), Nov. 20, 1954.

CASSANDRA   (V. Gnecchi; prolog and 2 parts, Italian, Bologna 1905). Philadelphia, Metropolitan Op. H., Feb. 26, 1914.

CASTLE AGRAZANT   (R. Lyford; 3 acts, American).   *Cincinnati, Music Hall, Apr. 29, 1926.

The CASTLE OF ANDALUSIA   (S. Arnold; 3 acts, English, London 1781). New York, John Street Th., Apr. 21, 1788, as "The Banditti."

The Castle of Otranto.   See The SICILIAN ROMANCE.

CASTOR ET POLLUX   (J. P. Rameau; 5 acts, French, Paris 1737). Poughkeepsie, N.Y., Students' Building (Vassar College), Mar. 6, 1937 (concert form, with piano acc.).

CATHERINE PARR (A. Collins; 1 act, English, London 1933). New
York, Columbia Broadcasting System, May 9, 1948 (radio perf.);
Hopkinton, N.H., Meadow Hearth Th., Aug. 4, 1950 (stage perf.).

CAVALLERIA RUSTICANA (P. Mascagni; 1 act, Italian, Rome
1890). Philadelphia, Grand Op. H., Sept. 9 (not 8), 1891.

La CENA DELLE BEFFE (U. Giordano; 4 acts, Italian, Milan 1924).
New York, Metropolitan Op. H., Jan. 2, 1926.

CENDRILLON (N. Isouard; 3 acts, French, Paris 1810). --New York,
Park Th., July 13, 1827 [New Orleans earlier (?)].

CENDRILLON (J. Massenet; 4 acts, French, Paris 1899). New Orleans,
French Op. H., Dec. 23, 1902.

La CENERENTOLA (G. Rossini; 2 acts, Italian, Rome 1817). New
York, Park Th., June 27, 1826.

Le CHALET (A. Adam; 1 act, French, Paris 1834). New York, Park
Th., Sept. 22, 1836, in English, as "The Swiss cottage;" New
Orleans, Théâtre d'Orléans, Nov. 22, 1840, in French.

La CHANSON DE FORTUNIO (J. Offenbach; 1 act, French, Paris
1861). New York, Pike's Op. H., Dec. 21, 1868.

CHANTICLEER (S. Barab; 1 act, American). *Aspen, Colo., Wheeler
Op. H., Aug. 4, 1956.

The CHAPLET (W. Boyce; 2 acts, English, London 1749). Philadelphia, Southwark Th., June 4, 1767.

CHARIVARI (P. Westergaard; "nine movements," American).
*Cambridge, Mass., Paine Hall Auditorium (Harvard Univ.), May
13, 1953.

CHARLES VI (J. Halévy; 5 acts, French, Paris 1843). New Orleans,
Théâtre d'Orléans, Apr. 22, 1847.

CHARLIE'S UNCLE (D. Ahlstrom; 1 act, American). *Columbus,
Ind., Apr. 23, 1954.

La CHATTE METAMORPHOSEE EN FEMME (J. Offenbach; 1
act, Paris 1858). New York, Théâtre Français, Nov. 21, 1859.

CHE ORIGINALI (S. S. Mayr; 1 act, Italian, Venice 1798). New
York, Bowery Th., Apr. 20, 1829, as "Il Trionfo della musica"
(pasticcio; music by V. Pucitta, J. S. Mayr and G. Pacini).

CHELM (R. Strassburg; 1 act, American). *White Plains, N.Y.,
Little Th. (Westchester Community Center), Dec. 11, 1955.

Le CHEMINEAU (X. Léroux; 4 acts, French, Paris 1907). New
Orleans, French Op. H., Feb. 11, 1911.

CHEREVICHKY (P. Tchaikovsky; 3 acts, Russian, Moscow 1887).
New York, New Amsterdam Th., May 26, 1922.

The CHEROKEE (S. Storace; 3 acts, English, London 1794). Boston,
Haymarket Th., June 24, 1799.

Le CHEVAL DE BRONZE (D. Auber; 3 acts, French, Paris 1835). New York, Bowery Th., Oct. 23, 1837, in English as a spectacle, as "The Bronze horse;" New York, Bowery Th., Jan. 31, 1842, in English (not French); New Orleans, Théâtre d'Orléans, 1845-46, in French.

CHIARA DI ROSEMBERGH (L. Ricci; 2 acts, Italian, Milan 1831). New Orleans, St. Charles Th., May 3, 1837.

Chicken Little. See MISS CHICKEN LITTLE.

The CHILD OF THE MOUNTAIN, or The Deserted mother (A. P. Heinrich; 3 acts, musical play, American). *Philadelphia, Walnut Street Th., Feb. 10, 1821.

A CHILDHOOD MIRACLE (N. Rorem; 1 act, American). *New York, Carl Fischer Concert Hall, May 10, 1955.

The CHILDREN IN THE WOOD (S. Arnold; 2 acts, English, London 1793). Philadelphia, Southwark Th., Nov. 24, 1794.

The Chimes of Normandy. See Les CLOCHES DE CORNEVILLE.

The Chocolate soldier. See Der TAPFERE SOLDAT.

CHOPIN (G. Orefice; 4 acts, Italian, Milan 1901). San Francisco, Central Th., Jan. 1907.

A CHRISTMAS CAROL (B. Herrmann; musical television play, American). *New York, Columbia Broadcasting System, Dec. 23, 1954.

A CHRISTMAS TALE (E. E. Freer; 1 act, American). *Chicago, Chicago Woman's Club, Dec. 19, 1936.

CHRISTOPHE COLOMB (D. Milhaud; 2 acts, French, Berlin 1930 in German; Paris 1953 in French). New York, Carnegie Hall, Nov. 6, 1952, in English (concert form); New York, Winter Garden Th., Jan. 30, 1957 (stage perf.).

CHRISTOPHER COLUMBUS (E. Zador; 1 act, Hungarian). *New York, National Broadcasting Company, Oct. 8, 1939, in English (radio perf.).

La CHULAPONA (F. M. Torroba; 2 acts, zarzuela, Spanish). New York, Greenwich Mews Th., Mar. 18, 1959, in English.

Il CICALAMENTO DELLE DONNE AL BUCATO E LA CACCIA (A. Striggio; madrigal play, Italian, 1567). Boston, Museum of Fine Arts, May 31, 1955 (concert form).

Le CID (J. Massenet; 4 acts, French, Paris 1885). New Orleans, French Op. H., Feb. 23, 1890.

CINDERELLA, or The Little glass slipper (M. Kelly; pantomime, English, London 1804). Philadelphia, New [Chestnut Street] Th., Jan. 1, 1806.

The CIRCUS (E. Chudacoff; 1 act, American). *Interlochen, Mich.,
National Music Camp, July 26, 1952.

Clara and the slave. See The SLAVE.

CLARI, THE MAID OF MILAN (H. R. Bishop; 3 acts, English,
London 1823). New York, Park Th., Nov. 12, 1823.

CLARISSA HARLOWE (N. Parelli; Italian, Vienna 1858). Philadelphia, Concert Hall, Feb. 6, 1866, in English (amateurs under the
composer).

The CLARKSTOWN WITCH (L. A. Nowak; 2 acts, American).
*Piermont, N.Y., Lyric Th., July 11, 1959.

La CLEMENZA DI TITO (W. A. Mozart; 2 acts, Italian, Prague
1791). New York, Mutual Broadcasting System, June 22 (Act I and
part of Act II) and June 29 (remainder), 1940, in Italian (radio perf.);
Tanglewood, Lenox, Mass., Theatre-Concert Hall (Berkshire Music
Center), Aug. 4, 1952, in English (stage perf.).

CLEOPATRA'S NIGHT (H. K. Hadley; 2 acts, American). *New
York, Metropolitan Op. H., Jan. 31, 1920.

CLEOPATRE (J. Massenet; 4 acts, French, Monte Carlo 1914).
Chicago, Auditorium, Jan. 10, 1916.

The Clever flirt. See La FINTA SEMPLICE.

Les CLOCHES DE CORNEVILLE (R. Planquette; 3 acts, French,
Paris 1877). New York, Fifth Avenue Th., Oct. 22 (not 27), 1877,
in English, as "The Chimes of Normandy;" New York, Park Th.,
May 13, 1878, in French.

La CLOCHETTE (H. Hérold; 3 acts, French, Paris 1817). --Philadel-
phia, Chestnut Street Th., Sept. 30, 1831 [New Orleans earlier (?)].

COCKCROW (J. Smith; 1 act, American). *Austin, Tex., Driskill
Hotel, Apr. 22, 1954.

COLLECTOR'S PIECE (J. McKee; 1 act, American). *Chicago,
Lyon & Healy Recital Hall, May 2, 1958.

La COLOMBE (C. Gounod; 2 acts, French, Baden-Baden 1860).
--Philadelphia, Amateur Drawing Room, Nov. 10, 1871, in English,
as "The Pet dove."

Columella. See Il RITORNO DI PULCINELLA.

Il COMBATTIMENTO DI TANCREDI E CLORINDA (C.
Monteverdi; Italian, Venice 1624). Northampton, Mass., Academy
of Music, May 12, 1928 (Smith College).

COMEDY ON THE BRIDGE [Komedie na Mosté] (B. Martinu; 1 act, Czech, Prague 1937). New York, Hunter Playhouse
(Hunter College), May 28, 1951, in English (Mannes Music School).

The COMMITTEE (M. Doran; 1 act, American). *New York, Mac-
Millin Th. (Columbia Univ.), Mar. 15, 1958.

The Commodore. See La CREOLE.

I COMPAGNACCI (P. Riccitelli; 1 act, Italian, Rome 1923). New York, Metropolitan Op. H., Jan. 2, 1924.

Le COMTE ORY (G. Rossini; 2 acts, French, Paris 1828). --New York, Park Th., Aug. 22, 1831 [New Orleans earlier (?)].

COMUS (H. Lawes; masque, English, Ludlow Castle, England, 1634; London 1738, adapted by T. A. Arne). Philadelphia, Southwark Th., Mar. 9, 1770; New York, Burton's Th., Sept. 11, 1848 (arr. by George Loder from music by Lawes, Handel and Arne).

The CONCERT (L. C. Marsh; 1 act, American). *Redlands, Cal., Watchorn Hall (Univ. of Redlands), Dec. 5, 1958.

CONCHITA (R. Zandonai; 4 acts, Italian, Milan 1911). San Francisco, Cort Th., Sept. 28, 1912.

The CONSPIRACY OF PONTIAC (C. Mayer; American). *Detroit, Brush Th., Jan. 27, 1887.

The CONSUL (G. C. Menotti; 3 acts, American). *Philadelphia, Shubert Th., Mar. 1, 1950.

La CONTADINA ASTUTE (G. B. Pergolesi; 1 act, Italian, Naples 1734). *Pottersville, N.Y., Schroon Crest, Aug. 15, 1952, in English, as "The Bargain."

Les CONTES D'HOFFMANN (J. Offenbach; prolog, 3 acts and epilog, French, Paris 1881). New York, Fifth Avenue Th., Oct. 16, 1882.

The CONTRABANDISTA (A. Sullivan; 2 acts, English, London 1867). --Philadelphia, Amateur Drawing Room, Feb. 16, 1870 (New York, Broadway Th., Mar. 3, 1879, as "I Ladroni").

Le CONTREBASSE (H. Sauget; 1 act, French, Paris 1932). *Aspen, Colo., Wheeler Op. H., July 27, 1962.

The CONTRIVANCES (H. Carey; 1 act, English, London 1715). Philadelphia, Southwark Th., Apr. 20, 1767.

Le COQ D'OR (N. Rimsky-Korsakov; 3 acts, Russian, Moscow 1909). New York, Metropolitan Op. H., Mar. 6, 1918, in French; New York, Mecca Temple Auditorium, Mar. 28, 1932, in Russian.

CORIOLANUS BEFORE ROME, or Filial love (C. Salvioni; scena, Italian). *New York, Italian Op. H., Feb. 1, 1834.

CORRADO D'ALTAMURA (F. Ricci; 2 acts, Italian, Milan 1841). Boston, Howard Athenaeum, Sept. 1847.

Der CORREGIDOR (H. Wolf; 4 acts, German, Mannheim 1896). New York, Carnegie Hall, Jan. 5, 1959, in English (semi-staged).

CORSICA (I. Berge; 1 act, American). *Kingston, N.Y., Kingston Op. H., Oct. 26, 1910.

The CORSICAN BRIDE (E.Mollenhauer 3 [?] acts, German-American). *New York, Winter Garden Th., June 15, 1863, in German.

La CORSICANA (J. L. Browne; 1 act, American). *Chicago, Playhouse, Jan. 4, 1923, as "The Corsican girl."

COSI FAN TUTTE (W. A. Mozart; 2 acts, Italian, Vienna 1790). New York, Metropolitan Op. H., Mar. 24, 1922.

COSIMO (E. P. Prévost; 2 acts, French, Paris 1835). --New York, Niblo's Graden, July 22, 1843, under the composer [New Orleans earlier (?)].

The Cossack and the volunteer. See Der KOSAK UND DER FREYWILLIGE.

COSSACKS BEYOND THE DANUBE [Zaporogetz za Dunayem] (S. Artemovsky; 3 acts, Ukrainian, St. Petersburg 1863). Philadelphia, May 26, 1932.

COSTANZA E FORTEZZA (J. J. Fux; 3 acts, Italian, Prague 1723). Northampton, Mass., John M. Greene Hall (Smith College), May 7, 1938, in English (abridged concert form).

THE COTTAGERS (J. Hewitt; 1 act, musical scene, American). *New York, Park Th., May 6, 1801.

The Country philosopher. See Il FILOSOFO DI CAMPAGNA.

The COWHERD AND THE SKY MAIDEN (J. Verrall; 1 act, American). *Seattle, University Playhouse (Univ. of Washington), Jan. 17, 1952.

COX AND BOX (A. Sullivan; 1 act, English, London 1867). --New York, Standard Th., Apr. 14, 1879.

The CRADLE WILL ROCK (M. Blitzstein; 2 parts, American). *New York, Venice Th., June 16 (not 15), 1937 (concert form); New York, Mansfield Th., Dec. 26, 1947 (stage premiere).

La CREOLE (J. Offenbach; 3 acts, French, Paris 1875). --New York, Casino Th., Oct. 4, 1886, in English, as "The Commodore."

CRESCENT EYEBROW (J. Dvorkin; 1 act, "concert opera," American). *New York, Town Hall, Jan. 8, 1956.

The Cricket on the hearth. See Das HEIMCHEN AM HERD.

CRISPINO E LA COMARE (L. and F. Ricci; 3 acts, Italian, Venice 1850). New York, Academy of Music, Oct. 24, 1865.

CRISTOFORO COLOMBO (A. Franchetti; 4 acts and epilog, Italian, Genoa 1892). Philadelphia, Metropolitan Op. H., Nov. 20, 1913.

The Crown diamonds. See Les DIAMANTS DE LA COURONNE.

The CRUCIBLE (R. Ward; 3 acts, American). *New York, City Center, Oct. 26, 1961.

CUMBERLAND FAIR (A. Wilder; 1 act, American). *Montclair, N.J., College High Auditorium (Montclair State Teachers College), May 22, 1953.

CUPID AND DEATH (C. Gibbons and M. Locke; masque, English, London 1653). Piermont, N.Y., Lyric Th., July 19, 1962.

CUPID AND PSYCHE (A. Vernon; 1 act, American). *Woodstock, N.Y., Byrdcliffe Th., July 27, 1956.

The CURIOUS FERN (M. Kupfermann; 1 act, American). *New York, Master Institute Th., June 5, 1957.

CYNTHIA PARKER (J. Smith; prolog and 1 act, American). *Denton, Tex., North Texas State Teachers College Auditorium, Feb. 16, 1939.

CYRANO (W. Damrosch; 4 acts, American). *New York, Metropolitan Op. H., Feb. 27, 1913.

CZAR UND ZIMMERMANN (A. Lortzing; 3 acts, German, Leipzig 1837). New York, Astor Place Op. H., Dec. 9, 1851.

The CZAR'S BRIDE (N. Rimsky-Korsakov; 3 acts, Russian, Moscow 1899). San Francisco, Columbia Th., Jan. 9, 1922.

- D -

DAELIA (H. Forrest; 1 act, American). *Interlochen, Mich., National Music Camp, July 21, 1954.

DALIBOR (B. Smetana; 3 acts, Czech, Prague 1868). Chicago, Národní Divadlo [Sokol Hall], Apr. 13, 1924.

La DAME BLANCHE (A. Boieldieu; 3 acts, French, Paris 1825). --New York, Park Th., Aug. 24, 1827 [New Orleans earlier (?)].

DAMN YANKEES (R. Adler and J. Ross; 2 acts, American). *New Haven, Conn., Shubert Th., Apr. 2, 1955 (New York, 46th Street Th., May 5, 1955; 1,019 perf.).

La DAMNATION DE FAUST (H. Berlioz; 4 parts, oratorio, French, Paris 1846 in concert form; Monte Carlo 1893 in operatic form). New York, Steinway Hall, Feb. 12, 1880, in English (concert form; Oratorio Society of New York); New York, Metropolitan Op. H., Dec. 7, 1906, in French (stage perf.) [New Orleans earlier (?)].

DAMON AND PHILLIDA (H. Carey; 1 act, English, London 1729). New York, Nassau Street Th., Feb. 18, 1751.

The DANAIDES, or Vice punished (V. Pelissier; 3 acts, pantomime, American). *Philadelphia, Southwark Th., Oct. 8, 1794.

DAPHNE (R. Strauss; 1 act, German, Dresden 1938). New York, Walt
Whitman Auditorium (Brooklyn College), Oct. 7, 1960 (concert form;
Little Orchestra Society; New York, Town Hall, Oct. 10, 1960).

DAPHNE, or The Pipes of Arcady (A. Bird; 3 acts, American).
* New York, Hotel Astoria, Apr. 1, 1895 (abridged concert form);
New York, Hotel Astoria, Dec. 13, 1897 (stage perf.).

DAPHNE AND AMINTOR (text, I. Bickerstaffe; 1 act, pasticcio,
English, London 1765). Charleston, S.C., "Theatre in the City
Exchange," May 29, 1785.

DARK SONNET (E. Chisholm; 1 act, English, Cape Town 1952). New
York, Cherry Lane Th., July 6, 1954.

DARK WATERS (E. Krenek; 1 act, American). * Los Angeles, Bovard
Auditorium (Univ. of Southern California), May 2, 1951.

Darlin' Corie. See MY DARLIN' CORIE.

The DAUGHTER OF ST. MARK (M. W. Balfe; 3 acts, English,
London 1844). New York, Niblo's Garden, June 18, 1855.

A DAUGHTER OF THE FOREST (A. F. Nevin; 1 act, American).
* Chicago, Auditorium, Jan. 5, 1918.

DAVID (D. Milhaud; 5 acts, French, Jerusalem 1954 in Hebrew, in
concert form; Milan 1955 in Italian, in operatic form). Los Angeles,
Hollywood Bowl, Sept. 22, 1956, in English.

DAVID RIZZIO (M. C. Moore; 2 acts, American). * Los Angeles,
May 26 (not 27), 1932, as "Rizzio."

The DAWN OF THE WEST (E. Enna; 4 acts, American). * Portland, Ore., Nov. 7, 1915 (privately).

Days of old. See The BATTLE OF HEXHAM.

The DEAD ALIVE (S. Arnold; 2 acts, English, London 1781). Philadelphia, Southward Th., Feb. 19, 1790.

The DEATH FETCH, or The Student of Göttingen (C. E.
Horn; English, London 1826). New York, Bowery Th., June 15, 1829.

DEBORAH (H. Millard; 4 acts, American). * New York, Apollo Hall,
Feb. 17, 1873 (Act III only, "in costume;" Amateur Operatic Club).

The DECORATOR (R. Woollen; 1 act, American). * New York,
National Broadcasting Company, May 24, 1959 (TV tape perf.;
Catholic Univ. of America).

The DEED OF GIFT (S. Woodward; 3 acts, American). * Boston,
Boston [Federal Street] Th., 1822.

DEEP RIVER (W. F. Harling; 3 acts, American). * Lancaster, Pa.,
Fulton Op. H., Sept. 18, 1926 (New York, Imperial Th., Oct. 4,
1926; 36 perf.).

DEIDAMIA (G. F. Handel; 3 acts, Italian, London 1741). Elmwood,
Conn., Talcott School Auditorium, Feb. 25, 1959 (Hartt College of
Music).

DEJANIRE   (C. Saint-Saëns; 4 acts, French, Monte Carlo 1911).
Chicago, Auditorium, Dec. 9, 1915.

Une DEMOISELLE EN LOTERIE   (J. Offenbach; 1 act, French,
Paris 1857). Schroon Lake, N. Y. , Aug. 6, 1954, in English, as
"A Lady to raffle. "

The DEMON   (A. Rubinstein; 3 acts, Russian, St. Petersburg 1875).
Los Angeles, Mason Op. H. , Feb 18, 1922 (not San Francisco, Jan.
17, 1922).

DES ADLERS HORST   (F. Glaser; 3 acts, German, Berlin 1832).
Baltimore, Washington Hall, 1856 (Baltimore Liederkranz).

Des LOEWEN ERWACHEN   (J. Brandl; 1 act, German, Vienna 1872).
New York, (Brooklyn) Athenaeum, Nov. 7, 1881.

DESERET   (L. Kastle; 3 acts, American). *New York, National Broadcasting Company, Jan. 1, 1961 (TV perf.).

DESERET, or A Saint's affliction   (D. Buck; 3 acts, American).
*New York, Fourteenth Street Th. , Oct. 11, 1880.

The DESERT FLOWER   (W. V. Wallace; 3 acts, English, London
1863). New York, Academy of Music, Jan. 13, 1868.

The DESERT SONG   (S. Romberg; 2 acts, American). *Wilmington,
Del. , Playhouse, Oct. 21, 1926, as "Lady fair" (New York, Casino
Th. , Nov. 30, 1926).

Le DESERTEUR   (P. A. Monsigny; 3 acts, French, Paris 1769). New
York, John Street Th. , June 8, 1787, in English, as "The Deserter"
(C. Dibdin's version); Charleston, S.C. , Charleston Th. , Dec. 12,
1794, in French, as a "grand comic ballet pantomime. "

Les DETTES   (C. Champein; 2 acts, French, Paris 1787). Charleston,
S.C. , Charleston Th. , July 21, 1795.

Les DEUX AVARES   (M. Grétry; 2 acts, French, Fontainebleau 1770).
New York, Brander Matthews Hall (Columbia Univ.), Dec. 8, 1943,
in English.

Les DEUX AVEUGLES   (J. Offenbach; 1 act, French, Paris 1855).
New York, Metropolitan Music Hall, Aug. 26, 1858.

Les DEUX CHASSEURS ET LA LAITIERE   (E. R. Duni; 1 act,
French, Paris 1763). New York, City Tavern, Nov. 10, 1790.

Les DEUX JOURNEES   (L. Cherubini; 3 acts, French, Paris 1800).
New Orleans, Théâtre St. Philippe, Mar. 12, 1811.

DEUX MOTS   (N. Dalayrac; 1 act, French, Paris 1806). Philadelphia,
Chestnut Street Th. , May 18, 1839, in English, as "Two words, or
A Night in the forest. "

Les DEUX PETITS SAVOYARDS   (N. Dalayrac; 1 act, French,
Paris 1789). Philadelphia, New [Chestnut Street] Th. , Jan. 16,
1797.

The DEVIL AND DANIEL WEBSTER (D. Moore; 1 act, American).
*New York, Martin Beck Th., May 18, 1939.

The Devil inventor. See VELNIAS ISRADEJAS.

The DEVIL TAKE HER (A. Benjamin; prolog and 1 act, English,
London 1931). New York, Brander Matthews Hall (Columbia Univ.),
Feb. 13, 1941.

The DEVIL TO PAY (text, C. Coffey; 1 act, ballad opera, London
1731). Charleston, S.C., New [Queen Street] Th., Mar. 16, 1736.

The DEVIL'S BRIDGE (J. Braham and C. E. Horn; 3 acts, English,
London 1812). New York, Park Th., July 4, 1815.

The Devil's daughter. See La TENTATION.

The DEVIL'S IN IT (M. W. Balfe; prolog and 3 acts, English,
London 1852). New York, Niblo's Garden, Dec. 17, 1852.

The Devil's share. See La PART DU DIABLE.

Le DEVIN DU VILLAGE (J. J. Rousseau; 1 act, French, Fontainebleau 1752). New York, City Tavern, Oct. 21, 1790.

Le DIABLE A QUATRE (J. P. Solié; 3 acts, French, Paris 1809).
--New York, Park Th., Aug. 17, 1827 [New Orleans earlier (?)].

Le DIABLE BOITEUX (J. Françaix; 1 act, French, Paris 1937).
New York, Carl Fischer Concert Hall, Nov. 19, 1950 (concert form).

Le DIABLE COUTURIER (J. G. M. Ropartz; 1 act, French, Paris
1894). San Francisco, La Gaité Française, Nov. 1926.

Le DIABLE EN VACANCES (P. Gaveaux; 1 act, French, Paris
1805). New Orleans, Théâtre d'Orléans, 1820-25.

DIALOGUES DES CARMELITES (F. Poulenc; 3 acts, French,
Zurich 1951 in German). San Francisco, War Memorial Op. H.,
Sept. 20, 1957, in English.

Les DIAMANTS DE LA COURONNE (D. Auber; 3 acts, French,
Paris 1841). --New York, Niblo's Garden, July 12 (not 14), 1843
[New Orleans earlier (?)].

DIAMOND CUT DIAMOND (A. Grisar; 1 act, English, London
185-). New York, French Th., Oct. 12, 1859.

DIANA VON SOLANGE (Ernest II, Duke of Saxe-Coburg-Gotha; 5
acts, German, Coburg 1858). New York, Metropolitan Op. H.,
Jan. 9, 1891.

Il DIBUC (L. Rocca; prolog and 3 acts, Italian, Milan 1934).
Detroit, Masonic Temple Auditorium, May 6, 1036, in English, as
"The Dybbuk."

DICK WHITTINGTON AND HIS CAT (J. Offenbach; 3 acts,
English, London 1874). Cleveland, Karamu House, Dec. 25, 1962.

DIDO (C. E. Horn; music arranged, mostly from Rossini, American).
*New York, Park Th., Apr. 9, 1828.

DIDO AND AENEAS (T. Beveridge; 1 act, American). *Boston, Fogg Art Museum, Feb. 14, 1958.

DIDO AND AENEAS (H. Purcell; 3 acts, English, London 1689 [?]). --New York, Hotel Plaza, Feb. 10, 1923 (Glee Club of Rosemary Hall, Greenwich, Conn.); New York, Town Hall, Jan. 13, 1924 (concert form, Bodanzky version).

Le DIEU ET LA BAYADERE (D. Auber; 2 acts, French, Paris 1830). New York, National Th., Oct. 3, 1836, in English, as "The Maid of Cashmere."

Dinorah. See Le PARDON DE PLOERMEL.

DIOCLESIAN (H. Purcell; 5 acts and epilog, English, London 1690). New York, Washington Square College (New York Univ.), Apr. 15, 1936 (concert form).

The DISAPPOINTED IMPRESARIO (K. Davis; 1 act, American). *Duxbury, Mass., Plymouth Rock Center of Music and Drama, July 15, 1955.

I DISPETTOSI AMANTI (A. Parelli; 1 act, American). *Philadelphia, Metropolitan Op. H., Mar. 6 (not 28), 1912.

DJAMILAH (G. Bizet; 1 act, French, Paris 1872). Boston, Boston Op. H., Feb. 24, 1913.

DOBRINYA NIKITICH (A. T. Gretchaninov; 3 acts, Moscow 1903). New York, Carnegie Hall, Jan. 23, 1954 (Act III, concert form).

The DOCTOR AND THE APOTHECARY (S. Storace, adapted from Dittersdorf's "Doctor und Apotheker" below; 2 acts, English, London 1788). Charleston, S.C., City [Church Street] Th., Apr. 26, 1796.

DR. HEIDEGGER'S EXPERIMENT (S. Raphling; 1 act, American). *New York, Greenwich House, Feb. 18, 1956.

DR. JEKYLL AND MR. HYDE (F. D. Fragale; 2 acts, American). *Berkeley, Cal., Garfield Th., Aug. 28, 1953.

The DOCTOR OF ALCANTARA (J. Eichberg; 2 acts, American). *Boston, Boston Museum [theatre], Apr. 7, 1862.

DOCTOR UND APOTHEKER (K. von Dittersdorf; 2 acts, German, Vienna 1786). New York, Terrace Garden, June 30, 1875. (See The DOCTOR AND APOTHECARY above.)

Dogs' heads. See PSOHLAVCI.

DOLORETES (A. Vives and Guislant; 1 act, zarzuela, Spanish, Madrid 1901). New York, Teatro Apolo, Mar. 2, 1930.

Le DOMINO NOIR (D. Auber; 3 acts, French, Paris 1837). New Orleans, Théâtre d'Orléans, 1838.

DON BUCEFALO (A. Cagnoni; 3 acts, Italian, Milan 1847). New York, Academy of Music, Oct. 18, 1867.

DON CARLOS (G. Verdi; 5 acts, French, Paris 1867; Milan 1884 in Italian, revised form). New York, Academy of Music, Apr. 12, 1877, in Italian (Paris version); New York, Metropolitan Op. H., Dec. 23, 1920 (Milan version).

DON FORTUNIO (H. Forrest; 1 act, American). *Interlochen, Mich., National Music Camp, July 22, 1952.

DON GIOVANNI (W. A. Mozart; 2 acts, Italian, Prague 1787). New York, Park Th., Nov. 7, 1817, in English (Bishop's London version); New York, Park Th., May 23, 1826, in Italian (through Da Ponte's efforts).

DON PASQUALE (G. Donizetti; 3 acts, Italian, Paris 1843). New Orleans, Théâtre d'Orléans, Jan. 7, 1845, in Italian.

DON PEDRO (H. Erissman, compiled from Mozart's "L'Oca del Cairo," "Lo Sposo deluso," and other works; 3 acts, German, Zurich 1952). New York, Greenwich Mews Playhouse, June 1, 1953, in English.

DON PERLIMPLIN (V. Rieti; prolog and 3 scenes, Spanish). *Urbana, Ill., Auditorium (Univ. of Illinois), Mar. 30, 1952, in English (concert form); New York, Hunter College Playhouse, Mar. 18, 1959, in English (stage perf.).

DON QUICHOTTE (J. Massenet; 5 acts, French, Monte Carlo 1910). New Orleans, French Op. H., Jan. 27, 1912.

DON QUIXOTE, DER RITTER VON DER TRAURIGEN GESTALT (A. Neuendorff; prolog and 3 acts, German-American). *New York, Germania Theater, Jan. 9, 1882, in German.

DON QUIXOTTE (H. Purcell, arranged; 1 act, English). New York, Wagner College, Dec. 17, 1937 (London Intimate Opera).

DON SEBASTIEN (G. Donizetti; 5 acts, French, Paris 1843). New York, Academy of Music, Nov. 25, 1864, in Italian; New Orleans, French Op. H., Mar. 11, 1875, in French.

DONNA CARITEA (S. Mercadante; 2 acts, Italian, Venice 1826). New Orleans, St. Charles Th., Apr. 26, 1837.

La DONNA DEL LAGO (G. Rossini; 2 acts, Italian, Naples 1819). --New York, Park Th., Aug. 26 (not 25), 1829, in French, as "La Dame du Lac" [New Orleans earlier (?)]; New York, Italian Op. H., Dec. 16, 1833, in Italian.

DONNA JUANITA (F. von Suppe; 3 acts, German, Vienna 1880). Boston, Boston Th., May 12, 1881, in English; New York, Thalia Theater, Sept. 27, 1881, in German.

Le DONNE CURIOSE (E. Wolf-Ferrari; 3 acts, Italian, Munich 1903, in German). New York, Metropolitan Op. H., Jan. 3 (not 4), 1912, in Italian (first perf. in that language).

DON'T WE ALL (B. Phillips; 1 act, American). *Rochester, N.Y., Kilbourn Hall (Eastman School of Music), May 9, 1949.

The DOOR (I. Mopper; 1 act, American). *Newark, N.J., Lauter
Auditorium, Dec. 5, 1954, as "The Sire de Maledroit's door."
Der DORFBARBIER (J. Schenk; 1 act, German, Vienna 1796). --New
Orleans, Deutsches Theater, Aug. 14, 1842.
DORIAN GRAY (C. L. Flick-Steger; 8 scenes, German-American).
*Aussiz, Bohemia, Stadttheater, Mar. 1, 1930, in German.
Double bill. See The CANDLE; and The BARGAIN.
The DOUBLE DISGUISE (J. Hook; 2 acts, English, London 1784).
New York, John Street Th., Apr. 29, 1795, with "the accompany-
ments by Mons. Pelisier" [Victor Pelissier].
La DOUBLE ECHELLE (A. Thomas; 1 act, French, Paris 1837). New
Orleans, Théâtre d'Orléans, Jan. 1841.
DOUBLE TROUBLE (R. Mohaupt; 1 act, American). *Louisville, Ky.,
Columbia Auditorium, Dec. 4, 1954.
DOWN IN THE VALLEY (K. Weill; 1 act, American). *Blooming-
ton, Ind., East Hall (Indiana Univ.), July 14, 1948.
DRAAGENFOOT GIRL (M. Kupferman; 2 acts, American). *Bronx-
ville, N.Y. Sarah Lawrence College, May 8, 1958.
The DRAGON (D. Taylor; 3 acts, American). *New York, Hall of
Fame Playhouse (New York Univ.), Feb. 6, 1958.
Les DRAGONS DE VILLARS (A. Maillart; 3 acts, French, Paris
1856). New Orleans, Théâtre d'Orléans, Jan. 17, 1859.
DREAMS IN SPADES (S. Hovey; 1 act, American). *Philadelphia,
Plays and Players Th., Dec. 15, 1949.
Die DREIGROSCHENOPER (K. Weill; prolog and 8 scenes, German,
Berlin 1928). New York, Empire Th., Apr. 13, 1933, in English, as
"The Threepenny opera;" Waltham, Mass., Adolph Ullman Amphi-
theatre (Brandeis Univ.), June 14, 1952, in English (Marc Blitzstein
version).
Das DREIMAEDERLHAUS (H. Berte; 3 acts, German, Berlin 1916).
New York, Irving Place Th., Oct. 10, 1917, in German; Atlantic
City, Globe Th., Mar. 22, 1921, in English, with additional music
by S. Romberg, as "Blossom time" (New York, Ambassador Th.,
Sept. 29, 1921).
The DRESS (M. Bucci; 1 act, American). *New York, Theresa
Kaufmann Concert Hall (Y.M. & Y.W.H.A.), Dec. 8, 1953.
A DRUMLIN LEGEND (E. Bacon; 3 acts, American). *New York,
Brander Matthews Hall (Columbia Univ.), May 9, 1949.
DUBROVSKY (E. Napravnik; 4 acts, Russian, St. Petersburg 1895).
San Francisco, Columbia Th., Jan. 8, 1922.
Il DUCA D'ALBA (G. Donizetti; 4 acts, Italian, Rome 1882). New
York, Carnegie Hall, Oct. 20, 1959 (concert form).

I DUE FOSCARI   (G. Verdi; 3 acts, Italian, Rome 1844). Boston,
Howard Athenaeum, May 10, 1847.

The DUENNA   (T. Linley sr. and T. Linley jr.; 3 acts, London 1775).
Savannah, Ga., Theatre, Feb. 21, 1786.

The Duenna (Prokofiev). See BETHROTHAL AT A
MONASTERY.

DVE VDOVY [The Two widows]   (B. Smetana; 2 acts, Czech,
Prague 1874). New York, T. J. Sokol Hall, Oct. 23, 1949.

The Dybbuk (Rocco). See Il DIBUC.

The DYBBUK   (D. Tamkin; 3 acts, American). *New York, City
Center, Oct. 4, 1951.

- E -

EARLY DAWN   (N. Lockwood; American). *Denver, Little Th. (Univ.
of Denver), Aug. 7, 1961.

EARTH-TRAPPED   (H. O. Reed; 1 act, American). *East Lansing,
Mich., Michigan State Univ. Music Auditorium, Feb. 24, 1962.

EASTWARD IN EDEN   (J. Meyerowitz; 4 acts, American). *Detroit,
Wayne Univ. Th., Nov. 16, 1951.

The ECHO   (F. Patterson; 1 act, American). *Portland, Ore., Civic
Auditorium, June 9, 1925.

L'ECLAIR   (J. Halévy; 3 acts, French, Paris 1835). New Orleans,
Théâtre d'Orléans, Feb. 16, 1837.

EDGAR   (G. Puccini; 4 acts, Italian, Milan 1889). New York, Waldorf-
Astoria Hotel, Apr. 12, 1956 (three scenes, in concert form, with
piano acc.).

EDIPO RE   (R. Leocavallo; 1 act, Italian). *Chicago, Auditorium,
Dec. 13, 1920.

EDUARDO E CRISTINA   (G. Rossini; 2 acts, Italian, Venice 1819).
New York, Italian Op. H., Nov. 25, 1834.

Une EDUCATION MANQUEE   (E. Chabrier; 1 act, French, Paris
1879). Tanglewood, Lenox, Mass., Theatre-Concert Hall (Berkshire
Music Center), Aug. 3, 1953, in English, as "An Incomplete education."

EDWIN AND ANGELINA   (V. Pelissier; 3 acts, American). *New
York, John Street Th., Dec. 19, 1796.

EGLE, ZALCIU KARALIENE [Egle, Queen of the Snakes]
(M. Petrauskas; 6 acts, Lithuanian-American). *South Boston,
Broadway Th., May 30, 1924, in Lithuanian.

EGON UND EMILIE   (E. Toch; 1 act, German, Mannheim 1928).
New York, Provincetown Playhouse, May 10, 1954, in English.

28

ELAINE (H. Bemberg; 4 acts, French, London 1892). New York,
Metropolitan Op. H., Dec. 17, 1894.

ELEKTRA (R. Strauss; 1 act, German, Dresden 1909). New York,
Manhattan Op. H., Feb. 1, 1910, in French; Philadelphia, Academy
of Music, Oct. 29, 1931, in German.

ELIJAH (F. Mendelssohn-Bartholdy; 2 parts, oratorio, English, Birming-
ham, England, 1846; Liverpool 1912 in a stage perf.). New York,
Tabernacle, Nov. 8, 1847 (concert form); New Haven, Conn.,
Hyperion Th., May 8, 1901 (stage perf.).

ELISA E CLAUDIO (G. Mercadante; 2 acts, Italian, Milan 1821).
New York, Richmond Hill Th., Oct. 18 (not 19), 1832.

L'ELISIR D'AMORE (G. Donizetti; 2 acts, Italian, Milan 1832).
New York, Park Th., June 18, 1838, in English, as "The Elixir of
love;" New Orleans, Théâtre d'Orléans, Mar. 30, 1842, in Italian.

ELIZABETH AND LEICESTER (E. S. Lindsey; American).
*Chattanooga, John A. Patten Memorial Chapel (Univ. of Chat-
tanooga), Apr. 21, 1936.

The EMERALD ISLE (A. Sullivan; 2 acts, English, London 1901).
New York, Herald Square Th., Sept. 1, 1902.

The EMPEROR JONES (L. Gruenberg; 1 act, American). *New
York, Metropolitan Op. H., Jan. 7, 1933.

The EMPEROR'S NEW CLOTHES (D. Moore; 2 acts, American).
*New York, Carnegie Hall, Feb. 19, 1949 (concert form).

The EMPTY BOTTLE (M. Kalmanoff; 3 acts, American). *New
York, Municipal Broadcasting System, Feb. 17, 1952 (excerpts in a
radio concert).

The ENCHANTED CANARY (N. S. Stevens; 1 act, American).
*Bemidji, Minn., Bemidji State College, Mar. 18, 1961.

The Enchanted fife. See Le SOLDAT MAGICIEN.

The ENCHANTED HORSE, or The Eastern lovers (J. Jones;
3 acts, American). *New York, Park Th., Sept. 30, 1844. (The
composer sang the tenor role of the Prince.)

The ENCHANTED KISS (R. R. Bennett; 1 act, American). *New
York, Mutual Broadcasting System, Dec. 30, 1945 (abridged radio
perf.).

The ENCHANTED PEAR TREE (H. Overton; 1 act, American).
*New York, Juilliard School of Music, Feb. 7, 1950.

The ENCHANTRESS (M. W. Balfe; 4 acts, English, London 1845).
Philadelphia, Walnut Street Th., Jan. 31, 1846.

L'ENFANCE DU CHRIST (H. Berlioz; 3 parts, oratorio, French,
Paris 1854). Los Angeles, Royce Hall (Univ. of California), Dec. 30,
1957, in English (stage perf.; Los Angeles Bureau of Music).

L'ENFANT ET LES SORTILEGES (M. Ravel; 2 acts, French, Monte
Carlo 1925). San Francisco, Civic Auditorium, Sept. 19, 1930.

L'ENFANT PRODIGUE (D. Auber; 5 acts, French, Paris 1850).
New York, Broadway Th., June 2, 1851, in English, as "Azael, the
prodigal" (Drury Lane version).

L'ENFANT PRODIGUE (C. Debussy; cantata, French, Paris 1884).
Chicago, Fine Arts Building, Mar. 3, 1910, in English (concert
form, with piano accomp.); Boston, Boston Op. H., Nov. 16, 1910,
in French (stage perf.).

Les ENFANTS DE BETHLEEM (G. Pierné; 2 parts, oratorio,
French, Amsterdam 1907). New York, Carnegie Hall, Dec. 19,
1908, in English (concert form), as "The Children of Bethlehem;"
New York, Carnegie Hall, Dec. 17, 1910, in English (stage perf.).

The ENGLISH FLEET (J. Braham; 3 acts, English, London 1803).
--New York, Park Th., Apr. 26, 1819.

L'ENLEVEMENT D'EUROPE (D. Milhaud; 8 scenes, French, Baden-
Baden 1927 in German). --San Francisco, Veteran's Auditorium, May
18, 1955, in English, as "The Abduction of Europa."

Die ENTFUEHRUNG AUS DEM SERAIL (W. A. Mozart; 3 acts,
German, Vienna 1782). New York, (Brooklyn) Athenaeum, Feb. 16,
1860 (New York, German Op. H. [Wallack's Th.], Oct. 10, 1862).

L'EPREUVE VILLAGEOISE (M. Grétry; 2 acts, French, Versailles
1784). New Orleans, Théâtre d'Orléans, 1815.

ERMINIE (E. Jakobowski; 2 acts, English, London 1885). New York,
Casino Th., May 10, 1886.

ERNANI (G. Verdi; 4 acts, Italian, Venice 1844). New York, Park Th.,
Apr. 15, 1847.

ERO E LEANDRO (L. Mancinelli; 3 acts, Italian, Norwich, England,
1896 in English in concert form; Madrid 1897 in Italian in operatic
form). New York, Metropolitan Op. H., Mar. 10, 1899.

ERRISINOLA (L. Lombard; 2 acts, Italian-American). *Lugano,
Italy, Trevano Castle (composer's estate), Aug. 25, 1907.

ERWARTUNG (A. Schonberg; 1 act, "minodrama," German, Prague
1924 in concert form). New York, Carnegie Hall, Nov. 15, 1951
(concert form); Washington, D.C., Lisner Auditorium, Dec. 28,
1960 (stage perf.).

ESCAPE FROM LIBERTY (R. Doellner; American). *Hartford,
Conn., Avery Memorial Hall, Apr. 1, 1948.

ESCLARMONDE (J. Massenet; prolog, 4 acts and epilog, French,
Paris 1889). New Orleans, French Op. H., Feb. 10, 1893.

ESCURIAL (M. D. Levy; 1 act, American). *New York, Theresa
Kaufmann Concert Hall (Y.M. & Y.W.H.A.), May 4, 1958.

La ESMERALDA   (E. Prévost; French).   *(?) New Orleans, Théâtre
d'Orléans, Mar. 2, 1842.

ESMERALDA   (A. G. Thomas; 4 acts, English, London 1883). New
York, Metropolitan Op. H., Nov. 19, 1900 (Damrosch Opera).

ESTHER   (J. Meyerowitz; 3 acts, American).   *Urbana, Ill., Lincoln
Hall Th. (Univ. of Illinois), Mar. 17, 1957.

El ESTUCHE DE MONERIAS   (J. Valverde jr.; 1 act, zarzuela,
Spanish).   --New York, 63rd Street Music Hall, Feb. 6, 1921.

The ETERNAL ROAD   (K. Weill; prolog and 3 acts, American
[originally German]).   *New York, Manhattan Op. H., Jan. 7, 1937.

L'ETOILE   (E. Chabrier; 3 acts, French, Paris 1877). New York, Broadway Th., Aug. 18, 1890, in English, as "The Merry monarch"
(with additional music by Woolson Morse; orchestrated by John Philip
Sousa).

L'ETOILE DU NORD   (G. Meyerbeer; 3 acts, French, Paris 1854).
New Orleans, French Op. H., Mar. 5, 1855.

EUGEN ONEGIN   (P. Tchaikovsky; 3 acts, Russian, Moscow 1879).
New York, Carnegie Hall, Feb. 1, 1908, in English (concert form);
New York, Metropolitan Op. H., Mar. 24, 1920, in Italian (stage
perf.); San Francisco, Columbia Th., Jan. 6, 1922, in Russian.

EURIDICE   (J. Peri; prolog and 6 scenes, Italian, Florence 1600). New
York, Berkeley Lyceum, Mar. 15, 1894, in English (scenes from
"Act I;" American Academy of Dramatic Arts); Saratoga Springs, N.
Y., Skidmore College, Apr. 9, 1941, in English (student project).

EURYANTHE   (C. M. von Weber; 3 acts, German, Vienna 1823).
New York, Metropolitan Op. H., Dec. 23, 1887.

EVANDRO   (S. Guerrieri; 1 act, Italian-American).   *New York,
Garden Th., Nov. 23, 1917, in Italian.

Der EVANGELIMANN   (W. Kienzl; 2 acts, German, Berlin 1895).
Chicago, Great Northern Th., Nov. 3, 1923.

EVANGELINE   (O. Luening; 3 acts, American).   *New York, Brander
Matthews Hall (Columbia Univ.). May 5, 1948.

The EVE OF ADAM   (J. Duffy; 1 act, American).   *Interlaken,
Mass., Stockbridge School, June 1, 1955.

Les EVENEMENTS IMPREVUES   (M. Grétry; 3 acts, French,
Versailles 1779). New York, Park Th., Nov. 10 (not 5), 1819, in
English, as "The Gay deceivers" (M. Kelly's London version).

The EXILE   (J. Mazzinghi and H. R. Bishop; 3 acts, English, London
1809). New York, Park Th., Apr. 27, 1810.

The EXPERIMENT   (P. Schwartz; 1 act, American).   *Gambier, O.,
Kenyon College, Jan. 27, 1956.

EZIO   (G. F. Handel; 3 acts, Italian, London 1732). New York, Gate
Th., May 11, 1959, in English.

Fact or fiction. See SPIEL ODER ERNST?

The FAIR AMERICAN (T. Carter; 3 acts, English, London 1782).
Albany, N.Y., Theatre, Jan. 27, 1786 (as a play without the music!);
New York, John Street Th., Nov. 9, 1789.

The FAIR AT SOROCHINSK (M. Moussorgsky; 3 acts, Russian,
Petrograd 1917). New York, Metropolitan Op. H., Nov. 29, 1930,
in Italian (Tcherepnin's version).

The Fair maid of Elizondo. See PEPITO.

The Fairies. See DAPHNE AND AMINTOR.

The FAIRY QUEEN (H. Purcell; prolog and 5 acts, English, London
1692). San Francisco, Palace of the Legion of Honor, Apr. 30, 1932.

FAIRYLAND (H. Parker; 3 acts, American). *Los Angeles, Clune's
Auditorium, July 1, 1915.

The FALL OF ALGIERS (H. R. Bishop; 3 acts, English, London 1825).
Philadelphia, New [Chestnut Street] Th., July 4, 1827.

The FALL OF THE CITY (J. Cohn; 1 act, American). *Athens, O.,
Ewing Auditorium (Ohio Univ.), July 29, 1955.

The FALL OF THE HOUSE OF USHER (C. Loomis; 6 scenes,
American). *Indianapolis, Block's Auditorium, Jan. 11, 1941 (three
scenes in concert form with piano acc.).

The FALL OF THE HOUSE OF USHER (M. H. Ruger; 1 act,
American). *Los Angeles, Wilshire Ebell Th., Apr. 15, 1953.

The False harlequin. See Il FINTO ARLECCHINO.

FALSTAFF (G. Verdi; 3 acts, Italian, Milan 1893). New York,
Metropolitan Op. H., Feb. 4, 1895.

Il Fanatico per la musica. See CHE ORIGINALI.

La FANCIULLA DEL WEST (G. Puccini; 3 acts, Italian). *New
York, Metropolitan Op. H., Dec. 10, 1910.

FANNY (H. Rome; 2 acts, American). *Boston, Shubert Th., Sept.
20, 1954 (New York, Majestic Th., Nov. 4, 1954).

FAR HARBOR (B. Bergersen; 2 acts, American). *New York, Hunter
College Playhouse, Jan. 22, 1948.

La FARCE DU CONTREBANDIER (C. Pascal; 1 act, French,
Mulhouse 1951). Interlochen, Mich., National Music Camp, July
22, 1952, in English.

FARINELLI (H. Zumpe; 3 acts, German, Hamburg 1886). New York,
Amberg Theater, Dec. 20, 1888.

The FARMER (W. Shield; 2 acts, English, London 1787). Richmond,
Va., New Th., Oct. 18, 1790.

The Farmer and the fairy. See La FEE ET LE CULTI-
VATEUR.

The FARMER'S WIFE   (H. R. Bishop, W. Reeve, J. Davy, J. Addison, T. Welsh and H. Condell; 3 acts, English, London 1814). New York, Park Th., Sept. 26, 1814.

FAT TUESDAY   (S. Berkowitz; 2 acts, American). *Tamiment, Pa., Tamiment Playhouse, Aug. 11, 1956.

The FATAL OATH   (B. Koutzen; 1 act, American). *New York, Hunter College Playhouse, May 25, 1955.

FATINITZA   (F. von Suppé; 3 acts, German, Vienna 1876). --San Francisco, California Th., Oct. 27, 1878, in German (New York, Thalia Theater, Apr. 14, 1879; New York, Fifth Avenue Th., Apr. 22, 1879, in English).

La FAUSSE MAGIE   (M. Grétry; 2 acts, French, Paris 1775). Charleston, S.C., Charleston Th., June 1, 1795.

Les FAUSSES APPARENCES   (M. Gretry; 3 acts, French, Versailles 1778). New Orleans, Théâtre d'Orléans, 1815.

FAUST   (C. Gounod; 5 acts, French, Paris 1859). Philadelphia, Academy of Music, Nov. 18, 1863, in German; New York, Academy of Music, Nov. 25 (not 26), 1863, in Italian; New Orleans, French Op. H., Nov. 12, 1866, in French.

La FAVORITE   (G. Donizetti; 4 acts, French, Paris 1840). New Orleans, Théâtre d'Orléans, Feb. 9, 1843, in French; New York, Astor Place Op. H., Feb. 9, 1849, in Italian.

A FAWN IN THE FOREST   (G. Cockshott; 1 act, English). *Westport, Conn., White Barn Th., Aug. 9, 1959.

FAY-YEN-FAH   (J. D. Redding; prolog and 3 acts, American). *Monte Carlo, Opéra, Feb. 25, 1925, in French; San Francisco, Columbia Th., Jan. 11, 1926, in French.

FEDORA   (U. Giordano; 3 acts, Italian, Milan 1898). New York, Metropolitan Op. H., Dec. 5, 1906.

La FEE AUX ROSES   (J. Halévy; 3 acts, French, Paris 1849). New Orleans, Théâtre d'Orléans, Jan. 1851.

La FEE ET LE CULTIVATEUR   (A. Tcherepnin; 2 scenes, French-American). *Aspen, Colo., Amphitheatre, Aug. 13, 1952, in English, as "The Farmer and the fairy."

Der FELDPREDIGER   (K. Millöcker; 3 acts, German, Vienna 1884). New York, Thalia Theater, May 1, 1885 (New York, Wallack's Th., May 4, 1885, in English, as "The Black hussar").

FERNAND CORTEZ   (G. Spontini; 3 acts, French, Paris 1809). New York, Metropolitan Op. H., Jan. 6 (not 16), 1888, in German.

FESTINO NELLA SERA DEL GIOVEDI GRASSO AVANTI CENA   (A. Banchieri; madrigal entertainment, Italian, Venice 1608). New York, Queen's College, May 20, 1952.

La FETE DU VILLAGE VOISIN (A. Boieldieu; 3 acts, French, Paris 1816). --New York, Park Th., July 16, 1827 [New Orleans earlier (?)].

FEUERSNOT (R. Strauss; 1 act, German, Dresden 1901). Philadelphia, Metropolitan Op. H., Dec. 1, 1927.

La FIAMMA (O. Respighi; 3 acts, Italian, Rome 1934). Chicago, Civic Op. H., Dec. 2, 1935.

FIAMMETTA (A. Hochman; 3 acts, American). *New York, Metropolitan Op. H., Apr. 6, 1913 (trial rehearsal of Acts I and II with the composer at the piano).

La FIANCEE (D. Auber; 3 acts, French, Paris 1829). --New York, Park Th., Aug. 21 (not 14), 1829 [New Orleans earlier (?)].

FIDELIO (L. van Beethoven; 2 acts, German, Vienna 1805). New York, Park Th., Sept. 9, 1839, in English; New York, Broadway Th., Dec. 29, 1856, in German.

The Fiend and the fairy. See JUSTINA.

FIESTA (D. Milhaud; 1 act, French). *Los Angeles, Univ. of California, Mar. 16, 1959, in English.

A FIFTH FOR BRIDGE (R. Sheldon; 1 act, American). *San Francisco, San Francisco Conservatory of Music, Dec. 3, 1961.

La FIGLIA DELL' ARIA (M. Garcia; 2 (?) acts, Italian). *New York, Park Th., Apr. 25, 1826.

La Figlia del reggimento. See La FILLE DU REGIMENT.

La FILLE DE MADAME ANGOT (C. Lecocq; 3 acts, French, Brussels 1872). New York, Broadway Th., Aug. 25, 1873.

La FILLE DU MEUNIER (L. Delibes; 1 act, French). New York, Koster and Bial's Th., Jan. 2, 1803, in French.

La FILLE DU REGIMENT (G. Donizetti; 2 acts, French, Paris 1840). New Orleans, Théâtre d'Orléans, Mar. 2 (not 6), 1843, in French; New York, Niblo's Garden, Jan. 10, 1853, in Italian.

Il FILO D'ARIANNA (P. Rubino; 3 acts, Italian-American). *New York, Guild Hall [Steinway Building], Nov. 15, 1932 (excerpts in concert form); New York, Town Hall, Sept. 24, 1938 (semi-staged).

Il FILOSOFO DI CAMPAGNA (B. Galuppi; 3 acts, Italian, Venice 1754). New York, Columbia Broadcasting System, Feb. 7, 1960, in English, as "The Country philosopher" (half-hour TV version); Boston, Boston Conservatory of Music, Feb. 26, 1960, in English (stage perf.).

Il FILTRO (P. H. Allen; 1 act, Italian-American). *Genoa, Politeama Genovese, Oct. 26, 1913, in Italian.

La FINTA GIARDINIERA (W. A. Mozart; 3 acts, Italian, Munich 1775). New York, Mayfair Th., Jan. 18 (not 17), 1927, in English.

La FINTA SEMPLICE (W. A. Mozart; 3 acts, Italian, Salzburg 1769). Boston, Jordan Hall, Jan. 27, 1961, in English, as "The Clever flirt. "

Il FINTO ARLECCHINO (G. F. Malipiero; 2 scenes, Italian, Mayence 1928 in German; San Remo 1933 in Italian). New York, Juilliard School of Music, Apr. 28, 1932, in English as "The False harlequin. "

FIORELLA (D. Auber; 3 acts, French, Paris 1826). --New York, Park Th., Aug. 22, 1829 [New Orleans earlier (?)].

The Firebird. See L'OISEAU DE FEU.

The FIREFLY (R. Friml; 3 acts, American). *Syracuse, N. Y., Empire Th., Oct. 14, 1912 (New York, Lyric Th., Dec. 2, 1912).

The FISHERMAN'S WIFE (L. Stein; 1 act, American). *Chicago, Eight Street Th., May 12, 1955.

FIT FOR A KING (M. Kalmanoff; 1 act, American). *New York, Municipal Broadcasting System (WNYC), Feb. 13, 1949 (radio perf.); New York, Master Th., June 21, 1950 (stage perf.).

FJELDEVENTYRET (V. Thrane; 2 acts, Norwegian, Christiania 1824 in concert form; 1850 in operatic form). Duluth, Orpheum-Strand Th., Apr. 7, 1916.

The FLAMING ARROW (M. C. Moore; 1 act, American). *San Francisco, Century Club, Mar. 27, 1922.

Il FLAMINO (P. Pergolesi; 3 acts, Italian, Naples 1735). New York, Theresa Kaufmann Concert Hall (Y. M. & Y. W. H. A), Mar. 9, 1953 (concert form).

Die FLEDERMAUS (J. Strauss; 3 acts, German, Vienna 1874). New York, Stadt Theater, Nov. 21, 1874, in German (--San Francisco, Tivoli Op H. , July 1880, in English).

Der FLIEGENDE HOLLAENDER (R. Wagner; 3 acts, German, Dresden 1843). Philadelphia, Academy of Music, Nov. 8, 1876, in Italian, as "Il Vascello fantasma"; New York, Academy of Music, Mar. 12, 1877, in German (with the same soprano!).

FLIS (S. Moniuszko; 1 act, Polish, Warsaw 1858). Philadelphia, Metropolitan Op. H. , Apr. 29, 1925.

The FLITCH OF BACON (W. Shield; 2 acts, English, London 1778). New York, Theatre Royal [John Street Th.], Oct. 30, 1780 (by the "Gentlemen of the Army, " during Lord Howe's occupation of the city); New York, John Street Th. , Sept. 27, 1785 (professional company).

FLORA, or Hob in the well (text, Colley Cibber; 2 acts, ballad opera, English, London 1729). Charleston, S. C., Courtroom, Feb. 18, 1735.

FLORENCE NIGHTINGALE (D. M. Williams; 3 acts, American). *New York, St. Bartholomew's Community House, May 4, 1943.

Florizel and Perdita. See The SHEEP SHEARING.

FLORODORA (L. Stuart; 2 acts, English, London 1899). New York,
Casino Th., Nov. 12, 1900.
FLOTTE BURSCHE (F. von Suppé; 1 act, German, Vienna 1863).
New York, Stadt Theater, Oct. 25, 1867.
FLOWER DRUM SONG (R. Rodgers; 2 acts, American). *Boston,
Shubert Th., Oct. 27, 1958 (New York, St. James Th., Dec. 1,
1958).
Die FLUT (B. Blacher; 1 act, German, Berlin 1946 in a radio perf.;
Dresden 1947 in operatic form). Boston, Boston Univ., Apr. 19,
1956, in English, as "The Tide. "
The Flying Dutchman. See Der FLIEGENDE HOLLAENDER.
Une FOLIE (E. N. Méhul; 1 act, French, Paris 1802). New Orleans,
Théâtre St. Philippe, Jan. 30, 1808.
Les FOLIES AMOUREUSES (F. Castil-Blaze; 3 acts, French, Paris
1823). Philadelphia, Chestnut Street Th., Oct. 3, 1828 [New
Orleans earlier (?)].
FONTAINEBLEAU (W. Shield; 3 acts, English, London 1784).
Charleston, S.C., Charleston Th., Mar. 9, 1795.
The FOREST ROSE (J. Davies; 2 acts, American). *New York
Chatham Garden Th., Oct. 7 (not 6), 1825.
Le FORET BLEUE (L. Aubert; 3 acts, French, Geneva 1913). Boston,
Boston Op. H., Mar. 8, 1913.
Forever Rembrandt. See X-MAL REMBRANDT.
The FORTUNE TELLER (V. Herbert; 3 acts, American). *Toronto,
Canada, Grand Op. H., Sept. 14, 1898; Buffalo, Star Th., Sept. 19,
1898 (U.S. premiere) (New York, Wallack's Th., Sept. 26, 1898).
FORTUNIO AND HIS SEVEN GIFTED SONS (F. T. Sully; 3
acts, American). *Philadelphia, Lyceum Th., Mar. 26 (not 25),
1883.
Forty winks. See Une NUIT BLANCHE.
La FORZA DEL DESTINO (G. Verdi; 4 acts, Italian, St. Petersburg
1862). New York, Academy of Music, Feb. 24, 1865.
The FOUNTAIN OF BAKHCHI-SARAI (A. S. Arensky; 1 act,
Russian, 1899). New York, Jolson Th., Jan. 11, 1926.
The Four ruffians. See I QUATTRO RUSTEGHI.
FOUR SAINTS IN THREE ACTS (V. Thomson; 4 acts, American).
*Ann Arbor, Mich., Hill Auditorium (Univ. of Michigan), May 20,
1933 (concert form); Hartford, Conn., Avery Memorial Auditorium,
Feb. 8 (not 7), 1934 (stage premiere).
FRA DIAVOLO (D. Auber; 3 acts, French, Paris 1830). --Philadelphia,
Chestnut Street Th., Sept. 16, 1831, in French [New Orleans earlier
(?)] (Boston, Tremont Th., Feb. 5, 1833, in English, John Howard

Payne translator; New York, Stadt Theater, Nov. 16, 1858, in
German; New York, Academy of Music, Dec. 21, 1864, in Italian).

FRA GHERARDO (I. Pizzetti; 3 acts, Italian, Milan 1928). New
York, Metropolitan Op. H., Mar. 21, 1929.

FRANCESCA DA RIMINI (R. Zandonai; 4 acts, Italian, Turin 1914).
New York, Metropolitan Op. H., Dec. 22, 1916.

FRANCOIS DE FOIX (H. M. Berton; 3 acts, French, Paris 1809).
New Orleans, Mar. 9, 1813.

FRANCOIS VILLON (M. Baron; 3 acts, American). *New York,
National Broadcasting Company (WJZ network), Apr. 14, 1940
(abridged radio perf.).

The FRANKLIN'S TALE (N. Sokoloff; 1 act, American). *Baton
Rouge, University Th. (Louisiana State Univ.), Nov. 10, 1961.

Lo FRATE 'NNAMORATO (G. B. Pergolesi; 3 acts, Italian, Naples
1732). New York, Municipal Broadcasting System (WNYC), May 23,
1948, in English, as "The Brother in love" (radio perf.; New York
College of Music).

FRAU ANNE, DIE DAME AM PUTZTISCH (S. Letovsky; 3
acts, German-American). *Posen, Stadttheater, Dec. 14, 1913, in
German.

Die FRAU OHNE SCHATTEN (R. Strauss; 3 acts, German, Vienna
1919). San Francisco, War Memorial Op. H., Sept. 18, 1959.

The Freebooters. See I FUORUSCITI DI FIRENZA.

Der FREISCHUETZ (C. M. von Weber; 3 acts, German, Berlin 1821).
New York, Park Th. Mar. 2 (not 12), 1825, in English; New Orleans,
circa 1827 (or earlier), in French; Philadelphia, Chestnut Street Th.,
Mar. 23, 1840, in German; New York, Astor Place Op. H., Oct. 21,
1850, in Italian.

Friquet. See Les DRAGONS DE VILLARS.

FRISCO MAME (G. Wehner; 1 act, American). *New York, Church
of the Neighbor, Feb. 12, 1959, as "Frisco belles"; New York,
Central Park Mall, July 25, 1961, in revised form, as "Frisco Mame."

FRITHIOF (E. E. Freer; 2 acts, American). --Chicago, Studebaker
Th., Feb. 1, 1931 (concert form).

Fritzchen und Lieschen. See LISCHEN ET FRITZCHEN.

FUGITIVES (C. Floyd; 3 acts, American). *Tallahassee, Opperman
Hall (Florida State Univ.), Apr. 17, 1951.

I FUORUSCITI DI FIRENZA (F. Paër; 2 acts, Italian, Dresden
1802). New York, Bowery Th., Dec. 24, 1827, in English, as "The
Freebooters" (William Hawes's London version).

Le FURIE DE ARLECCHINO (A. Lualdi; 1 act, Italian, Buenos Aires
1924). New York, Hotel Pennsylvania, Dec. 20, 1924.

Il FURIOSO NELL' ISOLA DI SAN DOMINGO (G. Donizetti; 2 acts, Italian, Rome 1833). New Orleans, Théâtre d'Orléans, Mar. 28, 1842.

- G -

GABRIELLA (E. Pizzi; 2 acts, Italian). *Boston, Music Hall, Nov. 25, 1893 (performed the same night, in English, in London, for copyright purposes).

GAGLIARDA OF A MERRY PLAGUE (L. Saminsky; 1 act, American). *New York, Times Square Th., Feb. 22, 1925.

GAINSBOROUGH'S DUCHESS (A. Coates; English). *Los Angeles, Royce Hall (Univ. of California), Apr. 20, 1941 (concert form).

GALATEE (V. Massé; 2 acts, French, Paris 1852). New Orleans, 1858 (New York, Théâtre Français, Nov. 30, 1866).

GALE (E. Leginska; 1 act, American). *Chicago, Civic Op. H., Nov. 23, 1935.

GALLANTRY (D. Moore; 1 act, American). *New York, Brander Matthews Hall (Columbia Univ.), Mar. 19, 1958.

La GALLINA CIEGA (M. Fernández-Caballero; zarzuela, Spanish, Madrid 1874). --San Francisco, Washington Square Th., [June ?] 1918.

The GAMBLER (S. Prokofiev; 4 acts, Russian, Brussels 1929 in French). New York, 85th Street Playhouse, Apr. 4, 1957, in English.

The GAME OF CARDS (Arnold Franchetti; 1 act, American). *Hartford, Conn., Hartt College of Music, Mar. 20, 1955 (concert form); Hartford, Conn., Burns School Auditorium, May 9, 1956 (stage premiere).

A GAME OF CHANCE (S. Barab; 1 act, American). *Rock Island, Ill., Potter Hall (Augustana College), Jan. 11, 1957.

The GARDEN OF MYSTERY (C. W. Cadman; 1 act, American). *New York, Carnegie Hall, Mar. 20, 1925.

GARRICK (A. Stoessel; 3 acts, American). *New York, Juilliard School of Music, Feb. 24, 1937.

GASTIBELZA (A. Maillart; 3 acts, French, Paris 1847). New Orleans, Théâtre d'Orléans, Nov. 1848.

The GATE (M. Brand; "scenic oratorio," American). *New York, Metropolitan Op. H., May 23, 1944.

Los GAVILANES (J. Guerrero; 3 acts, zarzuela, Spanish). *New York, Community Center, Apr. 21, 1956.

The Gay deceivers. See Les EVENEMENTS IMPREVUES.

La GAZZA LADRA   (G. Rossini; 2 acts, Italian, Milan 1817).
--Philadelphia, Chestnut Street Th., Sept. 14, 1829 (not Oct. 1827),
in French, as "La Pie voleuse" [New Orleans earlier (?)]; New York,
Italian Op. H., Nov. 18, 1833, in Italian.

The GEISHA   (S. Jones; 2 acts, English, London 1896). New York,
Fifth Avenue Th., Sept. 9, 1896.

Il GELOSO SCHERNITO   (att. to G. B. Pergolesi; 3 acts, Italian,
Naples 1731 or 1732). Indianapolis, John Herron Art Museum, Dec.
13, 1952, in English, as "The Jealous husband" (Indiana University).

GEMMA DI VERGY   (G. Donizetti; 2 acts, Italian, Milan 1834).
New York, Niblo's Garden, Oct. 2, 1843.

GENEVIEVE DE BRABANT   (J. Offenbach; 3 acts, French, Paris
1859 in 2 acts; Paris 1867 in 3 acts). New York, Théâtre Français,
Oct. 22, 1868.

The GENTLE SHEPHERD   (T. Linley; 1 act, English, London 1781).
New York, John Street Th., June 7, 1786.

GENTLEMEN PREFER BLONDES   (J. Styne; 2 acts, American).
* Philadelphia, Forrest Th., Nov. 17, 1949 (New York, Ziegfeld Th.,
Dec. 8, 1949).

GENTLEMEN'S ISLAND   (G. Snell; 1 act, American). * Westport,
Conn., White Barn Th., Aug. 9, 1959.

Les GEORGIENNES   (J. Offenbach; 3 acts, French, Paris 1864). New
York, Grand Op. H., Mar. 6, 1871.

GERMANIA   (A. Franchetti; prolog, 2 acts and epilog, Italian, Milan
1902). New York, Metropolitan Op. H., Jan. 22, 1910.

GETTYSBURG   (M. H. Ruger; 1 act, American). * Los Angeles,
Hollywood Bowl, Sept. 23, 1938.

The Ghost of Brittany.   See Les REVENANTS BRETONS.

GIANNI SCHICCHI   (G. Puccini; 1 act, Italian). * New York,
Metropolitan Op. H., Dec. 14, 1918.

The GIANT'S GARDEN   (S. Krane; 2 acts, American). * Norfolk,
Va., Blair Junior High School Auditorium, Mar. 12, 1960 (College
of William and Mary).

GIANTS IN THE EARTH   (D. Moore; 3 acts, American). * New
York, Brander Matthews Hall (Columbia Univ.), Mar. 28, 1951.

GILLES RAVISSEUR   (A. Grisar; 1 act, French, Paris 1848). San
Francisco, Adelphi Th., Oct. 30, 1853.

La GIOCONDA   (A. Ponchielli; 4 acts, Italian, Milan 1876). New
York, Metropolitan Op. H., Dec. 20 (not 21), 1883.

I GIOJELLI DELLA MADONNA   (E. Wolf-Ferrari; 3 acts, Italian,
Berlin 1911 in German). Chicago, Auditorium, Jan. 16, 1912, in
Italian (first perf. in that language).

GIONA (G. Carissimi; cantata, Italian). New York, Carnegie Hall,
Apr. 27, 1960, in English (semi-staged; Schola Cantorum).

Un GIORNO DI REGNO (G. Verdi; 2 acts, Italian, Milan 1840).
New York, Town Hall, June 18, 1960, in English, as "King for a
day" (semi-staged).

GIOVANNA PRIMA DI NAPOLI (M. Strakosch; 3 acts, Italian).
*New York, Astor Place Op. H., Jan. 6, 1851.

GIOVANNI GALLURESE (I. Montemezzi; 3 acts, Italian, Turin
1905). New York, Metropolitan Op. H., Feb. 19, 1925.

The GIPSY'S WARNING (J. Benedict; 3 acts, English, London
1838). New York, Park Th., Apr. 20, 1841.

GIRALDA (A. Adam; 3 acts, French, Paris 1850). Philadelphia,
Walnut Street Th., Dec. 5, 1850, in English (as a play "taken from
a French opera by Adam"); Boston, Globe Th., Apr. 3 (not Mar. 4),
1885, in English (stage perf.).

The Girl from Elizondo. See PEPITO.

The GIRL FROM SANJAK (A. Savine; 4 acts, American).
*Chicago, Blackstone Th., Oct. 3, 1943.

The Girl of the golden West. See La FANCIULLA DEL
WEST.

GIROFLE-GIROFLA (C. Lecocq; 3 acts, French, Brussels 1874).
Boston, Boston Th., Dec. 7, 1874, in English; New York, Park Th.,
Feb. 4, 1875, in French.

GISMONDA (H. Février; 3 acts, French). *Chicago, Auditorium,
Jan. 14, 1919.

La GITA IN CAMPAGNA (M. Peragallo; 1 act, Italian, Milan
1954). Baton Rouge, University Th. (Louisiana State Univ.), Nov.
8, 1956, in English, as "A Trip to the country."

GIUDITTA (Achille Peri; 3 acts, Italian, Milan 1860). New York,
Academy of Music, Nov. 11, 1863.

GIULIETTA E ROMEO (N. Vaccai; 2 acts, Italian, Milan 1825).
New York, Academy of Music, June 15, 1855 (the famous finale
only; usually introduced in Bellini's "I Capuletti e Mentecchi," and
probably heard in that connection in performances of the latter al-
ready in 1840s and later).

GIULIETTA E ROMEO (N. A. Zingarelli; 3 acts, Italian, Milan
1796). New York, Park Th., July 26, 1826.

GIULIO CESARE (G. F. Handel; 3 acts, Italian, London 1724).
Northampton, Mass., Academy of Music, May 14, 1927, in English
(Oskar Hagen's edition; Smith College).

GIULIO CESARE (G. F. Malipiero; 3 acts, Italian, Genoa 1936).
New York, Carnegie Hall, Jan. 13, 1937 (concert form; New York
Philharmonic-Symphony Society under the composer).

Il GIURAMENTO (G. S. Mercadante; 3 acts, Italian, Milan 1837). New York, Astor Place Op. H., Feb. 14, 1848.

The GLITTERING GATE (P. Glanville-Hicks; 1 act, American). *New York, Theresa Kaufmann Concert Hall (Y.M. & Y.W.H.A.), May 14, 1959.

GLORIANA (B. Britten; 3 acts, English, London 1953). Cincinnati, Music Hall, May 8, 1956 (concert form).

Die GLUECKLICHE HAND (A. Schonberg; 1 act, German, Vienna 1924). Philadelphia, Academy of Music, Apr. 11, 1930.

A GOAT IN CHELM (A. W. Binder; 1 act, American). *New York, Theresa Kaufmann Concert Hall (Y.M. & Y.W.H.A.), Mar. 20, 1960.

GOBI (A. Reiser; prelude and 3 scenes, American). *New York, Lewisohn Stadium, July 29, 1923 (excerpts in concert form).

GODFATHER DEATH (J. Meyerowitz; 3 parts, American). *New York, George Gershwin Th. (Brooklyn College), June 1, 1961.

The GOLDEN CHILD (P. Bezanson; 1 act, American). *New York, National Broadcasting Company (WNBC-TV), Dec. 18, 1960 (TV perf.; tape).

The GOLDEN LION (G. Kechley; 2 acts, American). *Seattle, University Playhouse (Univ. of Washington), Apr. 28, 1959; (Dec. 1, 1959, in revised form).

Das GOLDENE KREUZ (I. Brüll; 2 acts, German, Berlin 1875). New York, Terrace Garden, July 19, 1879.

The GOLEM (A. Ellstein; 4 acts, American). *New York, City Center, Mar. 22, 1962.

The GOLEM (L. Weiner; prolog, 2 scenes and epilog, American). *White Plains, N.Y., Jewish Community Center, Jan. 13, 1957.

GOLFO (G. Vitalis; 3 acts, Greek, Athens 1943). New York, Carnegie Hall, Jan. 1, 1949.

The GONDOLIERS (A. Sullivan; 2 acts, English, London 1889). New York, Park Th., Jan. 7, 1890 (New York, Palmer's Th., Feb. 18, 1890; London company).

The GOOD NEIGHBOR (V. Pelissier; 1 act, American). *New York, Park Th., Feb. 28, 1803.

The GOOD SOLDIER SCHWEIK (R. Kurka; 2 acts, American). *New York, City Center, Apr. 23, 1958.

GOODBYE TO THE CLOWN (E. Laderman; 1 act, American). *New York, Theresa Kaufmann Concert Hall (Y.M. & Y.W.H.A.), May 22, 1960.

The GOOSEHERD AND THE GOBLIN (J. Smith; prolog and 1 act). *New York, Municipal Broadcasting System (WNYC), Feb. 22, 1947 (radio perf.); New London, Conn., Buell Hall, Nov. 10, 1949 (stage premiere, with two-piano acc.); Hartford, Conn., Julius Hartt School of Music, Nov. 28, 1949 (with orch.).

El GORRO FRIGIO (M. Nieto; 1 act, zarzuela, Spanish). --New York, 63rd Street Music Hall, Feb. 6, 1921.

GOYESCAS (E. Gradados; 3 scenes, Spanish). *New York, Metropolitan Op. H., Jan. 28, 1916 (first Spanish-language opera there).

La GRAN VIA (F. Chueca and J. Valverde; 1 act, zarzuela, Spanish, Madrid 1886). --New York, Irving Place Th., June 17, 1911, in Italian.

The GRAND DUKE (A. Sullivan; 2 acts, English, London 1896). --New York, Heckscher Th., Apr. 7, 1937.

GRAND SLAM (V. Vernon; 1 act, American). *Stamford, Conn., Stamford Museum and Nature Center, June 25, 1955.

La GRANDE BRETECHE (A. Claflin; 1 act, American). *New York, Columbia Broadcasting System, Feb. 3, 1957 (radio perf.).

La GRANDE BRETECHE (S. Hollingsworth; 1 act, American). *New York, National Broadcasting Company (WNBC-TV), Feb. 10, 1957 (TV perf.).

La GRANDE DUCHESSE DE GEROLSTEIN (J. Offenbach; 3 acts, French, Paris 1867). New York, Théâtre Français, Sept. 24, 1867.

The GRAY MARE'S THE BEST HORSE (R. Taylor; 1 act, "burletta," English). Annapolis, Md., Assembly Room, Jan. 28, 1793.

GREEN MANSIONS (L. Gruenberg; radio opera, American). *New York, Columbia Broadcasting System, Oct. 17, 1937.

GRIFFELKIN (L. Foss; 3 acts, American). *New York, National Broadcasting Company, Nov. 6, 1955 (TV perf.); Tanglewood, Lenox, Mass., Theater-Concert Hall (Berkshire Music Center), Aug. 6, 1956 (stage premiere).

GRISELIDES (J. Massenet; prolog and 3 acts, French, Paris 1901). New York, Manhattan Op. H., Jan. 19 (not 9), 1910.

Il GUARANY (A. C. Gomes; 4 acts, Italian, Milan 1870). San Francisco, Grand Op. H., Aug. 27, 1884.

The GUARDIAN OUT-WITTED (T. A. Arne; 3 acts, English, London 1764). New York, John Street Th., May 7, 1794.

Guglielmo Tell. See GUILLAUME TELL.

A GUIDE TO THE LIFE EXPECTANCY OF A ROSE (V. Fine; 1 act, American). *New York, Donnell Library Center, Feb. 7, 1959.

GUIDO FERRANTI (J. Van Etten; 1 act, American). *Chicago, Auditorium, Dec. 29, 1914.

GUILLAUME TELL   (M. Grétry; 3 acts, French, Paris 1791). --New
York, Park Th., Aug. 12, 1831 [New Orleans earlier (?)].

GUILLAUME TELL   (G. Rossini; 4 acts, French, Paris 1829). New
Orleans, Théâtre d'Orléans, Dec. 13, 1842, in French (New York,
Academy of Music, Apr. 9, 1855, in Italian).

GULISTAN   (N. Dalayrac; 3 acts, French, Paris 1805). --New York,
Park Th., Aug. 1, 1827 [New Orleans earlier (?)].

GULNARE   (N. Dalayrac; 1 act, French, Paris 1798). New Orleans,
Théâtre d'Orléans, 1815.

GUSTAVE III   (D. Auber; 5 acts, French, Paris 1833). New York,
Park Th., July 21, 1834, in English (Cooke's Covent Garden version);
New York, National Th., Oct. 21, 1839, in English (with Auber's
music).

GUYS AND DOLLS   (F. Loesser; 2 acts, American). *Philadelphia,
Shubert Th., Oct. 14, 1950 (New York, 46th Street Th., Nov. 24,
1950).

- H -

H.M.S. PINAFORE   (A. Sullivan; 2 acts, English, London 1878).
Boston, Boston Museum [theatre], Nov. 25, 1878.

La HABANERA   (R. Laparra; 3 acts, French, Paris 1908). Boston,
Boston Op. H., Dec. 14, 1910.

HAENSEL UND GRETEL   (E. Humperdinck; 3 acts, German, Weimar
1893). New York, Daly's Th., Oct. 8, 1895, in English; New York,
Metropolitan Op. H., Nov. 25, 1905, in German.

Der Haeusliche Krieg. See Die VERSCHWORENEN.

HALKA   (S. Moniuszko; 4 acts, Polish, Wilno 1847; Warsaw 1858).
New York, People's Th., June 1903, in Russian; Milwaukee, Pabst
Th., May 13, 1923, in Polish.

HAMLET   (S. Kagen; 3 acts, American). *Baltimore, Peabody Conservatory of Music, Nov. 9, 1962.

HAMLET   (A. Thomas; 5 acts, French, Paris 1868). New York,
Academy of Music, Mar. 22, 1872, in Italian; New York, Metropolitan Op. H., Feb. 10, 1892, in French.

A HAND OF BRIDGE   (S. Barber; 1 act, American). *New York,
Fashion Institute of Technology Auditorium, Apr. 6, 1960 (Mannes
College of Music).

HANS, LE JOUEUR DE FLUTE   (L. Ganne; 3 acts, French, Monte
Carlo 1906). New York, Manhattan Op. H., Sept. 20, 1910, in
English.

HARLEQUIN'S TRIUMPH IN WAR AND PEACE (F. Traetta; 2 acts, pasticcio, Italian-American). *New York, City Hotel, Jan. 22, 1810.

The HARPIES (M. Blitzstein; 1 act, American). *New York, Manhattan School of Music, May 25, 1953.

HARTFORD-BRIDGE (W. Shield; 2 acts, English, London 1792). Philadelphia, New [Chestnut Street] Th., May 30, 1794.

The HARVEST (V. Giannini; 3 acts, American). *Chicago, Civic Op. H., Nov. 25, 1961.

The HARVEST (D. N. Lehner; 3 acts, American). *San Francisco, Palace of the Legion of Honor, Oct. 14, 1933.

HARY JANOS (Z. Kodaly; prolog, 5 parts and epilog, Hungarian, Budapest 1926). New York, Juilliard School of Music, Mar. 18, 1960, in English.

HASCHISCH (R. Delli Ponti and Else Gregori [of Michigan]; 3 acts, Italian-American). *Turin, Politeama Chiarella, Apr. 21, 1911.

The HAT MAN (R. Trogan; 1 act, American). *Interlochen, Mich., National Music Camp, Aug. 1, 1953.

The HAUNTED TOWER (S. Storace; 3 acts, English, London 1789). Charleston, S.C., Charleston Th., Apr. 24, 1793.

HAYDEE (D. Auber; 3 acts, French, Paris 1847). New Orleans, French Op. H., 1849.

HAZILA (G. A. Thomas; American). Los Angeles, Biltmore Th., Oct. 27, 1936 (second perf.).

HE WHO GETS SLAPPED (R. Ward; 3 acts, American). *New York, Juilliard School of Music, May 17, 1956, as "Pantaloon" (Columbia Univ. Workshop); New York, City Center, Apr. 12, 1959 (professional cast).

The HEADLESS HORSEMAN (D. Moore; 1 act, American). *Bronxville, N.Y., Bronxville High School, Mar. 5, 1937.

HECHALUTZ (J. Weinberg; 3 acts, Hebrew). *New York, Mecca Temple Auditorium, Nov. 25, 1934, in Hebrew (not English), under the title "The Pioneers."

Das HEIMCHEN AM HERD (C. Goldmark; 3 acts, German, Vienna 1896). Philadelphia, Metropolitan Op. H., Nov. 7, 1912, in English, as "The Cricket on the hearth."

Die HEIMKEHR AUS DER FREMDE (F. Mendelssohn-Bartholdy; 1 act, German, Berlin 1829). --Philadelphia, Amateur Drawing Room, Apr. 20, 1870, in English, as "Son and stranger" (H. F. Chorley's London version 1851).

HELLO OUT THERE (J. Beeson; 1 act, American). *New York, Brander Matthews Hall (Columbia Univ.), May 27, 1954.

De HERBERGPRINSES (J. Blockx; 3 acts, Flemish, Antwerp 1896).
New York, Manhattan Op. H., Mar. 10, 1909, in French, as "La
Princesse d'auberge."

Here and there. See HIN UND ZURUECK.

HERODIADE (J. Massenet; 4 acts, French, Brussels 1881). New
Orleans, French Op. H., Feb. 13, 1892.

HESTER PRYNNE (A. Claflin; 3 acts, American). *Hartford, Conn.,
Avery Memorial Auditorium, Dec. 15, 1935.

Une HEURE DE MARIAGE (N. Dalayrac; 1 act, French, Paris
1804). New Orleans, Le Spectacle de la Rue St. Pierre, ca. 1803-08.

L'HEURE ESPAGNOLE (M. Ravel; 1 act, French, Paris 1911).
Chicago, Auditorium, Jan. 5, 1920.

Das HEXENLIED (E. Pirani; 3 scenes, German, Prague 1902). New
York, Little Th. (Powell-Pirani Music Institute, Brooklyn), Dec. 9,
1909, in English, as "The Witch's song."

The HIGHLAND REEL (J. O'Keeffe; 3 acts, English, Dublin 1786).
Charleston, S.C., Charleston Th., Feb. 11, 1793.

HIN UND ZURUECK (P. Hindemith; 1 act, German, Baden-Baden
1927). Philadelphia, Broad Street Th., Apr. 22 (not 12), 1928.

HIPPOLYTE ET ARICIE (C. W. von Gluck; prolog and 5 acts,
French, Paris 1733). New York, Town Hall, Apr. 11, 1954 (concert
form).

The HIRED HAND (R. L. Milano; 1 act, American). *New York,
Carl Fischer Recital Hall, Mar. 23, 1959.

L'HISTOIRE DU SOLDAT (I. Stravinsky; 2 parts, French,
Lausanne 1918). New York, Klaw Th., Mar. 23, 1924 (concert
form); New York, Jolson Th., Mar. 25, 1928 (stage perf.).

Hob in the well. See FLORA, or Hob in the well.

Die HOCHZEIT DES CAMACHO (F. Mendelssohn-Bartholdy;
2 parts, German, Berlin 1827). Boston, Music Hall, Mar. 19, 1885,
in English, as "Camacho's wedding" (concert form; Cecilia Society).

HOLD THAT NOTE (W. C. Byrd; 1 act, American). *Philadelphia,
Mask and Wig Club, Dec. 10, 1954 (Co-Opera Company).

The HOLY DEVIL (N. Nabokob; 2 acts, American). *Louisville,
Ky., Columbia Auditorium, Apr. 16, 1958.

Der HOLZDIEB (H. Marschner; 1 act, German, Dresden 1825).
Rochester, N.Y., Eastman Th., May 27, 1935, in English, as "The
Poacher."

HOME, SWEET HOME! (H. R. Bishop; 2 acts, English, London
1829). New York, Park Th., May 25 (not 22), 1829.

The HONEST YORKSHIRE-MAN (H. Carey; 1 act, English,
London 1735). New York, Nassau Street Th., Mar. 4 (2?), 1752.

HONEYDEW (E. Zimbalist; 2 acts, American). *Stamford, Conn.,
Mar. 19, 1920 (New York, Casino Th., Sept. 6, 1920).

HOPITU (L. Albright; 1 act, American). *New York, Carnegie Hall,
Feb. 16, 1955.

HORUS (C. de Senez; 3 acts, Italian). *Philadelphia, Academy of
Music, Jan. 5, 1939.

HOSHI-SAN (W. Leps; 3 acts, American). *Philadelphia, Academy of
Music, May 21, 1909.

L'HOTELLERIE PORTUGAISE (L. Cherubini; 1 act, French, Paris
1798). San Francisco, War Memorial Op. H., Sept. 24, 1954, in
English, as "The Portuguese inn."

The HOUND OF HEAVEN (H. J. Stewart; scenic setting, American).
*San Francisco, Civic Auditorium, Apr. 24, 1924.

HRABINA (S. Moniuszko; 3 acts, Polish, Warsaw 1860). New York,
Manhattan Op. H., May 8, 1926.

HUBICKA (B. Smetana; 2 acts, Czech, Prague 1876). Chicago,
Blackstone Th., Apr. 17, 1921.

HUGH THE DROVER (R. Vaughan Williams; 2 acts, English, London
1924). Washington, D.C., Poli's Th., Feb. 21, 1928.

Les HUGUENOTS (G. Meyerbeer; 5 acts, French, Paris 1836). New
Orleans, Théâtre d'Orléans, Apr. 29, 1839.

HUNT THE SLIPPER (S. Arnold; 2 acts, English, London 1784).
New York, John Street Th., May 31, 1793.

The HUNTED (D. Gustafson; 1 act, American). *Greenville, S.C.,
Bob Jones Univ., May 26, 1960.

The HUNTED (M. Mailman; 1 act, American). *Rochester, N.Y.,
Eastman Th., Apr. 27, 1959.

The HUNTING OF THE SNARK (E. Laderman; 1 act, American).
*New York, Hunter College Assembly Hall, Mar. 25, 1961.

- I -

IDOMENEO (W. A. Mozart; 3 acts, Italian, Munich 1781). Tanglewood, Lenox, Mass., Theatre-Concert Hall (Berkshire Music Center),
Aug. 4, 1947.

IF MEN PLAYED CARDS AS WOMEN DO (C. Garland; 1 act,
American). *Chicago, American Conservatory of Music, May 22,
1952.

'ILE (B. Laufer; 1 act, American). *New York, Municipal Broadcasting
System (WNYC), Feb. 14, 1954 (radio perf.; tape); New York,
Brooklyn Museum, Apr. 28, 1957 (stage premiere).

L'ILE DE TULIPATAN (J. Offenbach; 1 act, French, Paris 1868).
--Louisville, Ky., Macauley's Th., Mar. 10, 1876, in English, as
"H. I. H. the Grand Duke, or The Island of Tulipatan."

ILLUSION FOR THREE (G. Muldoon; 2 acts, American). *San
Francisco, Contemporary Dancers Center, July 1, 1959.

The IMMORTAL HOUR (R. Boughton; 2 acts, English, Glastonbury,
England, 1914). New York, Grove Street Th., Apr. 6, 1926.

The IMPOSSIBLE FOREST (A. Wilder; American). *Westport,
Conn., White Barn Th., July 13, 1958.

The Impresario. See Der SCHAUSPIELDIREKTOR.

IN A GARDEN (M. Kupferman; 1 act, American). *New York, Finch
Junior College, Dec. 29, 1949.

IN PARADISE (H. Morris; 3 acts, American). *New York, Manhattan
School of Music (Act I; concert form).

IN THE NAME OF CULTURE (A. Bimboni; 1 act, American).
*Rochester, N.Y., Kilbourn Hall (Eastman School of Music), May 9,
1949.

IN THE PASHA'S GARDEN (J. L. Seymour; 1 act, American).
*New York, Metropolitan Op. H., Jan. 24, 1935.

L'INCANTESIMO (I. Montemezzi; 1 act, Italian). *New York,
National Broadcasting Company, Oct. 9, 1943 (radio perf.; stage
premiere, Verona 1951).

An Incomplete education. See Une EDUCATION
MANQUEE.

L'INCORONAZIONE DI POPPEA (C. Monteverdi; prolog and 2
acts, Italian, Venice 1642). Northampton, Mass., Academy of
Music, Apr. 27 (not 26), 1926 (Smith College).

Les INDES GALANTES (J. P. Rameau; prolog and 3 [later 4]
entrées, French, Paris 1735). New York, Town Hall, Mar. 1, 1961
(concert form).

The INDIAN PRINCESS (J. Bray; 3 acts, American). *Philadelphia, New [Chestnut Street] Th., Apr. 6, 1808.

The INFORMER (D. Sable; 1 act, American). *Columbus, O.,
Hughes Hall (Ohio State Univ.), Mar. 11, 1955.

L'INGANNO FELICE (G. Rossini; 1 act, Italian, Venice 1812).
New York, Bowery Th., May 11, 1833.

INKLE AND YARICO (S. Arnold; 3 acts, English, London 1787).
New York, John Street Th., July 6, 1789.

The Inspector general. See Der REVISOR.

The INTERRUPTED SERENADE (A. L. Scarmolin; 1 act,
American). Lindenhurst, L. I., N.Y., Lindenhurst High School
Auditorium, May 19, 1950.

INTERVALS   (D. Burge; 1 act, American).   *Evanston, Ill., Lutkin
    Hall (Northwestern Univ.), Nov. 13, 1962.
The INTRODUCTION   (R. R. Williams; 1 act, American).   *Green-
    castle, Ind., Speech Hall (De Pauw Univ.), Apr. 13, 1951.
INTRODUCTIONS AND GOODBYES   (L. Foss; 1 act, American).
    *New York, Carnegie Hall, May 6, 1960.
The INTRUDER   (R. Starer; 1 act, American).   *New York, Cherry
    Lane Th., Dec. 4, 1956.
The Involuntary thief.   See L'OCCASIONE FA IL LADRO.
IOLANTHE   (A. Sullivan; 2 acts, English, London 1882).   New York,
    Standard Th., Nov. 25, 1882 (same day with London premiere).
IOLANTHE   (P. Tchaikovsky; 1 act, Russian, St. Petersburg 1892).
    Scarborough-on-Hudson, Garden Th. (Sleepy Hollow Country Club),
    Sept. 10, 1933 (open-air perf.).
IONE   (E. Petrella; 4 acts, Italian, Milan 1858).   New York, Academy
    of Music, Apr. 6 (not Mar. 17), 1863.
IPHIGENIE EN AULIDE   (C. W. von Gluck; 3 acts, French, Paris
    1774).   Philadelphia, Academy of Music, Feb. 22, 1935.
IPHIGENIE EN TAURIDE   (C. W. von Gluck; 4 acts, French, Paris
    1779).   New York, Metropolitan Op. H., Nov. 25, 1916, in German;
    Poughkeepsie, N.Y., Skinner Recital Hall (Vassar College), Mar. 5,
    1938, in French (concert form).
L'IRATO   (E. Méhul; 1 act, French, Paris 1801).   New York, Brander
    Matthews Hall (Columbia Univ.), Feb. 6, 1947, in English, as "The
    Man with the terrible temper."
IRIS   (P. Mascagni; 3 acts, Italian, Rome 1898).   Philadelphia, Academy
    of Music, Oct. 14, 1902 (under the composer).
ISAAC LEVI   (F. Piket; 1 act, American).   * White Plains, N.Y.,
    Little Th. (Westchester Community Center), Dec. 11, 1955.
ISABEAU   (P. Mascagni; 3 acts, Italian, Buenos Aires 1911).   Chicago,
    Auditorium, Nov. 12, 1917.
Isidore de Merida.   See The PIRATES.
The ISLAND GOD   (G. C. Menotti; 1 act, American).   *New York,
    Metropolitan Op. H., Feb. 20, 1942.
L'ISOLA DISABITATA   (J. Haydn; 2 acts, Italian, Eszterhaz 1779).
    Washington, D.C., Elizabeth Sprague Coolidge Auditorium (Library
    of Congress), Mar. 9, 1936, in English, as "The Uninhabited
    island."
The ISRAELITES IN EGYPT   (M. R. Lacy; pasticcio, English,
    London 1833).   New York, Park Th., Oct. 31, 1842.
IT BEGAN AT BREAKFAST   (R. Elmore; 1 act, American).   *Phila-
    delphia, Bellevue-Stratford Hotel, Feb. 18, 1941.

L'ITALIANA IN ALGERI (G. Rossini; 2 acts, Italian, Venice 1813). New York, Richmond Hill Th., Nov. 5 (not 17), 1832.

L'ITALIANA IN LONDRA (D. Cimarosa; 2 acts, Italian, Rome 1778). New York, Hunter College Playhouse, May 25, 1955, in English, in one act, as "Love triumphant."

IVANHOE (G. Rossini; 3 acts, pasticcio, Italian, Paris 1826). New York, Park Th., Feb. 27, 1832, in English, as "The Maid of Judah" (M. R. Lacy's version 1829).

I'VE GOT THE TUNE (M. Blitzstein; musical play, American). * New York, Columbia Broadcasting System, Oct. 24, 1937 (radio perf.).

L'IVROGNE CORRIGE (C. W. von Gluck; 2 acts, French, Vienna 1760). Hartford, Conn., Hartt School of Music, Feb. 26, 1945, in English, as "The Marriage of the devil."

- J -

JACK AND THE BEANSTALK (L. Gruenberg; 3 acts, American). * New York, Juilliard School of Music, Nov. 19, 1931.

JACOB AND THE INDIANS (E. Laderman; 3 acts, American). * Woodstock, N.Y., Byrdcliffe Th., July 26, 1957.

JACQUELINE (J. Offenbach; 1 act, French, Paris 1862). --New York, Terrace Garden, Aug. 9, 1882, in German, as "Dorothea."

JACQUERIE (G. Marinuzzi; 3 acts, Italian, Buenos Aires 1918). Chicago, Auditorium, Nov. 17, 1920.

The JAILER (D. Gustafson; 1 act, American). * Greenville, S.C., Rodeheaver Auditorium (Bob Jones Univ.), May 27, 1954.

Le JARDINIER (E. Linden; 1 act, French-American). * New York, Princess Th., Jan. 31, 1916.

Der JA-SAGER (K. Weill; 2 acts, German, Berlin 1930). New York, Grand Street Playhouse, Apr. 25, 1933, in English.

JAUNIMO NUOTAIKA [The Humor of youth] (J. Bertulis; 1 act, Lithuanian-American). * Chicago, Jesuit Fathers House Hall, Mar. 12, 1961, in Lithuanian.

The Jealous husband. See Il GELOSO SCHERNITO.

JEAN DE PARIS (A. Boieldieu; 2 acts, French, Paris 1812). New York, Park Th., Nov. 25, 1816, in English, as "John of Paris;" New Orleans, Théâtre d'Orléans, 1819, in French.

JEAN LE SOT (A. Pilati; 1 act, French, Paris 1856). New York, Théâtre Français, Oct. 29, 1859.

JEANNE D'ARC AU BUCHER (A. Honegger; prolog and 11 scenes, dramatic oratorio, French, Basle 1938, in concert form; Zurich 1942, in German, in operatic form). New York, Carnegie Hall, Jan. 1,

1948, in French (concert form); San Francisco, War Memorial Op. H.,
Oct. 15, 1954, in English (stage perf.).

JEANNE QUI PLEURE ET JEAN QUI RIT (J. Offenbach; 1 act,
French, Ems 1864). --New Orleans, National Th., Dec. 15, 1871,
in German, as "Die Hanni weint und der Hansi lacht."

JEANNOT ET COLIN (N. Isouard; 3 acts, French, Paris 1814).
--New York, Park Th., Aug. 10, 1827 [New Orleans earlier (?)].

JENUFA [Jeji Pastorkyna] (L. Janáček; 3 acts, Czech, Brno
1904). New York, Metropolitan Op. H., Dec. 6, 1924, in German.

JEREMIAH (M. S. Fink; 4 acts, American). *Binghamton, N.Y.,
Harpur College Auditorium, May 25, 1962.

JERUSALEM (G. Verdi; 4 acts, French, Paris 1847). New Orleans,
Théâtre d'Orléans, Jan. 2, 1850.

JESSONDA (L. Spohr; 3 acts, German, Cassel 1823). Philadelphia,
Academy of Music, Feb. 15, 1864.

JESSY LEA (G. A. Macfarren; 2 acts, English, London 1863).
Williamsburgh, L.I., N.Y., Washington Hall, Oct. 8, 1868, as
"Jessie Lea."

Le JEU DE L'AMOUR ET DU HASARD (P. Petit; 1 act, French).
New York, Greenwich House Music School, May 26, 1953, in English,
as "Love is a game."

Le JEU DE ROBIN ET MARION (Adam de la Halle; French, Naples
ca. 1275 or 1285). Boston, Jordan Hall, Dec. 6, 1929, in English;
New York, Juilliard School of Music, Mar. 30, 1952, in English
(Milhaud's version). (Given in Quebec, Auditorium Th., May 24,
1928, in modern French, at the Canadian Folksong Festival.)

La JEUNE PRUDE (N. Dalayrac; 1 act, French, Paris 1804). --Phila-
delphia, Chestnut Street Th., Oct. 7, 1831 [New Orleans earlier (?)].

The JEWEL MERCHANTS (L. Cheslock; 1 act, American). *Baltimore, Peabody Conservatory of Music, Feb. 26, 1940.

The Jewels of the Madonna. See I GIOJELLI DELLA
MADONNA.

JOB (L. Dallapiccola; 1 act, "sacra rappresentazione," Italian, Rome
1950). New York, Juilliard School of Music, Dec. 19, 1958, in
English.

JOCONDE (N. Isouard; 3 acts, French, Paris 1814). --New York,
Park Th., July 27, 1827 [New Orleans earlier (?)].

JOHN BROWN'S BODY (W. Schumann; 2 acts, American). *Los
Angeles, Philharmonic Auditorium, Sept. 21, 1953.

John of Paris. See JEAN DE PARIS.

La JOLIE PARFUMEUSE (J. Offenbach; 3 acts, French, Paris 1873).
New York, Lyceum Th., Mar. 31, 1875.

Jonah (Carissimi). See GIONA.

Le JONGLEUR DE NOTRE DAME (J. Massenet; 3 acts, French,
Paris 1902). New York, Manhattan Op. H., Nov. 27, 1908.

JONNY SPIELT AUF (E. Krenek; 2 acts, German, Leipzig 1927).
New York, Metropolitan Op. H., Jan. 19, 1929.

JOSEPH (E. Mehul; 3 acts, French 1807). --Philadelphia, Chestnut
Street Th., Oct. 15, 1828 [New Orleans earlier (?)].

JUDGMENT DAY (P. Berl; 1 act, American). *New York, Hunter
College Playhouse, May 28, 1951.

JUDITH (R. N. C. Bochsa; 5 scenes, English). *New York, Astor
Place Op. H., Aug. 20, 1850.

JUDITH (G. W. Chadwick; 3 acts, dramatic oratorio, American).
*Worcester, Mass., Mechanics Hall, Sept. 26, 1901 (concert form).

JUDITH (E. Goossens; 1 act, English, London 1929). Philadelphia,
Academy of Music, Dec. 26, 1929.

JUDITH (A. Honegger; 3 acts, French, Monte Carlo 1926). Chicago,
Auditorium, Jan. 27, 1927.

JUGAR CON FUEGO (F. A. Barbieri; 3 acts, zarzuela, Madrid
1851). --San Francisco, Orpheum Th., Mar. 22, 1889.

Le JUGEMENT DE MIDAS (M. Grétry; 3 acts, French, Paris 1778).
New Orleans, Théâtre d'Orléans, June 11, 1808.

The JUGGLER (W. Graves; 1 act, American). *Washington, D.C.,
National Broadcasting Company (WNBC-TV), May 3, 1959 (TV
perf.; tape; Catholic Univ.).

The JUGGLER OF OUR LADY (U. Kay; 1 act, American). *New
Orleans, Xavier Univ. Auditorium, Feb. 23, 1962.

La JUIVE (F. Halévy; 5 acts, French, Paris 1835). New Orleans,
Théâtre d'Orléans, Feb. 13, 1844.

JULIEN (G. Charpentier; prolog and 4 acts, French, Paris 1913).
New York, Metropolitan Op. H., Feb. 26, 1914.

Julius Caesar (Handel). See GIULIO CESARE.

The JUMPING FROG OF CALAVERAS COUNTY (L. Foss;
1 act, American). *Bloomington, Ind., East Hall (Indiana Univ.),
May 18, 1950.

JUNIPERO SERRA (W. Hively; American). *Palma, Majorca,
Teatro Principal, Mar. 28, 1956, in Spanish.

El JURAMENTO (J. Gaztambide; 3 acts, zarzuela, Spanish, Madrid
1858). --Tucson, Levin's Hall, Aug. 16, 1884.

JUSTINA (J. Clemens; American). *Philadelphia, Walnut Street Th.,
May 18, 1830.

KAINTUCKEE (C. E. Eppert; 1 act, American). *North Yakima, Wash., North Yakima Th., Dec. 29, 1916.

Kakadu. See VERT-VERT.

KATINKA (R. Friml; 3 acts, American). *Morristown, N.J., Park Th., Dec. 2, 1915 (New York, 44th Street Th., Dec. 23, 1915).

KATYA KABANOVA (L. Janáček; 3 acts, Czech, Brno 1921). Cleveland, Karamu House, Nov. 26, 1957, in English (amateur); Harriman State Park, Bear Mountain, N.Y., Anthony Wayne Recreation Area, Aug. 2, 1960, in English (professional).

KATYDIDS (L. A. Nowak; 2 acts, American). *Piermont, N.Y., Lyric Th., July 26, 1962.

A KEKSZAKALLU HERCEG VARA [Bluebeard's Castle] (B. Bartok; 1 act, Hungarian, Budapest 1918). Dallas, Fair Park Auditorium, Jan. 8, 1946, in English, as "Prince Bluebeard's castle" (concert form; Dallas Symphony Orch.); New York, City Center, Oct. 2, 1952, in English, as "Bluebeard's castle" (stage perf.).

KHOVANTCHINA (M. Moussorgsky; 5 acts, Russian, St. Petersburg, 1886). Philadelphia, Metropolitan Op. H., Apr. 18, 1928, in English; New York, Mecca Temple Auditorium, Mar. 7, 1931, in Russian.

The KING AND I (R. Rodgers; 2 acts, American). *New Haven, Conn., Shubert Th., Feb. 27, 1951 (New York, St. James Th., Mar. 29, 1951; 1,246 perf.).

KING ARTHUR (H. Purcell; prolog, 5 acts and epilog, English, London 1691). New York, Park Th., Apr. 25 (not 24), 1800.

A King for a day (Adam). See SI J'ETAIS ROI.

A King for a day (Verdi). See Un GIORNO DI REGNO.

KING HARALD (E. Anders; 3 acts, American). *New York, Hunter College Playhouse, Jan. 7, 1948.

KING RENE'S DAUGHTER (J. Edwards; 1 act, American). *New York, Herrmann's Th., Nov. 23, 1893.

KING SOLOMON (J. H. Brown; 1 act, American). *Cleveland, Karamu House, Sept. 28, 1951.

King Theodore in Venice. See Il RE TEODORO IN VENEZIA.

KINGDOM COME (W. Mason; 1 act, American). *Boone, N.C., Administration Hall (Appalachian State Teachers College), Aug. 17, 1953.

The KING'S HENCHMAN (D. Taylor; 3 acts, American). *New York, Metropolitan Op. H., Feb. 17, 1927.

KISMET   (R. Wright and G. Forrest; 2 acts, American). * Los Angeles,
Philharmonic Auditorium, Aug. 17, 1953 (New York, Ziegfeld Th.,
Dec. 3, 1953; 583 perf.).

KISS ME KATE   (C. Porter; 2 acts, American). * Philadelphia,
Shubert Th., Dec. 2, 1948 (New York, Century Th., Dec. 30, 1948;
1,077 perf.).

Kitezh.   See The LEGEND OF THE INVISIBLE CITY OF
KITEZH AND THE MAIDEN FEVRONIA.

KITTIWAKE ISLAND   (A. Wilder; 2 acts, American). * Interlochen,
Mich., National Music Camp, Aug. 7, 1954.

Die KLUGE   (C. Orff; 1 act, German, Frankfurt a.M. 1943). Cleveland, Karamu House, Dec. 7, 1949, in English, as "The Wise
maiden" (amateur cast); San Francisco, War Memorial Op. H., Oct.
3, 1958, in English (professional cast).

KNICKERBOCKER HOLIDAY   (K. Weill; 2 acts, American).
* Hartford, Conn., Horace Bushnell Memorial Hall, Sept. 24, 1938
(New York, Ethel Barrymore Th., Oct. 19, 1938).

The Knight of Quadalquiver.   See The SPANISH CASTLE.

Die KOENIGIN VON SABA   (C. Goldmark; 4 acts, German, Vienna
1875). New York, Metropolitan Op. H., Dec. 2, 1885.

Die KOENIGSKINDER   (E. Humperdinck; 3 acts, German). * New
York, Metropolitan Op. H., Dec. 28, 1910.

Der KOSAK UND DER FREYWILLIGE   (J. Braun; 1 act, German,
Kinigsberg 1825). Philadelphia, New [Chestnut Street] Th., Feb. 7,
1828, in English, as "The Cossak and the volunteer."

KUAN YIN   (A. Avshalomov; Chinese, Pekin 1925). New York,
Neighborhood Playhouse, Mar. 16, 1925, in Chinese.

Der KUHREIGEN   (W. Kienzl; 3 acts, German Vienna 1911).
Philadelphia, Metropolitan Op. H., Feb. 21, 1913, in French, as
"Le Ranz des vaches."

- L -

Le LAC DES FEES   (D. Auber; 5 acts, French, Paris 1839). New
York, Olympic Th., Dec. 1, 1845, in English, as "The Fairies'
Lake."

I Ladroni.   See The CONTRABANDISTA.

LADY IN THE DARK   (K. Weill; 2 acts, American). * Boston,
Colonial Th., Dec. 30, 1940 (New York, Alvin Th., Jan. 23, 1941).

LADY MACBETH OF MZENSK   (D. Shostakovich; 4 acts, Russian,
Moscow 1934). Cleveland, Severance Hall, Jan. 31, 1935.

A Lady to raffle.   See Une DEMOISELLE EN LOTERIE.

La LAITIERE DE TRIANON (J. B. Weckerlin; 1 act, French, Paris 1858). --New York, Hotel Sherry, Mar. 7, 1911.

LAKME (L. Delibes; 3 acts, French, Paris 1883). Chicago, Grand Op. H., Oct. 4, 1883, in English; New York, Metropolitan Op. H., Feb. 22, 1892, in French.

LAMPLIGHT (J. Kern; 1 act, American). *New York, Mutual Broadcasting System, Aug. 25, 1941 (radio perf.).

The LAND BETWEEN THE RIVERS (C. Van Buskirk; 2 acts, American). *Bloomington, Ind., East Hall (Indiana Univ.), May 18, 1956.

LANDARA (E. Zimbalist; 3 acts, American). *Philadelphia, Academy of Music, Apr. 6, 1956.

LANZELOT (R. L. Herman; 3 acts, German-American). *Braunschweig, Hoftheater, Oct. 25, 1891, in German.

The Last of the Mohicans. See L'ULTIMO DEI MOICANI.

The LAUNCH (V. Pelissier; 1 act, American). *Boston, Haymarket Th., Sept. 20, 1797.

The LEGEND (J. C. Breil; 1 act, American). *New York, Metropolitan Op. H., Mar. 12, 1919.

The LEGEND OF RONSARD AND MADELON (M. W. Belcher; 2 acts, American). *Cleveland, Cleveland Art Museum, June 1918 (Mather College, Western Reserve Univ.).

The LEGEND OF SLEEPY HOLLOW (J. D. White; 3 acts, American). *Kent, O., Stump Th. (Kent State Univ.), Feb. 28, 1962.

A LEGEND OF SPAIN (E. E. Freer; 1 act, American). *Milwaukee, Marwood Studios, June 19, 1931 (concert form).

The LEGEND OF THE INVISIBLE CITY OF KITEZH AND THE MAIDEN FEVRONIA (N. Rimsky-Korsakov; 4 acts, Russian, St. Petersburg 1907). Ann Arbor, Mich., Hill Auditorium (Univ. of Michigan), May 21, 1932, in English (concert form); Philadelphia, Academy of Music, Feb. 4, 1936 (stage perf.).

The LEGEND OF THE PIPER (E. E. Freer; 1 act, American). *South Bend, Ind., Feb. 24 (not 28), 1925 (Progress Club).

The LEGEND OF WIWASTE (S. E. Blakeslee; American). *Ontario, Cal., Chaffey Junior College, Apr. 25, 1924.

Die LEGENDE VON DER HEILIGEN ELISABETH (F. Liszt; prolog and 4 scenes, oratorio, German, Pest 1865, in Hungarian, in concert form; Weimar 1881, in German, in operatic form). New York, Liederkranz Halle, Nov. 13, 1870 (concert form); New York, Metropolitan Op. H., Jan. 3, 1918 (stage perf.).

LEICHTE KAVALLERIE (F. von Suppé; 1 act, German, Vienna
1866). New York, Stadt Theater, Oct. 1, 1868.
LEIF ERIKSON (G. Tonning; 3 acts, Norwegian-American). *Seattle,
Moore Th., Dec. 10, 1910, in Norwegian.
LEON UND EDRITA (C. L. Flick-Steger; 4 acts, German-American).
*Krefeld, Stadttheater, Jan. 6, 1936, in German.
LEONCE UND LENA (E. Zeisl; 3 acts, German, Prague 1937). Los
Angeles College Auditorium, May 16, 1952, in English.
LEONORA (W. H. Fry; 3 acts, American). *Philadelphia, Chestnut
Street Th., June 4, 1845.
LESTOCQ (D. Auber; 4 acts, French, Paris 1834). New Orleans,
Théâtre d'Orléans, Feb. 10, 1835.
LET'S MAKE AN OPERA (B. Britten; 2 acts, English, Aldeburgh,
England, 1949). St. Louis, Kiel Auditorium, Mar. 22, 1950 (Music
Educators National Conference).
A LETTER TO EMILY (L. Johnson; 1 act, American). *Seattle,
Cornish School Th., Apr. 22, 1951.
La LETTRE DE CHANGE (R. N. C. Bochsa; 1 act, French, Paris
1815). New York, Park Th., Sept. 29, 1820, in English, as "The
Promissory note;" New York, Park Th., July 20, 1827, in French
[New Orleans earlier (?)].
Letty. See The DEVIL'S IN IT.
La LEYENDA DEL BESO (R. Soutullo Otero and J. Vert y Carbonell;
zarzuela, Spanish). New York, Cosmopolitan Th., Nov. 19, 1942.
The Libertine. See DON GIOVANNI.
A LIFE FOR THE CZAR (M. Glinka; 4 acts and epilog, Russian,
St. Petersburg 1836). New York, Steinway Hall, Nov. 14, 1871,
in Russian (fourteen excerpts; concert form); San Francisco, Veterans'
Auditorium, Dec. 12, 1936, in Russian (stage perf.).
A LIGHT FROM ST. AGNES (W. F. Harling; 1 act, American).
*Chicago, Auditorium, Dec. 26, 1925.
LILI-TSEE (F. Curti; 1 act, German, Mannheim 1896). New York,
Daly's Th., Feb. 17, 1898, in English.
The LILY OF KILLARNEY (J. Benedict; 3 acts, English, London
1862). Philadelphia, Academy of Music, Nov. 20, 1867.
LINDA (R. M. Fiore; 1 act, American). *Philadelphia, Society Hill
Playhouse, Mar. 13, 1961.
LINDA DI CHAMOUNIX (G. Donizetti; 3 acts, Italian, Vienna
1842). New York, Palmo's Op. H., Jan. 4 (not 2), 1847.
The LION (Arnold Franchetti; 2 acts, American). *New London,
Buell Hall (Williams Memorial Institute), Dec. 16, 1950.
LIONEL AND CLARISSA (C. Dibdin; 3 acts, English, London, 1768).
Philadelphia, Southwark Th., Dec. 14, 1772, as "The School for

fathers."

LISCHEN ET FRITZCHEN   (J. Offenbach; 1 act, French, Ems 1863).
--New York, Academy of Music, June 25, 1868.

LITTLE JO   (J. D. Robb; American). *Albuquerque, Albuquerque
Little Th., Jan. 18, 1950.

The Little match girl.   See PIGEN MED SVOVLSTIK-
KERNE.

The LITTLE PRINCE   (F. G. Parmentier; 1 act, American). *San
Francisco, Contemporary Dancers Center, Apr. 1, 1959.

The LOAFER AND THE LOAF   (H. L. Clarke; 1 act, American).
*Los Angeles, Schoenberg Hall (Univ. of California), May 1, 1956.

LOBETANZ   (L. Thuille; 3 acts, German, Carlsruhe 1898). New York,
Metropolitan Op. H., Nov. 18 (not 17), 1911.

The LOCK AND KEY   (W. Shield; 2 acts, English, London 1796).
Hartford, Conn., New Th., July 7, 1796.

LODOISKA   (S. Storace; 3 acts, English, London 1794). --Boston,
Boston [Federal Street] Th., Mar. 2, 1806.

LODOLETTA   (P. Mascagni; 3 acts, Italian, Rome 1917). New York,
Metropolitan Op. H., Jan. 12, 1918.

LOHENGRIN   (R. Wagner; 3 acts, German, Weimar 1850). New York,
Stadt Theater, Apr. 3, 1871.

I LOMBARDI   (G. Verdi; 4 acts, Italian, Milan 1843). New York,
Palmo's Op. H., Mar. 3, 1847 (first Verdi opera in the United States).

The LONG WAY   (A. Wilder; 2 parts, American). *Nyack, N. Y.,
Nyack High School Auditorium, June 3, 1955 (Rockland Lyric Theater).

LORD BYRON'S LOVE LETTER   (R. De Banfield; 1 act, American).
*New Orleans, Dixon Hall (Newcomb Memorial College, Tulane
Univ.), Jan. 17, 1955.

LORELEY   (A. Catalani; 3 acts, Italian, Turin 1890). Chicago, Auditorium, Jan. 17, 1919.

LORENZACCIO   (E. Moret; 4 acts, French, Paris 1920). Chicago,
Civic Op. H., Oct. 27, 1930.

The LOTUS TREE   (W. Prunty; American). *Morgantown, W. Va.,
May 13, 1960.

LOUIS XIV   (H. Moore; 3 acts, American). *St. Louis, Odeon, Feb.
16, 1917.

LOUISE   (G. Charpentier; 4 acts, French, Paris 1900). New York, Manhattan Op. H., Jan. 3, 1908.

The LOVE FOR THREE ORANGES   (S. Prokofiev; prolog and 4
acts, Russian). *Chicago, Auditorium, Dec. 30, 1921, in French,
as "L'Amour des trois oranges."

LOVE IN A CAMP   (W. Shield; 2 acts, English, London 1786). New
York, John Street Th., Apr. 9, 1787.

LOVE IN A VILLAGE   (T. A. Arne; 3 acts, English, London 1762).
Charleston, S.C., New [Queen Street] Th., Feb. 10, 1766.
Love is a game. See Le JEU DE L'AMOUR ET DU
HASARD.
LOVE LAUGHS AT LOCKSMITHS   (J. C. Breil; 1 act, American).
*Kingston, N.Y., Kingston Op. H., Oct. 26, 1910.
LOVE LAUGHS AT LOCKSMITHS   (M. Kelly; 2 acts, English,
London 1803). New York, Park Th., May 23, 1804.
The Love of three kings. See L'AMORE DEI TRE RE.
Love triumphant. See L'ITALIANA IN LONDRA.
A LOVER'S KNOT   (S. Buchhalter; 1 act, American). *Evanston,
Ill., July 15, 1915 (privately; concert form); Chicago, Auditorium,
Jan. 15 (not 16), 1916 (stage premiere).
A Lover's quarrel. See I DISPETTOSI AMANTI.
LOVE'S SACRIFICE   (G. W. Chadwick; 1 act, American). --Chicago,
Playhouse, Feb. 1, 1923.
The LOWLAND SEA   (A. Wilder; 1 act, American). *Montclair,
N.J., Hillside Junior High School Auditorium, May 8, 1952 (Mont-
clair State Teachers College).
LUCEDIA   (V. Giannini; prolog and 3 acts, American). *Munich,
Nationaltheater, Oct. 20, 1934, in German.
El LUCERO DEL ALBA   (M. Fernández Caballero; 1 act, zarzuela,
Spanish). New York, 63rd Street Music Hall, Feb. 13, 1921.
LUCIA DI LAMMERMOOR   (G. Donizetti; 3 acts, Italian, Naples
1835). New Orleans, Théâtre d'Orléans, Dec. 28, 1841, in French;
New Orleans, St. Charles Th., Feb. 27, 1842, in Italian.
LUCILLE   (S. G. Pratt; 5 acts, American). *Chicago, Columbia Th.,
Mar. 14 (not 4), 1887.
LUCREZIA BORGIA   (G. Donizetti; 3 acts, Italian, Milan 1834).
New Orleans, Théâtre d'Orléans, Apr. 27, 1844, in Italian.
LUISA FERNANDA   (F. M. Torroba; 3 acts, zarzuela, Spanish,
Madrid 1931). New York, Hunter College Assembly Hall, Dec. 16,
1956, in Spanish (semi-staged).
LUISA MILLER   (G. Verdi; 3 acts, Italian, Naples 1849). Philadelphia,
Walnut Street Th., Oct. 27, 1852, in English; New York, Castle
Garden, July 20, 1854, in Italian.
LULLY ET QUINAULT   (N. Isouard; 1 act, French, Paris 1812).
New Orleans, Théâtre d'Orléans, ca. 1820-25 (New York, Park Th.,
Sept. 1, 1827).
LURLINE   (W. V. Wallace; 3 acts, English, London 1869). Cambridge,
Mass., City Hall, June 1, 1863 (concert form); New York, Academy
of Music, May 13, 1869 (stage perf.).

Der LUSTIGE KRIEG (J. Strauss; 3 acts, German, Vienna 1881).
New York, Thalia Theater, Mar. 15, 1882.

Die LUSTIGE WITWE (F. Lehar; 3 acts, German, Vienna 1905).
New York, Zum Weissen Ross'l, and The Orpheum, Dec. 1907, in
German (unauthorized and truncated versions); Syracuse, N. Y.,
Wieting Op. H., Sept. 23, 1907, in English, as "The Merry widow"
(New York, Amsterdam Th., Oct. 21, 1907); New York, Irving
Place Th., June 7, 1911, in Italian, as "La Vedova allegra;" New
York, Irving Place Th., Nov. 15, 1911, in German.

Die LUSTIGEN WEIBER VON WINDSOR (O. Nicolai; 3 acts,
German, Berlin 1849). Philadelphia, Academy of Music, Mar. 16,
1863.

LYNEIA (W. C. Byrd; 2 acts, American). *Cincinnati, Wilbur Auditorium (Univ. of Cincinnati), Jan. 20, 1949.

- M -

MA TANTE AURORE (A. Boieldieu; 2 acts, French, Paris 1803).
New Orleans, Théâtre St. Phillippe, 1810.

MACBETH (E. Bloch; prolog and 3 acts, French, Paris 1910). Cleveland, Karamu House, Mar. 19, 1957, in English.

MACBETH (G. Verdi; 4 acts, Italian, Florence 1847). New York,
Niblo's Garden, Apr. 24, 1850.

Die MACCABAEER (A. Rubinstein; 3 acts, German, Berlin 1875).
New York, Educational Alliance, Dec. 1902, in Russian (Act III;
concert form).

Le MACON (D. Auber; 3 acts, French, Paris 1825). --New York,
Park Th., July 31 (not Aug. 3), 1827 [New Orleans earlier (?)].

MADAMA BUTTERFLY (G. Puccini; 3 acts, Italian, Milan 1904 in
2 acts; Brescia 1904 in 3 acts). Washington, D.C., Columbia Th.,
Oct. 15, 1906, in English; New York, Metropolitan Op. H., Feb. 11,
1907, in Italian.

MME. BUTTERFLY RECOVERS (L. Kroll; 1 act, American).
*New York, Pleasant Little Th., May 20, 1934.

MADAME CHRYSANTHEME (J. Massenet; prolog, 4 acts and epilog,
French, Paris 1893). Chicago, Auditorium, Jan. 19, 1920. (Given
in Quebec, Auditorium Th., Feb. 2, 1912.)

MADAME FAVART (J. Offenbach; 3 acts, French, Paris 1878).
New York, Park Th., May 12, 1879.

MADAME L'ARCHIDUC (J. Offenbach; 3 acts, French, Paris 1874).
New York, Lyceum Th., Dec. 29, 1874, in English; New York,
Lyceum Th., Sept. 6, 1875, in French.

MADAME SANS-GENE (U. Giordano; 4 acts, Italian). *New York, Metropolitan Op. H., Jan. 25, 1915.

MADAME SHERRY (C. L. Hoschna; 3 acts, American). *Blooming-ton, Ind., Chatterton Op. H., Apr. 7, 1910 (New York, New Amster-dam Th., Aug. 30, 1910).

MADELEINE (V. Herbert; 1 act, American). *New York, Metropoli-tan Op. H., Jan. 24, 1914.

MLLE. MODISTE (V. Herbert; 2 acts, American). *Trenton, Taylor Op. H., Oct. 7, 1905 (New York, Knickerbocker Th., Dec. 25, 1905).

MADONNA IMPERIA (F. Alfano; 1 act, Italian, Turin 1927). New York, Metropolitan Op. H., Feb. 8, 1928.

Il Maestro di cappella. See Le MAITRE DE CHAPELLE.

Il MAESTRO DI MUSICA (G. Pergolesi; 1 act, Italian, Naples 1731). Boston, Jordan Hall, May 20, 1936. (Loewenberg states: "revived in English by Columbia University students, New York, 17. iv. 1936;" on that day the Columbia University Symphonic Band played a concert.)

MAGDALENA (H. Villa-Lobos; 2 acts, American). *Los Angeles, Philharmonic Auditorium, July 26, 1948 (New York, Ziegfeld Th., Sept. 20, 1948).

MAGGIO FIORENTINO (E. Stramiello; 2 acts, Italian-American). *New York, (Brooklyn) Academy of Music, Apr. 29, 1940, in Italian.

The MAGIC MIRROR (W. Beckett; 3 acts, American). *Newark, N.J., Mosque Th., Apr. 27, 1955.

MAID MARIAN (H. R. Bishop; 3 acts, English, London 1822). New York, Park Th., Jan. 9, 1824.

The MAID OF ARTOIS (M. W. Balfe; 3 acts, English, London 1836). New York, Park Th., Nov. 5, 1847.

The MAID OF PSKOV (N. Rimsky-Korsakov; 4 acts, Russian, St. Petersburg 1873; Moscow 1898). [According to Baker, 4. and 5. eds., the prolog "Boyarynia Vera Sheloga" was performed in New York, May 9, 1922; on that day a touring Russian company gave the composer's opera "The Czar's Bride" at the New Amsterdam Th.]

The MAID OF SAXONY (C. E. Horn: 3 acts, American). *New York, Park Th., May 23, 1842.

The MAID OF THE MILL (S. Arnold; 3 acts, English, London 1765). New York, John Street Th., May 4, 1769.

The Maiden of Elizondo. See PEPITO.

Die MAIENKOENIGIN (C. W. von Gluck; 1 act, pasticcio, German, Vienna 1888). Philadelphia, Metropolitan Op. H., Dec. 1, 1927.

MAISON A VENDRE (N. Dalayrac; 1 act, French, Paris 1800). New York, Park Th., May 25, 1803, in English, as "A House to be sold" (M. Kelly's London version 1802); --New York, Park Th., July 13, 1827, in French [New Orleans earlier (?)].

La MAISON EN LOTERIE (A. Piccinni; 1 act, French, Paris 1820). --New York, Park Th., July 31 (not Aug. 3), 1827 [New Orleans earlier (?)].

Le MAITRE DE CHAPELLE (F. Paer; 2 acts, French, Paris 1821). --New York, Castle Garden, July 16, 1849 [New Orleans earlier (?)].

La MALA SOMBRA (J. Serrano; 1 act, zarzuela, Spanish). New York, 63rd Street Music Hall, Feb. 6, 1921.

The MALADY OF LOVE (L. Engel; 1 act, American). *New York, Brander Matthews Hall (Columbia Univ.), May 27, 1954.

The MALATROIT DOOR (S. Barab; 1 act, American). *New York, Hunter College Playhouse, Jan. 28, 1960.

Les MALHEURS D'ORPHEE (D. Milhaud; 3 acts, French, Brussels 1926). New York, Town Hall, Jan. 29, 1927 (concert form); New York, Hunter College Playhouse, May 22, 1958 (stage perf.).

Les MAMELLES DE TIRESIAS (F. Poulenc; prolog and 2 acts, French, Paris 1947). Waltham, Mass., Ullman Amphitheatre (Brandeis Univ.), June 13, 1953, in English.

MAMZELLE FIGARO (P. H. Allen; 1 act, American). *Lindenhurst, L.I., N.Y., Lindenhurst Junior-Senior High School, May 20, 1948.

The Man in the moon. See Il MONDO DELLA LUNA.

The MAN WITHOUT A COUNTRY (W. Damrosch; 2 acts, American). *New York, Metropolitan Op. H., May 12, 1937.

MANABOZO (T. W. Lester; 3 acts, American). *Chicago, Mar. 26, 1930 (excerpts; privately); Chicago, Curtis Hall, Feb. 17, 1931 (excerpts; concert form).

MANDRAGOLA (I. Waghalter; 3 acts, German, Berlin 1914). New York, Princess Th., Mar. 4, 1925, in English.

MANON (J. Massenet; 4 acts, French, Paris 1884). New York, Academy of Music, Dec. 23, 1885, in Italian; New Orleans, French Op. H., Jan. 4, 1894, in French.

MANON LESCAUT (G. Puccini; 4 acts, Italian, Turin 1893). Philadelphia, Grand Op. H., Aug. 29, 1894.

MANRU (I. Paderewski; 3 acts, German, Dresden 1901). New York, Metropolitan Op. H., Feb. 14, 1902.

La MARCHA DE CADIZ (J. Valverde and R. Estellès; 1 act, zarzuela, Spanish, Madrid 1902). --San Francisco, 1918.

MARCO BOZZARIS (P. Carrer; Greek-Italian, Athens 1858).
--Chicago, ca. 1938 (under the auspices of St. Basil Hellenic
Orthodox Church); Chicago, Civic Op. H., Jan. 21, 1940 (semi-
staged scenes).

MARDI GRAS (M. Kayden; 1 act, American). *New York, Municipal
Broadcasting System, May 22, 1958 (radio perf.).

Le MARECHAL FERRANT (F. Philidor; 1 act, French, Paris 1761).
Boston, New Exhibition Room, Mar. 25, 1783, in English, as "The
Blacksmith."

MARGUERITE D'ANJOU (G. Meyerbeer; 3 acts, French, Paris 1826).
New Orleans, Théâtre d'Orléans, Apr. 17, 1854.

Un MARI A LA PORTE (J. Offenbach; 1 act, French, Paris 1859).
--New York, Stadt Theater, May 15, 1867, in German, as "Der
Ehemann vor der Thür."

MARIA DI ROHAN (G. Donizetti; 3 acts, Italian, Vienna 1843).
New York, Astor Place Op. H., Dec. 10, 1849.

MARIA GOLOVIN (G. C. Menotti; 3 acts, American). *Brussels,
United States Pavilion (Brussels World's Fair), Aug. 20, 1958 (New
York, Martin Beck Th., Nov. 5, 1958).

MARIA MALIBRAN (R. R. Bennett; 3 acts, American). *New York,
Juilliard School of Music, Apr. 8, 1935.

Le MARIAGE AUX LANTERNES (J. Offenbach; 1 act, French,
Paris 1857). --New York, Stadt Theater, Mar. 18, 1860, in German,
as "Die Verlobung beim Laternenscheine;" New York, Théâtre
Français, Feb. 6, 1864, in French.

MARIAN (W. Shield; English, London 1788). Philadelphia, New
[Chestnut Street] Th., Apr. 21, 1798.

MARIE (L. Hérold; 3 acts, French, Paris 1826). --New York, Park Th.,
Aug. 18, 1829 [New Orleans earlier (?)].

MARINA (E. Arrieta; 3 acts, Spanish, Madrid 1855 in 2 acts; Madrid
1871 in 3 acts). New York, Lyceum Th., Nov. 8, 1875 (juvenile
cast); San Francisco, Orpheum Th., Feb. 1889 (adult cast).

MARINO FALIERO (G. Donizetti; 3 acts, Italian, Paris 1835).
New Orleans, St. Charles Th., Feb. 22, 1842, in Italian.

Les MARIS GARCONS (H. M. Berton; 1 act, French, Paris 1806).
--New York, Park Th., Oct. 26, 1827 [New Orleans earlier (?)].

MARITANA (W. V. Wallace; 3 acts, English, London 1845). Philadelphia, Walnut Street Th., Nov. 9, 1846.

The MARK OF KINGS (G. Wehner; 1 act, American). *New York,
Central Park Mall, June 24, 1961.

MAROUF (H. Rabaud; 5 acts, French, Paris 1914). New York,
Metropolitan Op. H., Dec. 19, 1917.

The MARRIAGE (B. Martinu; 1 act, Czech). *New York, National Broadcasting Company, Feb. 7, 1953, in English (TV perf.).

The MARRIAGE OF AUDE (B. Rogers; 1 act, American). *Rochester, N.Y., Eastman Th., May 22, 1932 (Eastman School of Music).

The Marriage of the devil. See L'IVROGNE CORRIGE.

MARTHA (F. von Flotow; 4 acts, German, Vienna 1847). New York, Niblo's Garden, Nov. 1, 1852, in English; Niblo's Garden, Mar. 13, 1855, in German.

The MARTYR (H. L. Freeman; 2 acts, American). *Denver, Deutsches Theater, Sept. 1893, in English (New York, Carnegie Hall, Sept. 21, 1947).

Le MARTYRE DE SAINT SEBASTIEN (C. Debussy; 5 acts, French, Paris 1911). New York, Carnegie Hall, Feb. 12, 1912 (excerpts; concert form; MacDowell Chorus); Boston, Boston Op. H., Mar. 30, 1912 (stage perf.).

Les MARTYRS (G. Donizetti; 4 acts, French, Paris 1840). New Orleans, Théâtre d'Orléans, Mar. 24, 1846.

MARUXA (A. Vives; 2 acts, Spanish, Madrid 1914). --Tampa, Fla., Centro Asturiano, Feb. 1919.

La MASCOTTE (E. Audran; 3 acts, French, Paris 1880). Boston, Gaiety Th., Apr. 11 (not 12), 1881, in English; New York, Park Th., Nov. 30, 1881, in French.

The MASK MAKER (O. Shimizu; Japanese, Tokyo 1954). Los Angeles, Schonberg Hall (Univ. of California), Apr. 6, 1962, in Japanese.

I MASNADIERI (G. Verdi; 4 acts, Italian, London 1847). New York, Winter Garden, May 31 (not 30, or June 2), 1860.

The Masque of Alfred. See ALFRED.

MASSIMILLIANO (E. E. Freer; 1 act, American). *Lincoln, Neb., Temple Th., Jan. 18, 1926.

Master Peter's puppet show. See El RETABLE DE MAESE PEDRO.

The MASTER THIEF (G. B. Williams; 3 acts, American). *Pasadena, Pasadena Community Playhouse, Nov. 28, 1933.

The MASTERPIECE (P. Nordoff; 1 act, American). *Philadelphia, Town Hall, Jan. 24, 1941.

MATASWINTHA (X. Scharwenka; 4 acts, German, Weimar 1896). New York, Chickering Hall, Feb. 13, 1896 (excerpts; concert form, before Weimar premiere); New York, Metropolitan Op. H., Apr. 1, 1907 (stage perf.).

MATHIS DER MALER (P. Hindemith; 7 scenes, German, Zurich 1938). Boston, University Th. (Boston Univ.), Feb. 17, 1956, in English.

A MATINEE IDYLL (H. Forrest; American). *Interlochen, Mich., National Music Camp, Aug. 17, 1954.

Il MATRIMONIO SEGRETO (D. Cimarosa; 2 acts, Italian, Vienna 1792). New York, Italian Op. H., Jan. 4 (not 6), 1834.

MATTEO FALCONE (H. Zöllner; 1 act, German-American). *New York, Irving Place Th., Dec. 18, 1893, in German.

MAVRA (I. Stravinsky; 1 act, Russian, Paris 1922 in French). Philadelphia, Academy of Music, Dec. 28, 1934, in English.

MAY DAY (R. Taylor; American). *Philadelphia, Vauxhall Garden, May 23, 1815 (amateur cast).

MAYERLING (H. S. Humphrey; 3 acts, American). *Cincinnati, Robert A. Taft High School, Nov. 16, 1957 (College-Conservatory of Music of Cincinnati).

The MAYPOLE (Arnold Franchetti; 1 act, American). *Westport, Conn., White Barn Th., July 6, 1952.

MAYTIME (S. Romberg; 4 acts, American). *Stamford, Conn., Stamford Th., Aug. 7, 1917 (New York, Shubert Th., Aug. 17, 1917).

MAZEPPA (P. Tchaikovsky; 3 acts, Russian, Moscow 1884). Boston, Boston Op. H., Dec. 14, 1922.

Medea (Cherubini). See MEDEE.

MEDEA (R. Di Giovanni; 2 acts, American). *New York, Brooklyn Museum, Feb. 13, 1955.

MEDEA (H. Farberman; 1 act, American). *Boston, Boston Conservatory, Mar. 26, 1961.

MEDEA (G. Pacini; 3 acts, Italian, Palermo 1843). New York, Niblo's Garden, Sept. 27, 1860.

Le MEDECIN MALGRE LUI (C. Gounod; 3 acts, French, Paris 1858). --Cincinnati, Odeon, Mar. 20, 1900, in English, as "The Mock doctor" (Cincinnati College of Music).

MEDEE (L. Cherubini; 3 acts, French, Paris 1797). New York, Town Hall, Nov. 8, 1955, in Italian, as "Medea" (concert form); San Francisco, War Memorial Op. H., Sept. 12, 1958, in Italian (stage perf.).

The MEDIUM (G. C. Menotti; 2 acts, American). *New York, Brander Matthews Hall (Columbia Univ.), May 8, 1946 (student cast); New York, Ethel Barrymore Th., May 1, 1947 (professional cast).

The MEETING   (J. Meyerowitz; 1 act [Originally Act II of his "Eastward in Eden, " q. v.], American). *Falmouth, Mass., Falmouth
Playhouse, Sept. 16, 1955.

MEFISTOFELE   (A. Boito; prolog, 4 acts and epilog, Italian, Milan
1868). Boston, Globe Th., Nov. 16, 1880, in English; New York,
Academy of Music, Nov. 24, 1880, in Italian.

Die MEISTERSINGER VON NUERNBERG   (R. Wagner; 3 acts, German, Munich 1868). New York, Metropolitan Op. H., Jan. 4, 1886.

MELODY IN "I"   (A. Moses; 1 act, American). *Baltimore, Maryland Th., May 2, 1939.

La MELOMANIE   (S. Champein; 1 act, French, Paris 1781). Charleston, S.C., Charleston Th., June 16, 1795.

MENELEK   (P. Lovingood; 3 acts, American). *New York, Central Op.
H., Nov. 16, 1936.

MER HAHN EN NEUE OBERKEET   (J. S. Bach; "cantate en bur-
lesque," German, 1742). New York, Hotel Barbizon-Plaza Concert
Hall, Mar. 11, 1914, in English, as "Peasant cantata" (stage perf.;
J. M. Diack's version).

MERLIN   (C. Goldmark; 3 acts, German, Vienna 1886). New York,
Metropolitan Op. H., Jan. 3, 1887.

MERRIE ENGLAND   (E. German; 2 acts, English, London 1902).
--New York, Hunter College Auditorium, Apr. 13, 1956 (concert
form; British Commonwealth Choir).

The Merry masquerade. See La FINTA GIARDINIERA.

The Merry monarch. See L'ETOILE.

MERRY MOUNT   (H. Hanson; 4 acts, American). *Ann Arbor, Mich.,
Hill Auditorium (Univ. of Michigan), May 20, 1933 (concert form);
New York, Metropolitan Op. H., Feb. 10, 1934 (stage premiere).

The Merry war. See Der LUSTIGE KRIEG.

The Merry widow. See Die LUSTIGE WITWE.

The Merry wives of Windsor. See Die LUSTIGEN
WEIBER VON WINDSOR.

Merrymount. See The MAYPOLE LOVERS.

MESE MARIANO   (U. Giordano; 1 act, Italian, Palermo 1910). New
York, Carnegie Recital Hall, June 6, 1955.

MESSALINE   (I. de Lara; 4 acts, French, Monte Carlo 1899). New
York, Metropolitan Op. H., Jan. 22, 1902.

MESSIAH   (G. F. Handel; 3 parts, oratorio, English, Dublin 1742).
Chicago, Auditorium, Mar. 20, 1933 (stage presentation).

MICHIGAN DREAM   (H. O. Read; 2 acts, American). *Lansing,
Mich., Michigan State College, May 13, 1955.

MIDAS   (text, Kane O'Hara; 2 [originally 3] acts, ballad opera, Dublin
1762). Philadelphia, Southwark Th., Nov. 24, 1769.

The MIDNIGHT DUEL (L. Kondorossy; 1 act, American). *Cleveland, Station WSRB, Mar. 20, 1955 (radio perf.).

The MIDNIGHT WANDERERS (W. Shield; 2 acts, English, London 1793). Philadelphia, New [Chestnut Street] Th., June 1, 1796.

A MIDSUMMER NIGHT'S DREAM (B. Britten; 3 acts, English, Aldeburgh 1960; London 1961). San Francisco, War Memorial Op. H., Oct. 10, 1961.

A MIDSUMMER NIGHT'S DREAM (F. Mendelssohn-Bartholdy; 5 acts, German, Potsdam and Berlin 1843). New York, Burton's Th., Feb. 3 (not 11), 1854, in English; New York, Stadt Theater, Jan. 20, 1864, in German.

The MIGHTY CASEY (W. Schuman; 1 act, American). *Hartford, Conn., Burns School Auditorium, May 4, 1953 (Hartt College of Music).

MIGNON (A. Thomas; 3 acts, French, Paris 1866). New Orleans, French Op. H., May 9, 1871.

The MIKADO (A. Sullivan; 2 acts, English, London 1885). Chicago, Chicago Museum [theatre], June 29, 1885 (garbled version); Chicago, Grand Op. H., July 6, 1885 (unauthorized); New York, Fifth Avenue Th., Aug. 19, 1885 (D'Oyly Carte).

MILDA (P. H. Allen; 1 act, American). *Venice, Teatro Rossini, Apr. 12, 1913, in Italian.

The MILLER AND HIS MEN (H. R. Bishop; 2 acts, English, London 1813). New York, Park Th., July 4, 1814.

Der MINSTREL (A. Neuendorff; 3 acts, German-American). *New York, Amberg Theater, May 18, 1892, in German.

The Miracle. See Das MIRAKEL.

The MIRACLE OF SAINT NICHOLAS (B. Britten; 9 scenes, dramatic cantata, English, London 1948). Dayton, O., Auditorium, Dec. 21, 1953 (stage perf.).

Das MIRAKEL (E. Humperdinck; 2 acts, pantomime, German, London 1911 in English as "The Miracle"). New York, Park Th., Feb. 17, 1913, in English (revived New York, Century Th., Jan. 15, 1924).

MIRANDA AND THE DARK YOUNG MAN (E. Siegmeister; 1 act, American). *Hartford, Conn., Burns School Auditorium, May 9, 1956 (Hartt College of Music).

MIREILLE (C. Gounod; 3 acts, French, Paris 1864). Philadelphia, Academy of Music, Nov. 17, 1864, in German (Act I and II); New York, (Brooklyn) Academy of Music, Dec. 18, 1884, in Italian; New York, Academy of Music, Dec. 20, 1884, in Italian; Boston, Jordan Hall, Apr. 25, 1916, in French (Hellenic Society of the New England Conservatory of Music).

A MIRROR IN THE SKY (G. Kubik; 1 act, American). *New York, City Center, May 12, 1947 (concert form); Eugene, Ore., Univ. of Oregon, May 23, 1938 (stage premiere).

The MISER KNIGHT (S. Rachmaninov; 3 scenes, Russian, Moscow 1906). Boston, Boston Op. H., Mar. 11, 1910 (Scene II only).

I MISERABILI (C. Bonsignore; 4 acts, Italian-American). *New York, (Brooklyn) Academy of Music, Oct. 24, 1925, in Italian.

MISS CHICKEN LITTLE (A. Wilder; 1 act, American). *New York, Columbia Broadcasting System, Dec. 27, 1953 (TV perf.); Piermont, N.Y., Lyric Th., Aug. 29, 1958 (stage premiere).

MISSISSIPPI LEGEND (J. Wolfe; 2 acts, American). *New York, Hotel Sutton Th., Apr. 24, 1951.

MR. PEPYS (M. Shaw; 3 acts, English, London 1926). New York, Earl Hall (Columbia Univ.), Feb. 22, 1940.

MISTRESS INTO MAID (V. Duke; 2 acts, American). *Santa Barbara, Campus Auditorium (Univ. of California), Dec. 12, 1958.

MOBY DICK (J. Low; 2 acts, American). *Idyllwild, Cal., Bowman Art Center (Idyllwild School of Music and Arts), Sept. 2, 1955.

The Mock doctor (Gounod). See Le MEDECIN MALGRE LUI.

The MOCK DOCTOR (text, Henry Fielding; 1 act and epilog, ballad opera, English, London 1732). New York, Nassau Street Th., Apr. 23, 1750.

MOHEGA (E. Sobolewski; 3 acts, German-American). *Milwaukee, Albany Hall, Oct. (not May), 11, 1859, in German.

MON AMI PIERROT (S. L. M. Barlow; 1 act, American). *Paris, Opéra-Comique, Jan. 11, 1935, in French.

MONA (H. Parker; 3 acts, American). *New York, Metropolitan Op. H., Mar. 14, 1912.

MONA LISA (M. von Schillings; prolog, 2 acts and epilog, German, Stuttgart 1915). New York, Metropolitan Op. H., Mar. 1, 1923.

La MONACA BIANCA (C. Giglio; prolog and 3 acts, Italian-American). *New York, Nation [late Fourteenth Street] Th., Feb. 11, 1926, in Italian (Patterson, N.J., Lyceum Th., Mar. 29, 1927, in English, as "The White sister;" New York, Wallack's Th., May 11, 1927).

The Monastery. See 'O MUNASTERIO.

Der MOND (C. Orff; 1 act, German, Munich 1939). New York, City Center, Oct. 16, 1956, in English, as "The Moon."

Il MONDO DELLA LUNA (J. Haydn; 3 acts, Italian, Esterház 1777). New York, Greenwich Mews Playhouse, June 7, 1949, in English, as "The Man in the moon."

The MONK OF TOLEDO (E. B. Knowlton; 3 acts, American).
*Portland, Ore., Auditorium, May 10, 1926.

The MONKEY'S PAW (C. Hamm; 1 act, American). *Cincinnati,
Cincinnati Conservatory of Music, May 2, 1952.

MONNA VANNA (H. Février; 4 acts, French, Paris 1909). Boston,
Boston Op. H., Dec. 5, 1913.

MONSIEUR BEAUCAIRE (A. Messager; prolog and 3 acts, French,
Birmingham, England, 1919 in English; Paris 1925 in French). New
York, New Amsterdam Th., Dec. 11, 1919, in English.

MONSIEUR CHOUFLEURI RESTERA CHEZ LUI (J. Offenbach;
1 act, French, Paris 1861). Boston, Boston Th., early 1869.

MONSIEUR DE CHIFFONNE (L. Caruso [?]; Italian). New Orleans,
St. Charles Th., Feb. 19, 1837.

MONSIEUR ET MADAME DENIS (J. Offenbach; 1 act, French,
Paris 1862). --New York, Terrace Garden, July 16, 1873, in German,
as "Herr und Madame Denis."

Montecchi e Capuleti. See I CAPULETI E MONTECCHI.

Les MONTENEGRINS (A. Limnander; 3 acts, French, Paris 1849).
New Orleans, Théâtre d'Orléans, Feb. 6, 1852.

The Moon. See Der MOND.

MORTE DELL' ARIA (G. Petrassi; 1 act, Italian, Rome 1950).
Urbana, Ill., Univ. of Illinois, Mar. 13, 1956, in English.

MOSE IN EGITTO (G. Rossini; 3 acts, Italian, Naples 1818). New
York, Masonic Hall, Dec. 22, 1832, in Italian (concert form); New
York, Italian Op. H., Mar. 2, 1835 (stage perf.).

MOSES (B. Hoff and O. Strock; 3 acts, German). *New York,
Brooklyn Museum, Feb. 26, 1850, in English (concert form).

MOSES (A. Rubinstein; 2 parts, German, 1888). New York, Liederkranz
Halle, Jan. 27, 1889 (excerpts; concert form).

The MOST HAPPY FELLA (F. Loesser; 3 acts, American). *Boston, Shubert Th., Mar. 13, 1956 (New York, Imperial Th., May 3,
1956).

The MOTHER (S. Hollingsworth; 1 act, American). *Philadelphia,
Curtis Institute, Mar. 29, 1954.

The MOTHER (J. Wood; 1 act, American). *New York, Juilliard
School of Music, Dec. 9, 1942.

The MOTHER OF US ALL (V. Thomson; 3 acts, American).
*New York, Brander Matthews Hall (Columbia Univ.), May 7, 1947.

The MOUNTAIN CHILD (E. Weigel; 1 act, American). *Missoula,
Mont., Montana Univ., July 27, 1958.

The MOUNTAIN SYLPH (J. Barnett; 2 acts, English, London 1834).
New York, Park Th., May 11, 1835.

The MOUNTAINEERS (S. Arnold; 3 acts, English, London 1793). Boston, Federal Street Th., Apr. 6, 1795.

MOZART AND SALIERI (N. Rimsky-Koraskov; 2 acts, Russian, Moscow 1898). Forest Park, Pa., Unity House, Aug. 6, 1933, in English; New York, Roerich Museum, Oct. 25, 1933, in Russian.

La MUETTE DE PORTICI (D. Auber; 5 acts, French, Paris 1828). New York, Park Th., Nov 9, 1829, in English; --New York, Park Th., Aug. 15, 1831, in French [New Orleans earlier (?)].

MUIRGHEIS (O. Butler; Irish, Dublin 1903). New York, Aeolian Hall, Apr. 19, 1915 (excerpts; concert form, with the composer at the piano).

La MULATA (G. Roig; 1 act, zarzuela, Cuban). New York, Teatro Apolo, Feb. 23, 1930.

'O MUNASTERIO (P. H. Allen; 2 parts, American). *Florence, Sala Filarmonica, Spring 1912; New York, Station WHOM, Jan. 11, 1948 (radio perf.).

Murder in the cathedral. See ASSASSINIO NELLA CATTEDRALE.

Murder in three keys. See BLACK ROSES; DARK SONNET; SIMOON.

MUSIC IN THE AIR (J. Kern; 2 acts, American). *Philadelphia, Garrick Th., Oct 17, 1932 (New York, Alvin Th., Nov. 8, 1932).

The MUSIC ROBBER (I. Van Grove; 2 acts, American). *Cincinnati, Zoological Gardens, July 7 (not 4), 1926.

MY DARLING CORIE (E. Siegmeister; 1 act, American). *Hempstead, L.I., N.Y., Calkin's Hall (Hofstra College), Feb. 18, 1954, as "Darlin' Corie."

MY FAIR LADY (F. Loewe; 2 acts, American). *New Haven, Conn., Shubert Th., Feb. 4, 1956 (New York, Mark Hellinger Th., Mar. 15, 1956; 2,717 perf.).

MY GRANDMOTHER (S. Storace; 2 acts, English, London 1793). Philadelphia, New [Chestnut Street] Th., Apr. 27, 1795.

MY MARYLAND (S. Romberg; 3 acts, American). *Atlantic City, N.J., Apollo Th., Jan. 10, 1927 (New York, Jolson Th., Sept. 12, 1927).

The MYSTERIOUS CHARACTERS OF MR. FU (B. Weber; American). *Oakland, Cal., Oakland Women's City Club, Oct. 7, 1932.

The MYSTERIOUS MARRIAGE (J. Hewitt; 3 acts, American). *New York, Park Th., June 5, 1799.

MYSTIC FORTRESS (L. Kondorossy; 1 act, American). *Cleveland, Station WSRS, June 12, 1955 (radio perf.).

NABUCODONOSOR [Nabucco] (G. Verdi; 4 acts, Italian, Milan
1842). New York, Astor Place Op. H., Apr. 4, 1848.
Das NACHTLAGER VON GRANADA (K. Kreutzer; 2 acts, Ger-
man, Vienna 1834). Hoboken, N.J., Vauxhall Garden, early Nov.
1853; also, Washington Hall, Nov. 26, 1853; Milwaukee, 1858
Musik Verein); New York, Mar. 1, 1859 (second perf.).
NADIR AND ZULEIKA (C. E. Horn; American). *New York, Park
Th., Dec. 27, 1832.
NAMIKO-SAN (Aldo Franchetti; 1 act, Italian-American). *Chicago,
Auditorium, Dec. 11, 1925, in Italian.
NARCISSA (M. C. Moore; 4 acts, American). *Seattle, Moore Th.,
Apr. 22, 1912.
NARCISSUS AND ECHO (H. Houseley; 1 act, American). *Denver,
El Jebel Temple, Jan. 30, 1912.
The National guard. See La FIANCEE.
NATIVE LAND (H. R. Bishop; 3 acts, English, London 1824). New
York, Park Th., Jan. 12, 1827.
NATOMA (V. Herbert; 3 acts, American). *Philadelphia, Metropoli-
tan Op. H., Feb. 25, 1911.
NAUGHTY MARIETTA (V. Herbert; 2 acts, American). *Syracuse,
N.Y., Wieting Op. H., Oct. 24, 1910 (New York, New York Th.,
Nov. 7, 1910).
NAUSICAA (P. Glanville-Hicks; 3 acts, American). *Athens, Greece,
Herodus Atticus Th., Aug. 19, 1961.
La NAVARRAISE (J. Massenet; 1 act, French, London 1894). New
York, Metropolitan Op. H., Dec. 11, 1895.
La NAVE (I. Montemezzi; prolog and 3 acts, Italian, Milan 1918).
Chicago, Auditorium, Nov. 18, 1919.
NE TOUCHEZ-PAS A LA REINE (X. Boisselot; 3 acts, French,
Paris 1847). New York, Castle Garden, Aug. 18 (not 20), 1852.
NEBRAHMA (N. L. Norden; 2 scenes, American). *Philadelphia,
Ethical Society Auditorium, Apr. 16, 1953 (concert form).
The NECKLACE (W. R. Bohrnstedt; 1 act, American). *Redlands,
Cal., Watchorn Hall (Univ. of Redlands), Mar. 12, 1956.
The NECKLACE OF THE SUN (D. N. Lehmer; American). *Oak-
land, Cal., Dec. 1934; San Francisco, War Memorial Op. H., Apr.
2, 1935.
A Neglected education. See Une EDUCATION MANQUEE.
NEPTUNE AND AMPHITRITE (T. A. Arne; masque, English, Lon-
don 1746). New York, John Street Th., June 3, 1773.
NERO (A. Rubinstein; 4 acts, German, Hamburg 1897). New York,
Metropolitan Op. H., Mar. 14, 1887, in English (National Opera
Company).

NEUES VOM TAGE   (P. Hindemith; 3 parts, German, Berlin 1929).
Santa Fe, Opera Th., Aug. 12, 1961, in English, as "News of the
day."

The NEW MOON   (S. Romberg; 2 acts, American).   *Philadelphia,
Chestnut Street Op. H., Dec. 22, 1927 (New York, Imperial Th.,
Sept. 19, 1928).

The NEW WORLD   (H. Moore; prolog and 4 acts, American).   *St.
Louis, Odeon Recital Hall, May 18, 1903 (excerpts; concert form).

News of the day.   See NEUES VOM TAGE.

NICHOLAS DE FLUE   (A. Honegger; 3 acts, French, Soleure,
Switzerland, 1939 in concert form).   New York, Carnegie Hall, May
8, 1941 (abridged concert form; Dessoff Choir).

La NIEGE   (D. Auber; 4 acts, French, Paris 1823).   New York, Park Th.,
July 30, 1827 [New Orleans earlier (?)].

The Night dancers.   See The WILLIS.

A NIGHT IN AVIGNON   (C. Loomis; 1 act, American).   *Indianapolis, Claypole Hotel, July 1932 (concert form).

A NIGHT IN OLD PARIS   (H. K. Hadley; 1 act, American).   *New
York, National Broadcasting Company, Feb. 22, 1933 (radio perf.).

A NIGHT IN ROME   (J. Eichberg; American).   --New York, New
French Th., June 25 (not 29), 1866.

A NIGHT IN THE PUSZTA   (L. Kondorossy; 1 act, Hungarian).
*Cleveland, Public Auditorium Music Hall, June 28, 1953, in
English.

The NIGHTINGALE   (B. Rogers; 1 act, American).   *New York,
Carl Fischer Concert Hall, May 10, 1955; Rochester, N.Y.,
Kilbourn Hall (Eastman School of Music), May 6, 1957.

The NIGHTINGALE AND THE ROSE   (G. Lessner; 1 act,
American).   *New York, National Broadcasting Company, Apr. 25,
1942 (radio perf.).

The NIGHTINGALE IS GUILTY   (R. Middleton; 1 act, American).
*Boston, Esquire Th., Mar. 5, 1954.

NIKOLA SUBIC ZRINSKI   (I. Zajc; 3 acts, Croatian, Zagreb 1876).
Chicago, Majestic Th., Apr. 21, 1929.

NINA   (N. Dalayrac; 1 act, French, Paris 1786).   Charleston, S.C.,
French Th. [late Sollee's Hall], July 23, 1794.

NINA   (A. C. Eggers; 2 acts, German-American).   *New York, Irving
Place Th., May 1, 1906.

NINA PAZZA PER AMORE   (P. A. Coppola; 2 acts, Italian, Rome
1835).   New York, Palmo's Op. H., Feb. 5, 1847.

NINA ROSA   (S. Romberg; 2 acts, American).   *Detroit, Shubert Th.,
Oct. [22], 1929 (New York, [Brooklyn] Majestic Th., Sept. 13, 1930;
New York, Majestic Th., Sept. 20, 1930).

NITA (W. L. Howland; 1 act, American). --Paris, Théâtre Nouveau, Jan. 31, 1898, in French.

The NITECAP (C. V. Burnham; 1 act, American). *New Orleans, Dixon Hall (Newcomb College, Tulane Univ.), Mar. 14, 1956.

NO, NO, NANETTE (V. Youmans; 3 acts, American). *Detroit, Garrick Th., Apr. 20 (not 21), 1924 (New York, Globe Th., Sept. 16, 1925).

NO SONG, NO SUPPER (S. Storace; 2 acts, English, London 1790). Philadelphia, Southwark Th., Nov. 30, 1792.

NOAH AND THE FLOOD (I. Stravinsky; dance-drama, American). *New York, Columbia Broadcasting System, June 14, 1962 (TV perf.).

NOAH AND THE STOWAWAY (M. Kalmanoff; 1 act, American). *New York, Municipal Broadcasting System (WNYC), Feb. 18, 1951 (radio perf.); New York, Provincetown Th., Oct. 12, 1952 (stage premiere).

The NOBLE PEASANT (W. Shield; 3 acts, English, London 1784). Philadelphia, New [Chestnut Street] Th., May 8, 1795.

Les NOCES DE JEANNETTE (V. Massé; 1 act, French, Paris 1853). New York, Niblo's Garden, Apr. 9, 1855, in English, as "The Marriage of Georgette" (concert form); Philadelphia, Academy of Music, Oct. 25, 1861, in French.

Les NOCES D'OLIVETTE (E. Audran; 3 acts, French, Paris 1870). New York, Bijou Op. H., Dec. 25, 1880, in English, as "Olivette;" New York, Abbey's Park Th., Dec. 6, 1881, in French.

Les NOCES D'OR (A. Maurage; 1 act, French). New Orleans, Tulane Th., Apr. 29, 1929.

Una NOCHE IN SEVILLA (A. Barili; 2 [?] acts, Spanish). New York, Wallack's Th., May 25, 1866.

NOEL (F. d'Erlanger; 3 acts, French, Paris 1910). Chicago, Auditorium, Jan. 8, 1913.

NORMA (V. Bellini; 2 acts, Italian, Milan 1831). New Orleans, St. Charles Th., Apr. 1, 1836, in Italian.

NOTRE DAME DE PARIS (W. H. Fry; 4 acts, American). *Philadelphia, Academy of Music, May 4 (not 9), 1864.

La NOTTE DI ZORAIMA (I. Montemezzi; 1 act, Italian, Milan 1931). New York, Metropolitan Op. H., Dec. 2, 1931.

Le NOUVEAU SEIGNEUR DU VILLAGE (A. Boieldieu; 1 act, French, Paris 1813). --New York, Park Th., Sept. 6, 1827 [New Orleans earlier (?)].

NOVELLIS, NOVELLIS (J. La Montaine; American). *Washington, D.C., Washington Cathedral, Dec. 24, 1961.

NOYE'S FLUDDE   (B. Britten; Chester miracle play, English,
    Aldeburgh, England, 1958). New York, James Memorial Chapel
    (Union Theological Seminary), Mar. 16, 1959.
Le NOZZE DI FIGARO   (W. A. Mozart; 4 acts, Italian, Vienna
    1786). New York, Park Th., May 10, 1824, in English (H. R.
    Bishop's version, London 1819); --New York, Chatham Th., Oct.
    24, 1831, in French [New Orleans earlier (?)]; New York, Academy
    of Music, Nov. 23, 1858, in Italian.
Une NUIT BLANCHE   (J. Offenbach; 1 act, French, Paris 1855).
    New Orleans, French Op. H., Nov. 1861.

- O -

OBERON   (C. M. von Weber; 3 acts, English, London 1826). New
    York, Park Th., Sept. 20, 1826 (T. S. Cooke's version, London
    1826); New York, Park Th., Oct. 9, 1828 (not 1829).
L'OCCASIONE FAL IL LADRO   (G. Rossini; 1 act, Italian, Venice
    1812). Columbia, Mo., Auditorium (Stephens College), Apr. 8,
    1954, in English, as "The Involuntary thief."
Die OCHSENMENUETTE   (I. X. von Seyfried; 1 act, Singspiel,
    German, Vienna 1823). New York Stadt Theater, Dec. 7, 1858.
OEDIPUS REX   (I. Stravinsky; 2 acts, Latin, Paris 1927). Boston,
    Symphony Hall, Feb. 24, 1928 (concert form); Philadelphia, Metro-
    politan Op. H., Apr. 10, 1931 (stage perf.).
OF AGE TO-MORROW   (M. Kelly; 2 acts, English, London 1800).
    Boston, Boston [Federal Street] Th., Jan. 31, 1806.
OF THEE I SING   (G. Gershwin; 2 acts, American). *Boston,
    Majestic Th., Dec. 8, 1931 (New York, Music Box, Dec. 26, 1931).
OH, KAY!   (G. Gershwin; 2 acts, American). *Philadelphia, Shubert
    Th., Oct. 18, 1926 (New York, Werba's Brooklyn Th., Nov. 1,
    1926; New York, Imperial Th., Nov. 8, 1926).
OH, LADY! LADY!   (J. Kern; 2 acts, American). *Albany, N.Y.,
    Harmanus Bleecker Hall, Jan. 7, 1918 (New York, Princess Th.,
    Jan. 31, 1918).
L'OISEAU BLEU   (A. Wolff; 4 acts, French). *New York, Metro-
    politan Op. H., Dec. 27, 1919.
OKLAHOMA!   (R. Rodgers; 2 acts, American). *New Haven, Conn.,
    Shubert Th., Mar. 11, 1943, as "Away we go" (New York, St.
    James Th., Mar. 31, 1943; 2,248 perf.).
OLAF   (H. Kirkpatrick; 2 acts, American). *Lincoln, Neb., Oliver
    Th., Mar. 5, 1912.

OLAV TRYGVASON   (E. Grieg, unfinished; 3 scenes, Norwegian, Christiania 1889 in concert form; Christiania 1908 in operatic form). Cincinnati, Music Hall, May 25, 1898, in English (concert form); Los Angeles, Biltmore Th., Feb. 14, 1934, in Norwegian.

The OLD MAID AND THE THIEF   (G. C. Menotti; 2 acts, American). *New York, National Broadcasting Company, Apr. 22, 1939 (radio perf.); Philadelphia, Academy of Music, Feb. 11, 1941 (stage premiere).

The OLD WOMAN OF EIGHTY-THREE   (R. Taylor; 1 act, American). *Annapolis, Md., Assembly Room, Feb. 28, 1793.

OLEANDER RED   (R. R. Williams; 1 act, American). *Cincinnati, Odeon, Apr. 1, 1953 (College of Music of Cincinnati).

OL-OL   (A. Tcherepnin; 3 acts, Russian, Weimar 1928 in German). New York, Casino Th., Feb. 7 (not 9), 1934, in Russian.

OMANO   (L. H. Southard; 4 acts, American). *Boston, Chickering Salon, Jan. 9, 1858 (excerpts; concert form).

L'OMBRE   (F. von Flotow; 3 acts, French, Paris 1870). New York, Academy of Music, Apr. 9, 1875, in Italian, as "L'Ombra;" New York, Lexington Avenue Op. H., May 18, 1875, in French (amateur cast).

OMBRE RUSSE   (C. Sodero; 3 acts, American). *New York, National Broadcasting Company, May 27 (Act I-II), June 3 (Act III), 1929, in English (radio perf.); Venice, Teatro La Fenice, June 19, 1930 (stage premiere).

ON NE S'AVISE JAMAIS DE TOUT   (P. A. Monsigny; 1 act, French, Paris 1761). New York, Hunter College Playhouse, June 7, 1957, in English, as "One never knows."

ON THE TOWN   (L. Bernstein; 2 acts, American). *Boston, Colonial Th., Dec. 13, 1944 (New York, Adelphi Th., Dec. 28, 1944).

L'ONCLE-VALET   (A. Duval; 1 act, French, Paris 1798). New Orleans, Théâtre d'Orléans, 1815.

135th STREET   (G. Gershwin; 1 act, American). *New Haven, Conn., Hyperion Th., Aug. 24, 1922, in "George White's Scandals of 1922" (New York, Globe Th., Aug. 28, 1922; 1 perf.).

One never knows.   See ON NE S'AVISE JAMAIS DE TOUT.

ONE TOUCH OF VENUS   (K. Weill; 2 acts, American). *Boston, Shubert Th., Sept. 17, 1943 (New York, Imperial Th., Oct. 7, 1943).

ONTEORA'S BRIDE   (D. D'Antalffy; 4 scenes, American). *New York, Radio City Music Hall, Nov. 15, 1934.

ONTI-ORA   (G. Hinrichs; 3 acts, American). *Philadelphia, Grand Op.
H., July 28, 1890.

The OPEN WINDOW   (D. Ahlstrom; 1 act, American). *Cincinnati,
Cincinnati Conservatory of Music, Mar. 1, 1953.

The OPERA CLOAK   (W. Damrosch; 1 act, American). *New York,
Broadway Th., Nov. 3, 1942.

OPERA, OPERA   (M. Kalmanoff; 1 act, American). *New York,
Finch College Auditorium, Feb. 22, 1956 (After Dinner Opera).

The Oracle (Bickerstaffe). See DAPHNE AND AMINTOR.

The ORACLE   (M. C. Moore; 3 acts, American). *San Francisco,
Golden Gate Hall, 1894.

The ORACLE   (H. J. Stewart; 1 act, American). *San Francisco,
Bohemian Club, Nov. 12, 1910.

L'ORACOLO   (F. Leoni; 1 act, Italian, London 1905). New York,
Metropolitan Op. H., Feb. 4, 1915.

The ORDEAL OF OSBERT   (A. Davis; 1 act, American). *Duxbury,
Mass., Plymouth Rock Center of Music and Drama, summer 1949.

ORFEO   (C. Monteverdi; prolog and 5 acts, Italian, Mantua 1607).
New York, Metropolitan Op. H., Apr. 14, 1912 (concert form);
Boston, Jordan Hall, Mar. 21, 1941 (stage perf.; G. F. Malipiero's
version).

ORFEO ED EURIDICE   (C. W. von Gluck; 3 acts, Italian, Vienna
1762). [Charleston, S.C., Théâtre Français (late Sollee's Hall),
June 24, 1794, as a French pantomime---Gluck's opera (?); see
Sonneck, "Early Opera," p. 206]; New York, Winter Garden, May 25,
1863, in English; Chicago, Auditorium, Nov. 11, 1891, in Italian.

ORLANDO PALADINO   (J. Haydn; 3 acts, Italian, Esterház 1782).
Boston, Oct. 25, 1961 (excerpts; concert form, privately under Karl
Geiringer).

ORPHEE AUX ENFERS   (J. Offenbach; 2 acts, French, Paris 1858).
New York, Stadt Theater, Mar. 1861, in German, as "Orpheus in der
Unterwelt;" New York, Théâtre Français, Jan. 17, 1867, in French
[New Orleans earlier (?)].

OSCAR AND MALVINA   (W. Shield and W. Reeve; ballet pantomime,
English, London 1791). Charleston, S.C., Charleston Th., Feb. 21,
1795.

OSCEOLA   (M. Campbell; American). *Los Angeles, 1944 (National
American Indian League).

OSSEO   (E. Noyes-Greene; 3 acts, American). *Brookline, Mass., Maud
Freshel's Th., 1917 (concert form).

OSTROLENKA   (J. H. Bonawitz; 4 acts, German-American). *Philadelphia, Academy of Music, May (not Dec.), 3, 1874, in English.

OTELLO (G. Rossini; 3 acts, Italian, Naples 1816). New York, Park
Th., Feb. 7 (not 11 or 27), 1826.

OTELLO (G. Verdi; 4 acts, Italian, Milan 1887). New York, Academy
of Music, Apr. 16, 1888.

The OTHER WISE MAN (I. Van Grove; 1 act, American).
*Bentonville, Ark., July 14, 1959 (Eureka Springs, Ark., Inspiration
Point Fine Arts Colony, July 24, 1959).

OTHERWISE, ENGAGED (A. Davis; 1 act, American). *New
York, Sullivan Street Playhouse, Apr. 23, 1958.

OTHO VISCONTI (F. G. Gleason; 3 acts, American). *Chicago,
College Th., June 4, 1907 (composed 1880).

OUANGA (C. C. White; 3 acts, American). *New York, Studio Th.
(New School of Social Research), June 18, 1941 (concert form);
South Bend, Ind., Central High School Auditorium, June 10, 1949
(stage premiere).

The OUTCASTS OF POKER FLAT (S. H. Adler; 1 act, American).
*Denton, Tex., North Texas State Univ. Th., June 8, 1962.

The OUTCASTS OF POKER FLAT (S. Beckler; 1 act, American).
*Stockton, Cal., College of the Pacific, Dec. 2, 1960.

The OUTCASTS OF POKER FLAT (J. Elkus; 1 act, American).
*Bethlehem, Pa., Grace Hall (Lehigh Univ.), Apr. 16, 1960.

- P -

The PADLOCK (C. Dibdin; 2 acts, English, London 1768). New
York, John Street Th., May 29, 1769.

Il PAESE DEI CAMPANELLI (V. Ranzato; 3 acts, Italian). New
York, Teatro Fourteenth Street and Sixth Avenue, Oct. 17, 1924.

PAGLIACCI (R. Leoncavallo; 2 acts, Italian, Milan 1892). Philadelphia, Grand Op. H., June 15, 1893.

PAINT YOUR WAGON (F. Loewe; 2 acts, American). *Philadelphia, Shubert Th., Sept. 17, 1951 (New York, Shubert Th., Nov.
12, 1951).

The Painted lady. See RAMONA (Strube).

The PAINTER OF DREAMS (C. E. Pemberton; prolog and 1 act,
American). *Los Angeles, Bovard Auditorium (Univ. of Southern
California), May 1934.

The PAJAMA GAME (R. Adler and J. Ross; 2 acts, American).
*New Haven, Conn., Shubert Th., Apr. 12, 1954 (New York, St.
James Th., May 13, 1954).

PAL JOEY (R. Rodgers; 2 acts, American). * Philadelphia, Forrest Th.,
Dec. 11, 1940 (New York, Ethel Barrymore Th., Dec. 25, 1940).

PAN (G. Hager; 1 act, American). * Seattle, Cornish School Th., Apr.
21, 1922.

PAN IN AMERICA (C. Venth; American). Asheville, N.C., June 13,
1923 (National Federation of Music Clubs).

PANAMA HATTIE (C. Porter; 2 acts, American). * New Haven,
Conn., Shubert Th., Oct. 3, 1940 (New York, 46th Street Th., Oct.
30, 1940).

PANFILO AND LAURETTE (C. Chavez; 3 acts, American). * New
York, Brander Matthews Hall (Columbi Univ.), May 9, 1957.

Pantaloon. See HE WHO GETS SLAPPED.

Les PANTINS DE VIOLETTE (A. Adam; 1 act, French, Paris
1856). --New York, Théâtre Français, Dec. 15, 1863.

PAOLETTA (P. Floridia; 4 acts, American). * Cincinnati, Music Hall,
Aug. 29, 1910.

PAOLO AND FRANCESCA (D. James; 3 acts, American). * Rochester, N.Y., Kilbourn Hall (Eastman School of Music), Apr. 2, 1931
(excerpts; concert form).

Le PARDON DE PLOERMEL [Dinorah] (G. Meyerbeer; 3 acts,
French, Paris 1859). New Orleans, French Op. H., Mar. 4, 1861
(New York, Academy of Music, Nov. 24, 1862, in Italian, as
"Dinorah").

A PARFAIT FOR IRENE (W. Kaufmann; 3 acts, American).
* Bloomington, Ind., East Hall (Indiana Univ.). Feb. 21, 1952.

PARIDE E ELENA (C. W. von Gluck; 5 acts, Italian, Vienna 1770).
New York, Town Hall, Jan. 15, 1954 (concert form).

PARISIANA (G. Donizetti; 3 a ts, Italian, Florence 1833). New
Orleans, St. Charles Th., June 4, 1837.

The PARK AVENUE KIDS (D. Gillis; 1 act, American). * Elkhart,
Ind., Elkhart High School Auditorium, May 12, 1957.

The PARROT (D. Peter; 1 act, American). * New York, National
Broadcasting Company, Mar. 24, 1953 (TV perf.; Armstrong Circle
Theater---first television opera commissioned by a commercial
sponsor).

PARSIFAL (R. Wagner; 3 acts, German, Bayreuth 1882). New York,
Metropolitan Op. H., Mar. 3, 1886 (concert form; Oratorio Society
of New York); Metropolitan Op. H., Dec. 24, 1903 (stage perf.).

La PART DU DIABLE (D. Auber; 3 acts, French, Paris 1843).
--New York, Niblo's Garden, May 10, 1852, in English, as "The
Devil's share."

Le PASSANT   (E. Paladilhe; 1 act, French, Paris 1872). New York,
    Hunter College Playhouse, June 7, 1957, in English, as "The Passerby. "
The PASSION OF JONATHAN WADE   (C. Floyd; 3 acts, Amer-
    ican). *New York, City Center, Oct. 11, 1962.
PASSIONNEMENT   (A. Messager; 3 acts, French, Paris 1926). New
    York, Jolson Th. , Mar. 7, 1929.
Il PASTOR FIDO   (G. F. Handel; 3 acts, Italian, London 1712). New
    York, Town Hall, Mar. 2, 1952 (concert form).
PATIENCE   (A. Sullivan; 2 acts, English, London 1881). St. Louis,
    Uhrig's Cave Th. , July 28, 1881 (New York, Standard Th. , Sept.
    22, 1881; D'Oyly Carte Company).
The PATRIOT   (J. Edwards; 1 act, American). New York, Keith &
    Proctor's Fifth Avenue Th. , Nov. 23, 1908 [Boston 1907 (?)].
The PATRIOT, or Liberty asserted   (J. Hewitt; 3 acts, Amer-
    ican). *New York, John Street Th. , June 5, 1794.
The PATRIOT, or Liberty obtained   (B. Carr; 3 acts, Amer-
    ican). *Philadelphia, New [Chestnut Street] Th. , May 16, 1796.
PAUL BUNYAN   (B. Britten; prolog and 2 acts, English). *New York,
    Brander Matthews Hall (Columbia Univ.), May 5, 1941.
PAUL ET VIRGINIE   (R. Kreutzer; 3 acts, French, Paris 1791).
    Boston, Federal Street Th. , May 10, 1797, in English (pantomime);
    New Orleans, Théâtre d'Orléans, 1815, in French.
PAUL ET VIRGINIE   (V. Massé; 3 acts, French, Paris 1876). New
    Orleans, Varieties Th. , Feb. 7, 1897, in English; New Orleans,
    French Op. H. , Jan. 31, 1881, in French.
PAULUS   (F. Mendelssohn-Bartholdy; 2 parts, oratorio, German,
    Dusseldorf 1836; Liverpool 1836 in English as "St. Paul"). New
    York, Chatham Street Chapel, Oct. 29, 1838, in English (concert
    form; New York Sacred Music Society); Chicago, New First Congre-
    gational Church, Mar. 22, 1923, in English (scenic presentation).
Le PAUVRE MATELOT   (D. Milhaud; 3 acts, French, Paris 1927).
    Philadelphia, Academy of Music, Apr. 1, 1937, in English; New
    York, Forty-fourth Street Th. , Nov. 10, 1937, in French.
The PEASANT BOY   (M. Kelly and P. von Winter; 3 acts, English,
    London 1811). --Washington, D.C., Washington Th. , summer 1811
    (New York, Park Th. , June 26, 1812).
Peasant cantata.   See MER HAHN EN NEUE OBERKEET.
Les PECHEURS DE PERLES   (G. Bizet; 3 acts, French, Paris 1863).
    Philadelphia, Grand Op. H. , Aug. 23 (not 25), 1893, in Italian;
    New Orleans, French Op. H. , season 1894-95, in French.
PEEPING TOM OF COVENTRY   (S. Arnold; 2 acts, English, London
    1784). Charleston, S.C., Charleston Th. , Feb. 18, 1793.

PEER GYNT (E. Grieg; 5 acts, Norwegian, Christiania 1876). Chicago, Grand Op. H., Oct. 29, 1906, in English (with Richard Mansfield; New York, New Amsterdam Th., Feb. 25, 1907).

PELLEAS ET MELISANDE (C. Debussy; 5 acts, French, Paris 1902). New York, Manhattan Op. H., Feb. 19, 1908.

PEP RALLY (D. Gillis; 1 act, American). *Interlochen, Mich., Kresge Assembly Hall (National Music Camp), Aug. 15, 1957.

PEPITO (J. Offenbach; 1 act, French, Paris 1853). --Chicago, Haverly's Th., Dec. 23, 1876, in English, as "Vertigo" (Philadelphia, Academy of Vocal Arts, 1914, in English, as "The Maid of Elizondo").

PEPITO'S GOLDEN FLOWER (M. E. Caldwell; 1 act, American). *Pasadena, Civic Auditorium, Mar. 13, 1955.

The PERFECT FOOL (G. Holst; 1 act, English, London 1923). --Wichita, Kan., Univ. of Wichita, Mar. 20, 1962.

The PERI (J. G. Maeder; 3 acts, American). *New York, Broadway Th., Dec. 13, 1852.

La PERICHOLE (J. Offenbach; 3 acts, French, Paris 1868 in two acts; Paris 1874 in three acts). New York, Pike's [later Grand] Op. H., Jan. 4, 1869.

PERINETTE (J. Offenbach; 1 act, French, Paris 1855). New York, Terrace Garden, July 2, 1873, in German, as "Paimpol und Per- inette."

Das PERLENHEMD (L. J. Kauffmann; 2 acts, German). Cleveland, Karamu House, Jan. 25, 1955, in English, as "The Robe of pearls."

PEROUZE (T. Sakellaridis; 2 acts, Greek, Athens 1911). New York, Terrace Garden, Sept. 27, 1925, in Greek.

La PERRUCHE (A. L. Clapisson; 1 act, French, Paris 1840). New York, Niblo's Garden, May 24, 1843 [New Orleans earlier (?)].

PERSEPHONE (I. Stravinsky; 3 parts, French, Paris 1934). Boston, Symphony Hall, Mar. 15, 1935 (concert form); Minneapolis, Cyrus Northrop Memorial Auditorium (Univ. of Minnesota), Nov. 23, 1956 (stage perf.).

The Pet dove. See La COLOMBE.

The PET OF THE PETTICOATS (J. Barnett; 3 acts, English, London 1831). Philadelphia, Walnut Street Th., Mar. 7, 1835.

The PET SHOP (V. Rieti; 1 act, American). *New York, Theresa Kaufmann Concert Hall (Y.M. and Y.W.H.A.), Apr. 14, 1958.

PETER GRIMES (B. Britten; prolog and 3 acts, English, London 1945). Tanglewood, Lenox, Mass., Theater-Concert Hall (Berkshire Music Center), Aug. 6, 1946 (student cast); New York, Metropolitan Op. H., Feb. 12, 1948 (professional cast).

PETER IBBETSON (D. Taylor; 3 acts, American). *New York,
Metropolitan Op. H., Feb. 7, 1931.

Le PETIT CHAPERON ROUGE (A. Boieldieu; 3 acts, French, Paris
1818). New Orleans, Théâtre d'Orléans, Jan. 1821.

Le PETIT MATELOT (P. Gaveaux; 1 act, French, Paris 1796).
--Philadelphia, Chestnut Street Th., Sept. 10, 1831 [New Orleans
earlier (?)].

PETRUCHIO (H. Groth; 2 acts, American). *Conway, Ark., Ida
Waldron Memorial Auditorium (Arkansas State Teachers College),
Mar. 29, 1954.

PHILEMON ET BAUCIS (C. Gounod; 3 acts, French, Paris 1860).
Chicago, Auditorium, Dec. 26, 1892, in English; New York, Metropolitan Op. H., Nov. 29, 1893, in French.

Le PHILTRE (D. Auber; 2 acts, French, Paris 1831). --New York,
Park Th., Aug. 9, 1833 [New Orleans earlier (?)].

Phoebus and Pan. See Der STREIT ZWISCHEN PHOEBUS
UND PAN.

PHRYNE (C. Saint-Saens; 2 acts, French, Paris 1893). New Orleans,
French Op. H., Feb. 3, 1914.

PIANELLA (F. von Flotow; 1 act, German, Schwerin 1857). New York,
Théâtre Français, Mar. 31, 1864, in French.

PIECES OF EIGHT (B. Wagenaar; 2 acts, American). *New York,
Brander Matthews Hall (Columbia Univ.), May 10, 1944.

PIERROT LUNAIRE (A. Schönberg; song cycle, German, Berlin 1912).
New York, Klaw Th., Feb. 4, 1923 (concert form); New York, Town
Hall, Apr. 16, 1933 (scenic presentation); New York, Fashion Institute
of Technology Auditorium, May 5, 1962 (ballet presentation).

PIERROT OF THE MINUTE (L. Engel; 1 act and epilog, American).
*Cincinnati, Cincinnati College of Music, Apr. 3, 1929.

PIERROT PUNI (H. M. Cieutat; 1 act, French). New York, Princess
Th., Dec. 28, 1915.

PIERROT QUI PLEURE ET PIERROT QUI RIT (J. Hubert; 1
act, French). New York, Princess Th., Jan. 27, 1916, in English.

La PIETRA DEL PAFAGONE (G. Rossini; 2 acts, Italian, Milan
1812). Hartford, Conn., Burns School Auditorium, May 4, 1955, in
English, as "The Touchstone" (Hartt College of Music).

PIGEN MED SVOVLSTIKERNE (A. Enna; 1 act, Danish, Copen-
hagen 1897). New York, McAlpin Hotel, Mar. 30, 1930, in
English, as "The Little match girl" (Minerva Club).

PIMPINONE (G. P. Telemann; 3 acts, German-Italian, Hamburg
1725). Chicago, Univ. of Chicago, Apr. 16, 1939, in English and
Italian (arias).

The Pioneers. See HECHALUTZ.

The PIPE OF DESIRE (F. S. Converse; 1 act, American). *Boston, Jordan Hall, Jan. 31 (not Jan. 1), 1906 (New York, Metropolitan Op. H., Mar. 18, 1910).

PIPELE (S. A. de Ferrari; 3 acts, Italian, Venice 1855). New York, Academy of Music, Dec. 10, 1869.

PIPPA'S HOLIDAY (J. P. Beach; 1 act, American). *Paris, Théâtre Réjane, Mar. 29, 1916, in French.

PIQUE DAME (P. Tchaikovsky; 3 acts, Russian, St. Petersburg 1890). New York, Metropolitan Op. H., Mar. 5, 1910, in German; Seattle, Metropolitan Th., Dec. 21, 1921, in Russian.

Il PIRATA (V. Bellini; 2 acts, Italian, Milan 1827). New York, Richmond Hill Th., Dec. 5, 1832.

The PIRATES (S. Storace; 3 acts, English, London 1792; London 1827 in revised form with additional music by J. Braham, as "Isidore de Merida"). New York, Park Th., June 9, 1828, as "Isidore de Merida" (music arr. by C. E. Horn, who sang in the production).

The PIRATES OF PENZANCE (A. Sullivan; 2 acts, English). *New York, Fifth Avenue Th., Dec. 31, 1897 (copyright perf., Paignton, England, Royal Bijou Th., Dec. 30, 1897; London, Opera Comique, Apr. 3, 1880).

PIZARRE (P. J. Candaille; 5 acts, French, Paris 1785). New Orleans, Théâtre St. Pierre, ca. 1803-10.

The PIZZA PUSHER (J. F. Goodman; 1 act, American). *San Francisco, Theatre Arts Playhouse, [Sept.] 1955.

PLANGO (W. C. Schad; 3 acts, American). *Islip, L.I., N.Y., 1938 (concert form).

The Poacher (Lortzing). See Der WILDSCHUETZ.

The Poacher (Marschner). See Der HOLZDIEB.

The Poachers (Offenbach). See Les BRACONNIERS.

El POBRE VALBUENA (J. Valverde; 1 act, Spanish, zarzuela, Mexico City ca. 1904). New York, Amsterdam Op. H., Dec. 22, 1916.

POCAHONTAS (W. Patton; American). *Minneapolis, Hotel Radison, Jan. 4, 1911 (concert form).

The POET'S DILEMMA (D. Lee; 1 act, American). *New York, Institute of Musical Art, Apr. 12, 1940.

POIA (A. F. Nevin; 3 acts, American). *Pittsburgh, Carnegie Music Hall, Jan. 16, 1907 (concert form); Berlin, Königliches Opernhaus, Apr. 23, 1910, in German.

The POISONED KISS (R. Vaughan Williams; 3 acts, English, Cambridge, England, 1936). New York, Juilliard School of Music, Apr. 21, 1937.

Der POLE UND SEIN KIND (A. Lortzing; 1 act, German, Osnabrück 1832). --Philadelphia, Franklin Hall, Jan. 14, 1850 (New York, Turnhalle, Feb. 22, 1867).

POLICHINELLE (A. Montfort; 1 act, French, Paris 1839). New Orleans, 1843 (New York, Niblo's Garden, May 19, 1843).

POLIFEMO (G. Bononcini; 1 act, Italian, Berlin 1702). Hartford, Conn., Hartt Auditorium (Julius Hartt School of Music), May 11, 1949, in English, as "Polifem."

The Polish Jew. See Der POLNISCHE JUDE.

Il Poliuto. See Les MARTYRS.

POLLY (J. C. Pepusch; 3 acts, English, London 1777). New York, Cherry Lane Playhouse, Oct. 10, 1925.

Der POLNISCHE JUDE (K. Weiss; 2 acts, German, Prague 1901). New York, Metropolitan Op. H., Mar. 9, 1921, in English.

POMME D'API (J. Offenbach; 1 act, French, Paris 1873). New York, Academy of Music, May 20, 1880.

Le PONT DES SOUPIRS (J. Offenbach; 4 acts, French, Paris 1861 in two acts; Paris 1868 in four acts). New York, Lina Edwin's Th., Nov. 27, 1871.

The POOR SOLDIER (W. Shield; 2 acts, English, Dublin 1783). New York, John Street Th., Dec. 2, 1785.

POOR VULCAN (C. Dibdin; 2 acts, English, London 1778). Charleston, S.C., Charleston Th., Feb. 22, 1793.

PORGY AND BESS (G. Gershwin; 3 acts, American). *Boston, Colonial Th., Sept. 30, 1935 (New York, Alvin Th., Oct. 10, 1935).

PORT TOWN (J. Meyerowitz; 1 act, American). *Tanglewood, Lenox, Mass., Music Shed (Berkshire Music Center), Aug. 4, 1960.

The PORTER AT THE DOOR (R. Mayer; 2 acts, American). *Winston-Salem, N.C., Reynolds Memorial Auditorium, Feb. 26, 1954.

Le PORTRAIT DE MANON (J. Massenet; 1 act, French, Paris 1894). New York, Waldorf Astoria Hotel, Dec. 13, 1897.

Le POSTILLON DE LONGJUMEAU (A. Adam; 3 acts, French, Paris 1836). New York, Park Th., Mar. 30, 1840, in English; New York, Niblo's Garden, June 16, 1843, in French [New Orleans earlier (?)].

The POT OF FAT (T. W. Chanler; 6 scenes, American). *Cambridge, Mass., Sanders Th., May 9, 1955 (concert form; Longy School of Music); New York, Finch College Auditorium, Feb. 22, 1956 (stage premiere; After Dinner Opera).

La POULE NOIRE (M. Rosenthal; 1 act, French, Paris 1937). New
York, Boylan Hall (Brooklyn College), Apr. 2, 1954, in English, as
"The Black hen."

La POUPEE (E. Audran; 4 acts, French, Paris 1896). New York,
Lyric Th., Oct. 21, 1897, in English.

La POUPEE DE NUREMBERG (A. Adam; 1 act, French, Paris
1852). --New York, Union Square Th., June 3, 1889, in English,
as "Ardiell" (translated from the German"); --New York, Princess
Th., Dec. 28, 1915, in French.

The PRANKSTER (R. Wykes; 1 act, American). *Bowling Green, O.,
Gate Th. (Bowling Green State Univ.), Jan. 12, 1952.

Le PRE AUX CLERCS (L. Herôld; 3 acts, French, Paris 1832).
--Baltimore, Holliday Street Th., Oct. 14, 1833 [New Orleans
earlier (?)].

PRECIOSA (C. M. von Weber; 4 acts, German, Berlin 1821). Philadelphia, New [Chestnut Street] Th., Oct. 31, 1829, in English; New
York, Franklin Th., Mar. 9, 1840, in German.

PRELUDE AND FUGUE (Arnold Franchetti; 1 act, American).
*Elmwood, Conn., Talcott School Auditorium, Apr. 21, 1959
(Hartt College of the Univ. of Hartford).

Les PRES SAINT-GERVAIS (C. Lecocq; 3 acts, French, Paris
1874). New York, Brooklyn Th., Sept. 27, 1875, in English, as
"Prince Conti."

Le PREZIOSE RIDICOLE (F. Lattuada; 1 act, Italian, Milan 1929).
New York, Metropolitan Op. H., Dec. 10, 1930.

Il PRIGIONIERO (L. Dallapiccola; prolog and 1 act, Italian, Turin
1949 in a radio perf.; Florence 1950 in operatic form). New York,
Juilliard School of Music, Mar. 15, 1951, in English, as "The
Prisoner."

PRIMA DONNA (A. Benjamin; 1 act, English, London 1949). Philadelphia, Mid-town Y.W.C.A., Dec. 5, 1953 (piano acc.); Evanston, Ill., Kahn Auditorium, Northwestern Univ.), Feb. 26, 1954
(orchestra acc.).

The Prima donna of [for] a night. See MONSIEUR
CHOUFLEURI.

The PRINCE AND THE PAUPER (A. Black; American). *Duxbury, Mass., Plymouth Rock Center of Music and Drama, Aug. 26,
1955.

Prince Conti. See Les PRES SAINT-GERVAIS

PRINCE IGOR (A. Borodin; prolog and 4 acts, Russian, St. Petersburg
1890). New York, Metropolitan Op. H., Dec. 30, 1915, in Italian;
Philadelphia, Academy of Music, Dec. 23, 1935, in Russian.

The PRINCE OF PILSEN (G. Luders; 2 acts, American). *Boston,
Tremont Th., May 21, 1902 (New York, Broadway Th., Mar. 17,
1903).
The PRINCESS (Arnold Franchetti; 1 act, American). *Hartford,
Conn., Hartt College of Music, Mar. 16, 1952.
The PRINCESS AND THE FROG (F. McClain; 1 act, American).
*Yankton, S.D., Forbes Hall Auditorium (Yankton College), June
13, 1959.
The PRINCESS AND THE SPINDLE (S. Virzi; 3 acts, American).
*New York, Bronx Winter Garden, May 6, 1955.
The PRINCESS AND THE VAGABOND (I. Freed; 2 acts,
American). *Hartford, Conn., Hartt School of Music, May 13, 1948.
PRINCESS IDA (A. Sullivan; prolog and 2 acts, English, London 1884).
New York, Fifth Avenue Th., and Boston, Boston Museum [theatre],
Feb. 11, 1884 (simultaneously).
La Princesse d'auberge. See De HERBERGPRINSES.
La PRINCESSE DE TREBIZONDE (J. Offenbach; 3 acts, French,
Baden-Baden 1869 in two acts; Paris 1869 in three acts). New York,
Wallack's Th., Sept. 11, 1871, in English; --New York, Lyceum
Th., Sept. 10, 1874, in French.
PRINZ METHUSALEM (J. Strauss; 3 acts, German, Vienna 1877).
San Francisco, California Th., Aug. 29, 1880, in German (New York,
Thalia Theater, Oct. 29, 1880, in German).
Die PRINZESSIN AUF DER ERBSE (E. Toch; 1 act, German,
Baden-Baden 1927). New York, Biltimore Th., June 9, 1936, in
English, as "The Princess on the pea."
The PRISONER (T. Attwood; 3 acts, English, London 1792). Philadel-
phia, New [Chestnut Street] Th., May 29, 1795.
The Prisoner (Dallapiccola). See Il PRIGIONIERO.
Le PRISONNIER (P. A. D. Della Maria; 1 act, French, Paris 1798).
--New York, Park Th., Sept. 12, 1827 [New Orleans earlier (?)].
The PRIZE (S. Storace; 2 acts, English, London 1793). Philadelphia,
New [Chestnut Street] Th., May 26, 1794.
PRODANA NEVESTA [The Bartered bride] (B. Smetana;
3 acts, Czech, Prague 1866). Chicago, Haymarket Th., Aug. 20,
1893, in Czech (New York, Metropolitan Op. H., Feb. 19, 1909,
in German).
The Prodigal son (Debussy). See L'ENFANT PRODIGUE.
The PRODIGAL SON (F. Jacobi; 3 acts, American). *Stanford,
Cal., Stanford Univ., Aug. 1949 (Act II; concert form); London,
England, Central Music Library, Apr. 10, 1951 (concert form).
The Promissory note. See La LETTRE DE CHANGE.

Le PROPHETE (G. Meyerbeer; 5 acts, French, Paris 1849). New
Orleans, Théâtre d'Orléans, Apr. 1 (not 2), 1850.

A PROVINCIAL EPISODE (M. Wald; 1 act, American). *Athens,
O., Ewing Auditorium (Ohio Univ.), July 17, 1952.

Der PROZESS (G. von Einem; 2 acts, German, Salzburg 1953). New
York, City Center, Oct. 22, 1953, in English.

Pskovitanka. See The MAID OF PSKOV.

PSOHLAVCI [Dogs' heads] (K. Kovarovic; 3 acts, Czech, Prague
1898). Cicero, Ill., Sterling Norton High School Auditorium, Nov.
8, 1936 (second perf., Nov. 15, 1936).

The PUMPKIN (L. Kondorossy; 1 act, American). *Cleveland,
Severance Chamber Music Hall, May 15, 1954 (concert form).

El PUNAO DE ROSAS (R. Chapi; 1 act, zarzuela, Spanish, Madrid
1910). New York, Amsterdam Op. H., Dec. 20, 1916.

PURGATORY (H. Weisgall; 1 act, American). *Washington, D.C.,
Coolidge Auditorium (Library of Congress), Feb. 17, 1961.

I PURITANI (V. Bellini; 3 acts, Italian, Paris 1835). Philadelphia,
Chestnut Street Th., July (not Nov.), 22, 1843.

The PURITAN'S DAUGHTER (M. W. Balfe; 3 acts, English,
London 1861). New York, Theatre Francais [sic], Sept. 11, 1869.

The PURSE (W. Reeve; 1 act, English, London 1794). Philadelphia,
New [Chestnut Street] Th., Jan. 7, 1795 (with additional music by
A. Reinagle).

PUSS IN BOOTS (C. Cui; Russian). New York, Frolic Th. [New
Amsterdam Roof Th.], Sept. 10, 1923 (V. Podrecca's Teatro dei
Piccoli).

PYGMALION (J. P. Rameau; 1 act, French, Paris 1748). New York,
Grace Rainy Rogers Auditorium (Metropolitan Museum of Art), Feb.
7, 1959 (concert form); Boston, Boston Conservatory, Feb. 17, 1961
(stage perf.).

PYGMALION (J. J. Rousseau; 1 act, French, Lyons 1770). New York,
City Tavern, Nov. 10, 1790.

- Q -

The QUAKER (C. Dibdin; 2 acts, English, London 1775). Fredericksburg, Va., Market House, Sept. 16, 1791.

The QUARTETTE, or Interrupted harmony (C. E. Horn;
1 act, American). *New York, Bowery Th., Apr. 27, 1829.

I QUATTRO RUSTEGHI (E. Wolf-Ferrari; 4 acts, Italian, Munich
1906 in German). New York, City Center, Oct. 18, 1951, in
English, as "The Four ruffians."

The Queen of Sheba. See Die KOENIGIN VON SABA.

The Queen's lace handkerchief. See Das SPITZENTUCH
DER KOENIGIN.

The QUIET DON (I. Dzerzhinsky; 4 acts, Russian, Leningrad 1935).
Detroit, Masonic Temple Auditorium, Mar. 25, 1945.

A QUIET GAME OF CRIBBLE (M. Kalmanoff; 1 act, American).
*New York, Greenwich House Music School, June 8, 1954.

QUO VADIS? (J. Nouguès; 5 acts, French, Nice 1909). Philadelphia,
Metropolitan Op. H., Mar. 25, 1911.

- R -

RAFFAELO (A. Mildenberg; 1 act, American). *Naples, 1910, in
Italian (concert form).

The RAJAH'S RUBY (S. Barab; 1 act, American). *New York,
Sullivan Street Playhouse, Apr. 19, 1958.

The RAKE'S PROGRESS (I. Stravinsky; 3 acts, American).
*Venice, Teatro La Fenice, Sept. 11, 1951, in English (New York,
Metropolitan Op. H., Feb. 14, 1953).

RAMONA (G. Strube; 3 acts, American). *Baltimore, Lyric Th.,
Feb. 28, 1938.

RAMUNTCHO (D. Taylor; 3 acts, American). *Philadelphia,
Academy of Music, Feb. 10, 1942.

Le Ranz des vaches. See Der KUHREIGEN.

RAOUL, SIRE DE CREQUI (N. Dalayrac; 3 acts, French, Paris
1789). New Orleans, 1810.

The RAPE OF LUCRETIA (B. Britten; 2 acts, English, Glyndebourne, England, 1946). Chicago, Shubert Th., June 1, 1947.

RAPUNZEL (L. Harrison; 1 act, American). *New York, Theresa
Kaufmann Concert Hall (Y.M. and Y.W.H.A.), May 14, 1959.

Der RATTENFAENGER VON HAMELN (V. Nessler; 5 acts,
German, Leipzig 1879). New York, Thalia Theater, Apr. 28, 1886.

Il RE PASTORE (J. J. Quantz, H. Graun, C. Nichelmann, and
Frederick the Great; pasticcio, Italian, Charlottenburg 1747).
[Grove, 5th ed., art., Frederick II, says: "revived...as 'Moltke-
Feier' (!), at the Metropolitan Opera, New York, on 27 Oct. 1890."
Midway in a program of music and speeches in honor of the German
field marshall Graf von Moltke, Anton Seidl conducted an item
listed as "Il Re Pastore von Friedrich dem Grossen"---presumably an
instrumental excerpt.]

Il RE TEODORE IN VENEZIA (G. Paisiello; 2 acts, Italian,
Vienna 1784). Tanglewood, Lenox, Mass., Theatre-Concert Hall
(Berkshire Music Center), Aug. 7, 1961, in English (two piano acc.);

New York, Juilliard School of Music, Sept. 10, 1961, in English (orchestra acc.).

A REAL STRANGE ONE (B. Holton; 1 act, American). *New York, Sullivan Street Playhouse, Apr. 23, 1958.

The REBEL (C. Venth; 5 scenes, American). *Fort Worth, Tex., May 29, 1926.

The RECRUITING SERJEANT (C. Dibdin; 1 act, English, Ranelagh 1769). Boston, Federal Street Th., Mar. 15, 1799.

The RED MILL (V. Herbert; 2 acts, American). *Buffalo, N.Y., Star Th., Sept. 3, 1906 (New York, Knickerbocker Th., Sept. 24, 1906).

REGINA (M. Blitzstein; 3 acts, American). *New Haven, Conn., Shubert Th., Oct. 6, 1949 (New York, 46th Street Th., Oct. 31, 1949).

REHEARSAL CALL (V. Giannini; 3 acts, American). *New York, Juilliard School of Music, Feb. 15, 1962.

La REINE DE CHYPRE (J. Halévy; 5 acts, French, Paris 1841). New Orleans, Théâtre d'Orléans, Mar. 25, 1845.

La REINE DE SABA (C. Gounod; 4 acts, French, Paris 1862). New Orleans, French Op. H., Jan. 12, 1889.

La REINE FIAMMETTE (X. Leroux; 4 acts, French, Paris 1903). New York, Metropolitan Op. H., Jan. 24, 1919.

El RELAMPAGO (F. A. Barbieri; 3 acts, zarzuela, Spanish, Madrid). --Tucson, Ariz., Levin's Hall, early Aug. 1884 (Spanish Mexican Opera Bouffe Combination).

RENARD (I. Stravinsky; 1 act, Russian, Paris 1922 in French). New York, Vanderbilt Th., Dec. 2, 1923, in French (concert form); New York, Hunter College Playhouse, Jan. 13, 1947, in English (stage perf.).

RENAUD D'AST (N. Dalayrac; 2 acts, French, Paris 1787). New Orleans, Sept. 3, 1799.

La RENCONTRE IMPREVUE (C. W. von Gluck; 3 acts, French, Vienna 1764). Cleveland, Karamu House, June 8, 1951, in English, as "The Caravan to Mecca."

Les RENDEZ-VOUS BOURGEOIS (N. Isouard; 1 act, French, Paris 1807). --New York, Park Th., July 25, 1827 [New Orleans earlier (?)].

El RETABLO DE MAESE PEDRO (M. de Falla; 1 act, Spanish, Seville 1923). New York, Town Hall, Dec. 29, 1925 (with marionettes); Chicago, Goodman Th., Feb. 8, 1931, in English (with marionettes); Boston, Esquire Th., Mar. 5, 1954, in English, as "Master Peter's puppet show" (Boston Univ.); New York, Grace

Rainey Rogers Auditorium (Metropolitan Museum of Art), Feb. 23, 1957, in Spanish (with marionettes).

The Return of the roamer. See Die HEIMKEHR AUS DER FREMDE.

Les REVENANTS BRETONS (J. B. Weckerlin; 1 act, French). --New York, Barbizon Plaza Hotel, Feb. 25, 1933, in English, as "The Ghost of Brittany."

The REVIEW, or The Wags of Windsor (S. Arnold; 2 acts, English, London 1801). Baltimore, New Th., May 1, 1802.

Der REVISOR (W. Egk; 3 acts, German, Schwetzingen 1957). New York, City Center, Oct. 19, 1960, in English, as "The Inspector General."

REVIVAL (C. Loomis; 1 act, choral opera, American). *Los Angeles, Station KFWB (Warner Bros.), Apr. 1942 (radio perf.).

El REY QUE RABIO (R. Chapi; 3 acts, zarzuela, Spanish, Madrid 1891). --New Orleans, Academy of Music, May 3, 1897 (Spanish Juvenile Opera).

Das Rheingold. See Der RING DES NIBELUNGEN.

The RIBBON (E. Kahn; 1 act, American). *Montclair, N.J., Hillside Junior High School, May 8, 1952.

RICHARD III (G. Salvayre; 4 acts, French, St. Petersburg 1883 in Italian; Nice 1891 in French). New Orleans, French Op. H., Jan. 5, 1895.

RICHARD COEUR-DE-LION (M. Grêtry; 3 acts, French, Paris 1784). Boston, New Exhibition Room, May 23, 1793, in English (as a pantomime); Boston, Federal Street Th., Jan. 23, 1797, in English ("with all the original music...composed by Gretry; the orchestra accompaniments entirely new, composed by Mons. [Trille] Labarre"); New Orleans, Le Spectacle de la Rue St. Pierre, ca. 1803-08, in French.

RIDERS TO THE SEA (R. Vaughn Williams; 1 act, English, London 1937). --Cleveland, Engineers Building Auditorium, Feb. 26, 1950 (Western Reserve Univ.).

RIENZI (R. Wagner; 5 acts, German, Dresden 1842). New York, Academy of Music, Mar. 4, 1878.

RIGOLETTO (G. Verdi; 3 acts, Italian, Venice 1851). New York, Academy of Music, Feb. 19, 1855.

Der RING DES NIBELUNGEN (R. Wagner; tetralogy, German, Bayreuth 1876). New York, Metropolitan Op. H., Mar. 4-5, 8, 11, 1889. Separately---
  Das RHEINGOLD (Munich 1869): New York, Metropolitan Op. H., Jan. 4, 1889.

Die WALKUERE (Munich 1870): New York, Academy of Music, Apr. 2, 1877.

SIEGFRIED (Bayreuth 1876): New York, Metropolitan Op. H., Nov. 9, 1887.

Die GOETTERDAEMMERUNG (Bayreuth 1876): Cincinnati, Music Hall, May 16, 1878 (Act III; concert form); New York, Metropolitan Op. H., Jan. 25, 1888 (stage perf., without the scenes of the Norns and Waltraute).

Der RING DES POLYKRATES (E. Korngold; 1 act, German, Munich 1916). Philadelphia, Metropolitan Op. H., Feb. 10, 1927.

RIP VAN WINKLE (G. F. Bristow; 3 acts, American). *New York, Niblo's Garden, Sept. 27, 1855.

RIP VAN WINKLE (R. DeKoven; 3 acts, American). *Chicago, Auditorium, Jan. 2, 1920.

RIP VAN WINKLE (J. Jordan; 3 acts, American). *Providence, R.I., Providence Op. H., May 25, 1897.

RIP VAN WINKLE (E. Manning; 3 acts, American). *New York, Town Hall, Feb. 12, 1932.

RISURREZIONE (F. Alfano; 4 acts, Italian, Turin 1904). Chicago, Auditorium, Dec. 31, 1925, in French.

RITA (G. Donizetti; 1 act, French, Paris 1860). New York, Hunter College Playhouse, May 14, 1957, in English (Manhattan School of Music).

Il Ritorno di Columella. See Il RITORNO DI PULCINELLA.

Il RITORNO DI PULCINELLA DAGLI STUDI DI PADOVA (V. Fioravanti; 2 acts, italian, Naples 1837). Philadelphia, Academy of Music, Apr. 4, 1857 (one scene, as "Columella"; same, New York, Niblo's Garden, May 8, 1857).

Il RITORNO D'ULISSE IN PATRIA (C. Monteverdi; prolog and 5 acts, Italian, Venice 1641). New York, Baron de Rothschild Foundation of the Arts and Sciences, May 15, 1956 (three scenes; semi-staged).

The RIVAL CANDIDATES (C. T. Carter; 2 acts and epilog, English, London 1775). Philadelphia, Southwark Th., June 13, 1791.

The RIVAL SOLDIERS (W. Shield; 2 acts, English, London 1793 as "Sprigs of laurel"). Philadelphia, New [Chestnut Street] Th., Apr. 5, 1799.

Rizzio. See DAVID RIZZIO.

ROB ROY MACGREGOR (H. R. Bishop and J. Davy; 3 acts, English, London 1818). New York, Park Th., June 8, 1818.

The ROBBERS (N. Rorem; 1 act, American). *New York, Theresa
   Kaufmann Concert Hall (Y.M. and Y.W.H.A.), Apr. 14, 1958.
The Robe of pearls. See Das PERLENHEMD.
ROBERT LE DIABLE (G. Meyerbeer; 5 acts, French, Paris 1831).
   New York, Park Th., Apr. 7, 1834, in English (M. R. Lacy's London
   version); New Orleans, Théâtre d'Orléans, Dec. 24, 1836.
ROBERTA (J. Kern; 2 acts, American). *Philadelphia, Forrest Th.,
   Oct. 22, 1933, as "Gowns by Roberta" (New York, New Amsterdam
   Th., Nov. 18, 1933).
ROBERTO DEVEREAUX (G. Donizetti; 3 acts, Italian, Naples 1837).
   New York, Astor Place Op. H., Jan. 15, 1849.
Robin and Marion. See Le JEU DE ROBIN ET DE MARION.
ROBIN HOOD (R. DeKoven; 3 acts, American). *Chicago, Chicago
   Op. H., June 9, 1890 (New York, Standard Th., Sept. 28, 1891).
ROBIN HOOD (J. Hewitt; 2 acts, American). *New York, Park Th.,
   Dec. 24, 1800.
ROBIN HOOD (W. Shield; 3 acts, English, London 1784). Charleston,
   S.C., Charleston Th., Feb. 16, 1793.
ROBINSON (F. A. Barbieri; 3 acts, zarzuela, Spanish, Madrid 1870).
   New York, Fifth Avenue Th., Sept. 6, 1875, as "Robinson Crusoe"
   (Mexican Juvenile Opera).
ROBINSON CRUSOE (J. Offenbach; 3 acts, French, Paris 1867).
   --New York, Wallack's Th., Sept. 12, 1877, in English (burlesque
   version).
RODELINDA (G. F. Handel; 3 acts, Italian, London 1725). North-
   hampton, Mass., Academy of Music, May 9, 1931, in English
   (Smith College).
Le ROI CAROTTE (J. Offenbach; 4 acts, French, Paris 1872). New
   York, Grand Op. H., Aug. 26, 1872, in English.
Le ROI DE LAHORE (J. Massenet; 5 acts, French, Paris 1877). New
   Orleans, French Op. H., Dec. 1883.
Le ROI D'YS (E. Lalo; 3 acts, French, Paris 1888). New Orleans,
   French Op. H., Jan. 23, 1890.
Le ROI D'YVETOT (J. Ibert; 4 acts, French, Paris 1930). Tangle-
   wood, Lenox, Mass., Theatre-Concert Hall (Berkshire Music Center),
   Aug. 7, 1950, in English.
ROKEBY (F. H. F. Berkeley; American). *New York, Park Th., May
   17, 1830.
ROLAND A RONCEVAUX (A. Mermet; 4 acts, French, Paris 1864).
   New Orleans, French Op. H., ca. 186- (as late as Oct. 1892).

A ROMANCE WITH A DOUBLE BASS [Roman s contrabsom]
(A. Dubensky; prolog, 3 acts and epilog, Russian, Moscow 1916).
New York, True Sisters Auditorium, Oct. 31, 1936, in Russian.
ROMEO ET JULIETTE (C. Gounod; 5 acts, French, Paris 1867).
New York, Academy of Music, Nov. 15 (not Dec. 14), 1867, in
Italian; New Orleans, French Op. H., Feb. 24, 1870, in French.
ROMEO ET JULIETTE (D. Steibelt; 3 acts, French, Paris 1793).
New Orleans, Théâtre St. Pierre, Aug. 6, 1810.
ROMEO UND JULIA (B. Blacher; 1 act, German, Salzburg 1950).
Urbana, Ill., Lincoln Hall Th. (Univ. of Illinois), Jan. 14, 1953, in
English.
ROMILDA (S. N. Cardillo; 1 act, American). New York, Carnegie
Lyceum, Oct. 4, 1913.
The ROMP (C. Dibdin; 2 acts, English, London 1778). Fredericksburg,
Va., Market House, Aug. 5, 1790.
La RONDINE (G. Puccini; 2 acts, Italian, Monte Carlo 1917). New
York, Metropolitan Op. H., Mar. 10, 1928.
ROOM NO. 12 (E. Kanitz; 1 act, American). *Los Angeles, Schön-
berg Hall (Univ. of California), Feb. 26, 1958.
The ROPE (L. Mennini; 1 act, American). *Tanglewood, Lenox,
Mass., Theatre-Concert Hall (Berkshire Music Center), Aug. 8, 1955.
ROSALIND (F. Wickham; prolog and 2 acts, American). *Carmel,
N.Y., Rockridge Th., Aug. 5, 1938; Dresden, Theater des Volkes,
Nov. 6, 1938, in German.
ROSAMUNDA VON CYPERN (F. Schubert; incidental music,
German, Vienna 1823). *Auburndale, Mass., Levi F. Warren High
School, July 31, 1928, in an American adaptation of the music by
Alexander Dean, as a school operetta (also, New York, National
Broadcasting Company, Nov. 18, 1928, in a radio perf.).
The ROSE AND THE RING (E. Leginska; 3 acts, American). *Los
Angeles, Wilshire Ebell Th., Feb. 23, 1957.
La ROSE DE SAINT-FLOUR (J. Offenbach; 1 act, French, Paris
1856). --Charleston, S.C., Charleston Th., Mar. 5, 1860.
ROSE-MARIE (R. Friml and H. Stothart; 2 acts, American).
*Atlantic City, Apollo Th., Aug. 18, 1924 (New York, Imperial
Th., Sept. 2, 1924).
The Rose of Auvergne. See La ROSE DE SAINT-FLOUR.
The ROSE OF CASTILE (M. W. Balfe; 3 acts, English, London
1857). New York, Olympic Th., July 27, 1864.
The ROSE OF DESTINY (C. Heckscher; 3 acts, American).
* Philadelphia, Metropolitan Op. H., May 2, 1918.

The ROSE OF PERSIA   (A. Sullivan; 2 acts, English, London 1899).
New York, Daly's Th., Sept. 6, 1900 (not 1901).

The ROSE OF TYROL   (J. Eichberg; American).   *Boston, 1865.

Der ROSENKAVALIER   (R. Strauss; 3 acts, German, Dresden 1911).
New York, Metropolitan Op. H., Dec. 9, 1913.

La ROSIERE DE SALENCY   (M. Grétry; 3 acts, French, Fontainebleau 1773 in four acts; Paris 1774 in three acts).   --New Orleans,
1815.

ROSINA   (W. Shield; 2 acts, English, London 1782).   New York, John
Street Th., Apr. 19, 1786.

Le ROSSIGNOL   (L. S. Lebrun; 1 act, French, Paris 1816).   --New
York, Chatham Th., Sept. 12, 1828 [New Orleans earlier (?)].

Le ROSSIGNOL   (I. Stravinsky; 3 acts, Russian, Paris 1914 in French).
New York, Metropolitan Op. H., Mar. 6 (not 7), 1926, in French.

ROYAL AUCTION   (E. Kanitz; 1 act, American).   *Los Angeles,
Schonberg Hall (Univ. of California), Feb. 26, 1958.

Los RUBIOS   (M. C. Moore; 3 acts, American).   *Los Angeles, Greek
Th., Sept. 10, 1931 (in English).

The RUBY   (N. Dello Joio; 1 act, American).   *Bloomington, Ind.,
East Hall (Indiana Univ.), May 13, 1955.

RUDDIGORE   (A. Sullivan; 2 acts, English, London 1887).   New York,
Fifth Avenue Th., Feb. 21, 1887.

RUIDO DE CAMPANAS   (V. Lleó; 1 act, zarzuela, Spanish).   New
York, 63rd Street Music Hall, Feb. 20, 1921.

RUSALKA   (A. S. Dargomyzhsky; 4 acts, Russian, St. Petersburg 1856).
New York, Educational Alliance, Dec. 1902 (Act III; concert form);
Seattle, Metropolitan Th., Dec. 23, 1921 (stage perf.).

RUSALKA   (A. Dvořák; 3 acts, Czech, Prague 1901).   Chicago, Sokal
Slav Hall, Mar. 10 (and 17), 1935.

RUSSLAN AND LUDMILA   (M. Glinka; 5 acts, Russian, St. Petersburg 1842).   New York, Town Hall, Dec. 26, 1942 (concert form).

RUTH   (K. Garland; 6 scenes, American).   *Fredericksburg, Va.,
George Washington Auditorium (Mary Washington College), May 4,
1952.

RUY BLAS   (F. Marchetti; 4 acts, Italian, Milan 1869).   New York,
Academy of Music, Oct. 14, 1874.

- S -

The SACRED TREE OF THE OMAHA   (H. P. Eames; 1 act,
American).   *Lincoln, Nebr., Nebraska University Open-Air Th.,
Spring 1917.

The SACRIFICE (F. S. Converse; 3 acts, American). *Boston,
    Boston Op. H., Mar. 3, 1911 (not Nov. 16, 1910).
SADKO (N. Rimsky-Korsakov; 7 scenes, Russian, Moscow 1898 [O. S.
    1897]. New York, Metropolitan Op. H., Jan. 25, 1930, in French;
    Swathmore, Pa., Collection Hall (Swathmore College), Apr. 11,
    1930, in Russian (excerpts; concert form).
SAFFO (G. Pacini; 3 acts, Italian, Naples 1840). Boston, Howard
    Athenaeum, May 4, 1847.
SAFIE (H. K. Hadley; 1 act, American). *Mayence, Germany,
    Stadttheater, Apr. 6, 1909, in German.
The SAILING OF THE NANCY BELL (A. Davis; 1 act,
    American). *Duxbury, Mass., Plymouth Rock Center of Music and
    Drama, Aug. 3, 1955.
The SAINT OF BLEECKER STREET (G. C. Menotti; 3 acts,
    American). *New York, Broadway Th., Dec. 27, 1954.
St. Paul. See PAULUS.
SAKAHRA (S. Bucharoff; 3 acts, American). *Frankfurt-am-Main,
    Stadtisches Opernhaus, Oct. 29, 1924, in German.
SAKURA (C. Lapham; American). *Los Angeles, Hollywood Bowl,
    June 24, 1933, in Japanese (first Japanese-language opera in the
    United States).
SALAMMBO (E. Reyer; 5 acts, French, Brussels 1890). New Orleans,
    French Op. H., Jan. 25, 1900.
The SALESGIRL (C. Hamm; 1 act, American). *Bristol, Va.,
    Drama Hall (Virginia Intermont College), Mar. 1, 1955.
SALLY BACK AND FORTH (S. F. Park; 1 act, American). *Tam-
    pa, Fla., Centro Asturiano, Oct. 6, 1959 (Univ. of Tampa).
SALOME (R. Strauss; 1 act, German, Dresden 1905). New York,
    Metropolitan Op. H., Jan. 22, 1907 (public rehearsal; withdrawn);
    New York, Manhattan Op. H., Jan. 28, 1909, in French; Los Angeles,
    Auditorium, Nov. 14, 1912, in Italian; San Francisco, Civic Audi-
    orium, Sept. 12, 1930, in German.
SAMSON ET DALILA (C. Saint-Saens; 3 acts, French, Weimar 1877
    in German in concert form; Paris 1892 in French in operatic form).
    New York, Music Hall [Carnegie Hall], Mar. 25, 1892, in English
    (concert form); New Orleans, French Op. H., Jan. 4, 1893, in
    French (stage perf.).
SAMUEL (J. Hopkins; 3 acts, American). *New York, Academy of
    Music, May 3, 1877.
SANCTA SUSANNA (P. Hindemith; 1 act, German, Frankfurt-am-
    Main 1922). --San Francisco, San Francisco Conservatory of Music,
    Mar. 19, 1961, in English.

92

SAPHO (J. Massenet; 5 acts, French, Paris 1897). New York, Manhattan
Op. H., Nov. 17 (not 15 or 18), 1909.

SARAH (E. Laderman; American). *New York, Columbia Broadcasting
System (CBS-TV), Nov. 30, 1958 (TV perf.).

El SARGENTO FEDERICO (F. A. Barbieri and J. Gaztambide; 4
acts, zarzuela, Spanish, Madrid 1855). --Tucson, Ariz., Levin's
Hall, Aug. 17, 1884 (Spanish Mexican Opera Bouffe Combination).

SARRONA (W. L. Howland; prolog and 1 act [2 acts], American).
*New York, Carnegie Lyceum, Dec. 5, 1901.

SATANELLA (M. W. Balfe; 4 acts, English, London 1858). New
York, Niblo's Garden, Feb. 23, 1863.

SATAN'S TRAP (F. Piket; 3 acts, American). *New York, Clark
Auditorium (West Side Y.W.C.A.), Nov. 26, 1960.

Le SAUTERIOT (S. Lazzari; 3 acts, French). *Chicago, Auditorium,
Jan. 19, 1918.

SAVITRI (G. Holst; 1 act, English, London 1916). --Chicago, Palmer
House, Jan. 23, 1934.

The SAVOYARD (A. Reinagle; 2 acts, American). *Philadelphia,
New [Chestnut Street] Th., July 12, 1797.

The SAW MILL (M. Hawkins; 2 acts, American). *New York,
Chatham Garden, Nov. 29, 1824.

The SCANDAL AT MULFORD INN (W. C. Byrd; 1 act,
American). *Cincinnati, Odeon, Apr. 1, 1953 (College of Music
of Cincinnati).

The SCARECROW (N. Lockwood; 2 acts, American). *New York,
Brander Matthews Hall (Columbia Univ.), May 9 (not 19), 1945.

The SCARF (L. Hoiby; 1 act, American). *Spoleto, Italy, Teatro
Calo Melisso, June 20, 1958; New York, City Center, Apr. 5, 1959
(U. S. premiere).

The SCARLET LETTER (W. Damrosch; 3 acts, American). *Boston, Boston Th., Feb. 10, 1896.

The SCARLET LETTER (V. Giannini; 2 acts, American). *Hamburg, Germany, Staatsoper, June 2, 1938, in German.

The SCARLET LETTER (W. Kaufmann; 3 acts, American).
*Bloomington, Ind., East Hall (Indiana Univ.), May 6, 1961.

The SCENT OF SARSAPARILLA (C. Hamm; 1 act, American).
*San Francisco, Sir Francis Drake Hotel, Sept. 5, 1954.

Die SCHOENE GALATEA (F. von Suppé; 1 act, German, Berlin
1865). New York, Stadt Theater, Sept. 6, 1867.

The SCHOOL FOR WIVES (R. Liebermann; German). *Louisville,
Ky., Columbia Auditorium (Univ. of Louisville), Dec. 3, 1955.

Schwanda. See SVANDA DUDAK.

Die SCHWEIGSAME FRAU (R. Strauss; 3 acts, German, Dresden 1935). New York, City Center, Oct. 7, 1958, in English.

Die SCHWEIZERFAMILIE (J. Weigl; 3 acts, German, Vienna 1809). Philadelphia, Arch Street Th., May 5, 1840.

Die SCHWESTERN VON PRAG (W. Müller; 2 acts, German, Vienna 1794). New York, Stadt Theater, Nov. 30, 1859.

The SECOND HURRICANE (A. Copland; 2 acts, American). *New York, Grand Street Playhouse, Apr. 21, 1937.

The SECRET LIFE OF WALTER MITTY (C. Hamm; 1 act, American). *Athens, O., Ewing Hall (Ohio Univ.), July 30, 1953.

The Seraglio (Dibdin). See The SULTAN.

The SERENADE (V. Herbert; 3 acts, American). *Cleveland, Euclid Avenue Op. H., Feb. 17, 1897 (New York, Knickerbocker Th., Mar. 16, 1897).

SERSE (G. F. Handel; 3 acts, Italian, London 1738). Northampton, Mass., Academy of Music, May 12, 1928, in English (Smith College).

La SERVA PADRONA (G. Paisiello; 2 acts, Italian, St. Petersburg 1781). New York, Academy of Music, Nov. 13, 1858.

La SERVA PADRONA (G. B. Pergolesi; 2 acts, Italian, Naples 1733). Baltimore, New Th., June 14, 1790, in French, as "La Servante maîtresse" (first French-language opera in the United States); New York, Lyceum Th., May 7, 1917, in English, as "The Maid mistress;" New York, Metropolitan Op. H., Feb. 23, 1935, in Italian.

SETTE CANZONI (G. F. Malipiero; 7 parts, Italian, Paris 1920 in French; Turin 1926 in Italian). New York, Times Square Th., Mar. 29, 1925, in French (concert form); Philadelphia, Penn Athletic Club, May 15, 1930, in Italian (stage perf.).

SHAMUS O'BRIEN (C. V. Stanford; 2 acts, English, London 1896). New York, Broadway Th., Jan. 5, 1897.

SHANEWIS (C. W. Cadman; 2 acts, American). *New York, Metropolitan Op. H., Mar. 23, 1918.

The SHEEP SHEARING (T. A. Arne; prolog, 2 acts and epilog, English, London 1754). Philadelphia, Theatre in the Northern Liberties, Dec. 20, 1791, as "Florizel and Perdita."

The SHEPHERDS OF THE DELECTABLE MOUNTAINS (R. Vaughan Williams; 1 act, English, London 1922). Cincinnati, St. Bernard Auditorium, Dec. 16, 1949.

Shinbone Alley. See ARCHY AND MEHITABEL.

The SHIPWRECK (S. Arnold; 2 acts, English, London 1796). Philadelphia, New [Chestnut Street] Th., Mar. (not May), 2, 1798.

SHOW BOAT   (J. Kern; 2 acts, American).   *Washington, D.C.,
    National Th., Nov. 15, 1927 (New York, Ziegfeld Th., Dec. 27,
    1927).
SI J'ETAIS ROI   (A. Adam; 3 acts, French, Paris 1852).   New Orleans,
    Théâtre d'Orléans, Apr. 10, 1856.
SIBERIA   (U. Giordano; 3 acts, Italian, Milan 1903).   New Orleans,
    French Op. H., Jan. 13 (not 31), 1906, in French; New York, Man-
    hattan Op. H., Feb. 5, 1908, in Italian.
The SICILIAN ROMANCE   (W. Reeve; 3 acts, English, London
    1794).   Boston, Federal Street Th., Apr. 10, 1796.
Le SIEGE DE CORINTHE   (G. Rossini; 3 acts, French, Paris 1826).
    New York, Italian Op. H., Feb. 6, 1835, in Italian, as "L'Assedio
    di Corinto. "
The SIEGE OF BELGRADE   (S. Storace; 3 acts, English, London
    1791).   New York, John Street Th., Dec. 30, 1796.
The SIEGE OF ROCHELLE   (M. W. Balfe; 3 acts, English, London
    1835).   New York, Park Th., Apr. 9, 1838.
Siegfried.   See Der RING DES NIBELUNGEN.
Il SIGNOR BRUSCHINO   (G. Rossini; 1 act, Italian, Venice 1813).
    New York, Metropolitan Op. H., Dec. 9, 1932.
SIGURD   (E. Reyer; 4 acts, French, Brussels 1884).   New Orleans, French
    Op. H., Dec. 24, 1891.
SILVAIN   (M. Grétry; 1 act, French, Paris 1770).   New Orleans, May
    27, 1796.
SIMONE BOCCANEGRA   (G. Verdi; prolog and 3 acts, Italian,
    Venice 1857).   New York, Metropolitan Op. H., Jan. 28, 1932.
SIMOON   (E. Chisholm; 1 act, English).   *New York, Cherry Lane Th.,
    July 6, 1954.
SIMOON   (J. Meyerowitz; 1 act, American).   *Tanglewood, Lenox,
    Mass., Theatre-Concert Hall (Berkshire Music Center). Aug. 2, 1949.
SING OUT, SWEET LAND!   (E. Siegmeister; 2 acts, American).
    *Hartford, Conn., Horace Bushnell Memorial Auditorium, Nov. 9,
    1944 (New York, International Th., Dec. 27, 1944).
SINGIN' BILLY   (C. F. Bryan; 2 acts, American).   *Nashville, Tenn.,
    Vanderbilt University Th., Apr. 23, 1952.
SIR JOHN IN LOVE (R. Vaughan Williams; 4 acts, English, London
    1929).   New York, Brander Matthews Hall (Columbia Univ.), Jan. 20,
    1949.
The SIRE DE MALEDROIT   (J. Duke; American).   *Schroon Lake,
    N.Y., Oscar Seagle Memorial Th., Aug. 15, 1958.
The Sire de Maledroit's door.   See The DOOR.
La SIRENE   (D. Auber; 3 acts, French, Paris 1844).   New Orleans,
    Théâtre d'Orléans, 1845.

The SISTERS (N. Flagello; 1 act, American). *New York, Manhattan School of Music, Feb. 22, 1961.

SIX CHARACTERS IN SEARCH OF AN AUTHOR. (H. Weisgall; 3 acts, American). *New York, City Center, Apr. 26, 1959.

Sixty-six. See Les SOIXANTE SIX!

The SLAVE (H. R. Bishop; 3 acts, English, London 1816). New York,
Park Th., July 4, 1817.

SLAVES IN ALGIERS (A. Reinagle; prolog and 3 acts, American).
*Philadelphia, New [Chestnut Street] Th., June 30, 1794.

The SLEEPING BEAUTY (B. Rubinstein; 3 acts, American). *New
York, Juilliard School of Music, Jan. 19, 1938.

SLEEPY HOLLOW (M. Maretzek; 3 acts, American). *New York,
Academy of Music, Sept. 25, 1879.

SLOW DUSK (C. Floyd; 1 act, American). *Syracuse, N.Y., Crouse
Auditorium (Syracuse Univ.), May 2, 1949.

The Smuggler. See Une NUIT BLANCHE.

The SNACK SHOP (F. McClain; 1 act, American). *Yankton, S.
D., Forbes Hall Auditorium (Yankton College), June 12, 1958.

SNEGOUROTCHKA (N. Rimsky-Korsakov; prolog and 4 acts,
Russian, St. Petersburg 1882). New York, Metropolitan Op. H.,
Jan. 23, 1922, in French; Los Angeles, Mason Op. H., Feb. 13,
1922, in Russian.

SNEGOUROTCHKA (P. Tchaikovsky; 4 acts, Russian, Moscow
1873). Swarthmore, Pa., Clothier Memorial Hall (Swarthmore
College), Jan. 12, 1941, in English (excerpts; concert form).

The SNOW QUEEN (K. Gaburo; 3 acts, American). *Lake Charles,
La., Lake Charles Little Th. (McNeese State College), May 5, 1952.

SNOWBIRD (T. P. Stearns; 1 act, American). *Chicago, Auditorium,
Jan. 13, 1923 (Dresden, Staatsoper, Nov. 7, 1928, in German).

SO SINGS THE BELL (G. Wehner; 1 act, American). *New York,
Central Park Mall, June 24, 1961.

Les SOIXANTE SIX! (J. Offenbach; 1 act, French, Paris 1856).
--New York, Wood's Museum and Theatre, Aug. 31, 1868, in
English, as "Sixty-six."

Le SOLDAT MAGICIEN (J. Offenbach; 1 act, French, Ems 1864;
Paris 1868 as "La Fifre enchanté."). Rochester, N.Y., Eastman Th.,
May 23, 1933, in English, as "The Enchanted fife."

The SOLDIER (L. Engel; 1 act, American). *New York, Carnegie
Hall, Nov. 25, 1956 (concert form); Jackson, Miss., Millsaps
College Auditorium, Nov. 24, 1958 (stage premiere).

The SOLDIER'S LEGACY (G. A. Macfarren; 1 act, English, London
1864). --Philadelphia, Dec., 1871.

The SOLDIER'S RETURN (J. Hook; 2 acts, English, London 1805). Philadelphia, New [Chestnut Street] Th., 1807.

Le SOLITAIRE (M. E. Carafa; 3 acts, French, Paris 1822). --Philadelphia, Chestnut Street Th., Oct. 19, 1829 [New Orleans earlier (?)].

SOLOMON AND BALKIS (R. Thompson; 1 act, American). *New York, Columbia Broadcasting System, Mar. 29, 1942 (radio perf.); Cambridge, Mass., Lowell House, Apr. 14, 1942 (stage premiere).

The SON-IN-LAW (S. Arnold; 2 acts, English, London 1779). Charleston, S.C., Charleston Th., Mar. 8, 1793.

SONATA ALLEGRO (J. Gottlieb; 1 act, American). *Urbana, Ill., Smith Music Hall (Univ. of Illinois), Mar. 9, 1958.

The SONG OF DAVID (I. B. Arnstein; 2 acts, American). *New York, Aeolian Hall, May 17, 1925 (concert form).

SONG OF NORWAY (R. Wright and G. Forrest; 2 acts, American). *Los Angeles, Philharmonic Auditorium, June 12, 1944 (New York, Imperial Th., Aug. 21, 1944).

SONG OF THE FLAME (H. Stothart and G. Gershwin; prolog, 2 acts and epilog, American). *Wilmington, Del., Playhouse, Dec. 10, 1925 (New York, 44th Street Th., Dec. 30, 1925).

Le SONGE D'UNE NUIT D'ETE (A. Thomas; 3 acts, French, Paris 1850). New Orleans, Théâtre d'Orléans, Jan., 1851.

The Songstress. See La CANTERINA.

La SONNAMBULA (V. Bellini; 2 acts, Italian, Milan 1831). New York, Park Th., Nov. 13, 1835, in English; New Orleans, Théâtre d'Orléans, Jan. 14, 1840, in Italian.

The SONS OF AARON (S. Landau; 2 acts, American). *Scarsdale, N.Y., Scarsdale Junior High School, Feb. 28, 1959.

SOPHIE ARNOULD (G. Pierné; 1 act, French, Paris 1927). Fishcreek, Wis., Gibralter High School, Aug. 18, 1961, in English (Peninsula Arts Ass'n).

The SORCERER (A. Sullivan; 2 acts, English, London 1877). New York, Broadway Th., Feb. 21, 1879.

SOTOBA KOMACHI (M. D. Levy; 1 act, American). *New York, Theresa Kaufmann Concert Hall (Y.M. and Y.W.H.A.), Apr. 7, 1957.

Les SOULIERS MORS-DORES (A. Fridzeri; 2 acts, French, Paris 1776). Philadelphia, Pantheon, Dec. 24, 1796.

Le SOURD (A. Adam; 3 acts, French, Paris 1853). --New York, Théâtre Français, Feb. 18, 1870.

SOURWOOD MOUNTAIN (A. Kreutz; 1 act, American). *Clinton, Miss., Univ. of Mississippi, Jan. 8, 1959.

SOUTH PACIFIC (R. Rodgers; 2 acts, American). *New Haven, Conn., Shubert Th., Mar. 7, 1949 (New York, Majestic Th., Apr. 7, 1949; 1,925 perf.).

The SPANISH BARBER (S. Arnold; 3 acts, English, London 1777). Philadelphia, New [Chestnut Street] Th., July 7, 1794.

The SPANISH CASTLE (J. Hewitt; American). *New York, Park Th., Dec. 5, 1800.

SPANISH DOLLARS (J. Davy; 1 act, English, London 1805). Philadelphia, New [Chestnut Street] Th., 1806-07.

SPEAKEASY (D. Lee; 1 act, American). *New York, Cooper Union, Feb. 8, 1957 (concert form).

The SPECTRE BRIDEGROOM (W. D. Armstrong; American). *St. Louis, Fourteenth Street Th., 1899.

The SPECTRE KNIGHT (A. Cellier; 1 act, English, London 1878). New York, Bijou Op. H., May 11, 1880.

Lo SPEZIALE (J. Haydn; 3 acts, Italian, Eszterhaz 1768). New York, Neighborhood Playhouse, Mar. 16, 1926, in English, as "The Apothecary."

SPIEL ODER ERNST? (E. Reznicek; 1 act, German, Dresden 1930). Philadelphia, Academy of Music, Feb. 11, 1941, in English, as "Fact or fiction."

SPIELMANNSGLUECK (R. L. Herman; 1 act, German-American). *Cassel, Hoftheater, Jan. 1, 1894, in German.

The Spinnery. See SZEKELY FONO.

Das SPITZENTUCH DER KOENIGIN (J. Strauss; 3 acts, German, Vienna 1880). New York, Casino Th., Oct. 21, 1882, in English, as "The Queen's lace handkerchief;" New York, Thalia Theater, Oct. 1, 1883, in German.

STACKED DECK (R. Maxfield; 1 act, "electronic opera," American). *New York, Theresa Kaufmann Concert Hall (Y.M. and Y.W.H.A.), Apr. 30, 1960.

STAR IN THE NIGHT (G. Wehner; 2 acts, American). *New York, Central Park Mall, Aug. 22, 1961.

STEAL AWAY (G. Allen; 1 act, American). *New York, Y.W.C.A. (138th Street), July 26, 1934.

STERLINGMAN (K. G. Roy; 1 act, American). *Boston, WGBH Educational Foundation, Apr. 18, 1957 (TV perf.).

STERNE'S MARIA, or The Vintage (V. Pelissier; 2 acts, American). *New York, Park Th., Jan. 14, 1799.

STORM GATHERING (S. F. Park; 5 scenes, American). *Tampa, Fla., Centro Asturiano, Oct. 6, 1959.

Stradella. See ALESSANDRO STRADELLA.

The STRANGER OF MANZANO   (J. Smith; prolog and 1 act,
   American).   *Dallas, Tex., McFarlin Memorial Auditorium
   (Southern Methodist Univ.), May 6, 1947.
La STRANIERA   (V. Bellini; 2 acts, Italian, Milan 1829). New York,
   Italian Op. H., Nov. 10, 1834.
STRASZNY DWOR [The Haunted castle]   (S. Moniuszko; 4
   acts, Polish, Warsaw 1858). New York, Mecca Temple Auditorium,
   Apr. 24, 1927.
STRATONICE   (E. N. Méhul; 1 act, French, Paris 1792). New York,
   Brander Matthews Hall (Columbia Univ.), Feb. 6, 1947, in English.
STREET SCENE   (K. Weill; 2 acts, American). *Philadelphia,
   Shubert Th., Dec. 16, 1946 (New York, Adelphi Th., Jan. 9, 1947).
Der STREIT ZWISCHEN PHOEBUS UND PAN   (J. S. Bach; 1
   act, German, Leipzig 1731). --Newark, N.J., South Side High
   School, Apr. 24, 1925, in English (concert form); New York,
   (Brooklyn) Little Th., Feb. 11, 1929, in English (stage perf.).
The STRING QUARTET   (L. Kondorossy; 1 act, American). *Cleve-
   land, Station WSRS, May 8, 1955 (radio perf.).
The STRONGER   (H. Weisgall; 1 act, American). *Lutherville, Md.,
   Hillton Th., Aug. 6, 1952.
The STUDENT PRINCE   (S. Romberg; prolog and 4 acts, American).
   *Atlantic City, N.J., Apollo Th., Oct. 27, 1924 (New York, Jolson
   Th., Dec. 2, 1924).
Der STURM   (F. Martin; 9 scenes and epilog, German, Vienna 1956).
   New York, City Center, Oct. 11, 1956, in English, as "The Tempest."
SULAMITA   (S. Virzi; 1 act, Italian-American). *New York, Munici-
   pal Broadcasting System (WNYC), Dec. 19, 1948, in English (radio
   perf.).
The SULTAN, or A Peep into the seraglio   (text, I. Bicker-
   staffe; 2 acts, ballad opera, English, London 1775). New York, John
   Street Th., May 3, 1794.
Le SULTAN DE ZANZIBAR   (A. de Konski; 3 acts, French). *New
   York, Academy of Music, May (not Apr.), 8, 1886.
A Summer night's dream. See Le SONGE D'UNE NUIT
   D'ETE.
The SUN BRIDE   (C. S. Skilton; 1 act, American). *New York,
   National Broadcasting Company, Apr. 17, 1930 (radio perf.).
The SUN DANCE   (W. F. Hanson; 5 acts, American). *Vernal, U.,
   Orpheus Hall, Feb. 20, 1913.
SUN-UP   (T. Z. Kassern; 1 act, American). *New York, Provincetown
   Playhouse, Nov. 10, 1954.

SUNDARI (R. L. Herman; 3 acts, German-American). *Cassel, Hoftheater, Mar. 30, 1911, in German.

SUNDAY COSTS FIVE PESOS (C. Haubiel; 1 act, American). *Charlotte, N.C., Piedmont Junior High School Auditorium, Nov. 6, 1950.

SUNDAY EXCURSION (A. Wilder; 1 act, American). --Interlochen. Mich., National Music Camp, July 18. 1953.

The SUNSET TRAIL (C. W. Cadman; 1 act, American). *San Diego, Cal., Spreckels Th., Aug. 23, 1920.

SUOR ANGELICA (G. Puccini; 1 act, Italian). *New York, Metropolitan Op. H., Dec. 14, 1918.

La SURPRISE DE L'AMOUR (F. Poise; 2 acts, French, Paris 1877). New York, Carnegie Lyceum, Nov. 17, 1906.

The SURRENDER OF CALAIS (S. Arnold; 3 acts, English, London 1791). Charleston, S.C., Charleston Th., Apr. 29, 1793.

SUSANNAH (C. Floyd; 2 acts, American). *Tallahassee, Fla., Westcott Auditorium (Florida State Univ.), Feb. 24, 1955 (student cast); New York, City Center, Sept. 27, 1956 (professional cast).

SVANDA DUDAK [Schwanda] (J. Weinberger; 2 acts, Czech, Prague 1927). New York, Metropolitan Op. H., Nov. 7, 1931, in German, as "Schwanda, der Dudelsackpfeifer."

SWEENY AGONISTES (R. Winslow; 1 act, American). *New York, Brander Matthews Hall (Columbia Univ.), May 20, 1953.

SWEET BETSY FROM PIKE (M. Bucci; 1 act, American). *New York, Theresa M. Kaufmann Concert Hall (Y.M. and Y.W.H.A.), Dec. 8, 1953.

The SWEET BYE AND BYE (J. Beeson; 3 acts, American). *New York, Juilliard School of Music, Nov. 22, 1957.

SWEETHEARTS (V. Herbert; 2 acts, American). *Baltimore, Academy of Music, Mar. 24, 1913 (New York, New Amsterdam Th., Sept. 8, 1913).

The SWEETWATER AFFAIR (R. Beadell; 2 acts, American). *Lincoln, Nebr., Howell Memorial Th. (Univ. of Nebraska), Feb. 8, 1961.

The SWING (L. Kastle; 1 act, American). *New York, National Broadcasting Company, June 11, 1956 (TV perf.).

SWING LOW (E. Wad; 1 act, American). *Baltimore, Lehmann Hall, Dec. 13, 1933 (Baltimore Civic Opera).

SYBIL (V. Jacobi; 3 acts, American). *Washington, D.C., National Th., Dec. 27, 1915 (New York, Liberty Th., Jan. 10, 1916).

SZEKELY FONO (Z. Kodaly; 1 act, Hungarian, Budapest 1932). Cleveland, Severance Hall, Apr. 29, 1939, in English, as "The Spinnery."

Il TABARRO (G. Puccini; 1 act, Italian). *New York, Metropolitan Op. H., Dec. 14, 1918.

Le TABLEAU PARLANT (M. Grétry; 1 act, French, Paris 1769). Charleston, S.C., Théâtre Français [late Sollee's Hall], June 17, 1794.

A TALE FOR A DEAF EAR (M. Bucci; 1 act, American). *Tanglewood, Lenox, Mass., Theatre Concert Hall (Berkshire Music Center), Aug. 5, 1957.

The TALE OF THE TSAR SALTAN (N. Rimsky-Korsakov; prolog and 4 acts, Russian, Moscow 1900). New York, St. James Th., Dec. 27, 1937, in English, as "The Bumble Bee Prince."

A TALE OF TWO CITIES (A. Benjamin; prolog and 3 acts, English, London 1953 in a radio perf.; London 1957 in operatic form). San Francisco, Main Th. (San Francisco State College), Apr. 2, 1960.

The Tales of Hoffmann. See Les CONTES D'HOFFMANN.

The Tales of Vertigo. See PEPITO.

The TALISMAN (M. W. Balfe; 3 acts, English, London 1874 in Italian). New York, Academy of Music, Feb. 10, 1875, in English (first perf. in that language).

The Taming of the shrew (Goetz). See Der WIDER-SPAENSTIGEN ZAEHMUNG.

The TAMING OF THE SHREW (V. Giannini; 3 acts, American). *Cincinnati, Music Hall, Jan. 31, 1953.

TAM-MAN-NACUP (W. F. Hanson; 3 acts, American). *Provo, U., Paramount Th., May 3, 1928.

TAMMANY (J. Hewitt; 3 acts, American). *New York, John Street Th., Mar. 3, 1794.

La TANCIA, ovvero Il Potesta di Colognole (J. Melani; 3 acts, Italian, Florence 1656). Chapel Hill, N.C., Hill Hall (Univ. of North Carolina), Dec. 28, 1953, in Italian (excerpts; concert form).

TANCREDI (G. Rossini; 2 acts, Italian, Venice 1813). New York, Park Th., Dec. 31, 1825.

Tancredi. See also IVANHOE.

TANNHAEUSER (R. Wagner; 3 acts, German, Dresden 1845). New York, Stadt Theater, Apr. 4, 1859 (first Wagner opera in the United States).

TANTE SIMONA (E. Dohnányi; 1 act, German, Dresden 1913). Rochester, N.Y., Eastman Th., May 27, 1935, in English, as "Aunt Simona" (Eastman School of Music).

Der TAPFERE SOLDAT (O. Straus; 3 acts, German, Vienna 1908). Philadelphia, Lyric Th., Sept. 6, 1909, in English, as "The Chocolate soldier" (New York, Lyric Th., Sept. 13, 1909).

TARAS BULBA (N. V. Lissenko; 5 acts, Ukrainian, Kiev 1890).
New York, Mecca Temple Auditorium, Apr. 21, 1940.

The TELEPHONE (G. C. Menotti; 1 act, American). *New York,
Heckscher Th., Feb. 18, 1947.

La TEMPESTAD (R. Chapi; 3 acts, zarzuela, Spanish, Madrid 1882).
--San Francisco, New Bush Street Th., 1888.

The TEMPLE DANCER (J. A. Hugo; 1 act, American). *New York,
Metropolitan Op. H., Mar. 12, 1919.

Der TEMPLER UND DIE JUEDIN (H. Marschner; 3 acts, German,
Leipzig 1829). New York, Stadt Theater, Jan. 29, 1872.

The TENDER LAND (A. Copland; 1 act, American). *New York,
City Center, Apr. 1, 1954.

TENNESSEE PARTNER (Q. Maganini; 1 act, American). *New
York, Mutual Broadcasting System, May 28, 1942 (radio perf.).

The TENOR (H. Weisgall; 1 act, American). *Baltimore, Peabody
Conservatory of Music, Feb. 11, 1952.

La TENTATION (J. Halévy and C. Gide; 5 acts, French, Paris 1832).
New York, Bowery Th., Oct. 5, 1835, in English, as "Temptation,
or The Devil's daughter. "

The TENTS OF THE ARABS (P. Tietjens; 2 acts, American).
*New York, McMillin Academic Th. (Columbia Univ.), Aug. 7,
1935 (rehearsal).

Le TESTAMENT DE LA TANTE CAROLINE (A. Roussel; 3 acts,
French, Olomouc 1936 in Czech; Paris 1937 in French). New York,
Cherry Lane Th., Aug. 10, 1954, in English, as "Aunt Caroline's
will. "

The TESTAMENT OF FRANCOIS VILLON (E. Pound; American). *Paris, Théâtre des Champs Elysées, Jan. 1924 (London,
British Broadcasting Corporation, Oct. 26, 1931, in revised form in
a radio perf.).

Die TEUFELSMUEHLE AM WIENERBERG (W. Müller; 4 acts,
German, Vienna 1799). --New Orleans, American Th., July 7,
1850, in German.

THAIS (J. Massenet; 3 acts, French, Paris 1894). New York, Manhattan Op. H., Nov. 25, 1907.

THAMOS (W. A. Mozart; 5 acts, incidental music, German, 1773).
New York, Mutual Broadcasting System, June 1, 1940 (radio perf.).

THEODORA (W. W. Furst; 2 acts, American). *San Francisco,
Tivoli Op. H., Sept. 16, 1889.

THEODORA (G. F. Handel; oratorio, English, London 1750). Chicago,
Field Museum, June 29, 1935 (open-air operatic presentation).

There and back. See HIN UND ZURUECK.

THESPIS (F. Miller; 2 acts, American). *New York, Joan of Arc
Center, Jan. 16, 1953.

The THIEF AND THE HANGMAN (A. Ellstein; 1 act, American).
*Athens, O., Ewing Auditorium (Ohio Univ.), Jan. 17, 1959.

The THIRTEEN CLOCKS (M. Bucci; 1 act, American). *New
York, American Broadcasting Company, Dec. 29, 1953 (TV perf.).

The THIRTEEN CLOCKS (M. Johnson; 2 acts, American). *New
York, Hunter College Playhouse, Mar. 8, 1958.

THIS EVENING (J. Serulnikoff; 1 act, American). *Bennington, Vt.,
Bennington College, June 20, 1960.

THOMAS AND SALLY (text, I. Bickerstaffe; 2 acts, ballad opera,
English, London 1760). Philadelphia, Southwark Th., Nov. 14, 1766.

The THREE AND THE DEUCE! (S. Storace; 3 acts, English,
London 1795). Boston, Haymarket Th., May 26, 1797.

THREE BLIND MICE (J. Verrall; 1 act, American). *Seattle,
University Playhouse (Univ. of Washington), May 20, 1955.

The 3-Penny opera. See Die DREIGROSCHENOPER.

The THREE SISTERS WHO ARE NOT SISTERS (D. Ahlstrom;
1 act, American). *Cincinnati, Cincinnati Conservatory of Music,
Mar. 1, 1953.

Der THURM ZU BABEL (A. Rubinstein; 1 act, German, Königsberg
1870). Cincinnati, Music Hall, June 1879, in German (Part II; concert form); Chicago, Central Music Hall, Dec. 7, 1880, in English
(complete; concert form).

The TICKET (S. Honigman; 1 act, American). *Woodstock, N. Y.,
Byrdcliffe Th., July 11, 1958.

The Tide. See Die FLUT.

TIEFLAND (E. d'Albert; prolog and 2 acts, German, Prague 1903).
New York, Metropolitan Op. H., Nov. 23, 1908.

TIRSI E CLORI (C. Monteverdi; Italian, Mantua 1616). Boston,
Museum of Fine Arts, May 10, 1960 (concert form).

Titus. See La CLEMENZA DI TITO.

The TOLEDO WAR (D. Broekmann; American). *New York,
Columbia Broadcasting System, May 4, 1956 (radio perf.).

TOM JONES (E. German; 3 acts, English, London 1907). *Plainfield,
N.J., New Plainfield Th., Oct. 31, 1907 (New York, Astor Th.,
Nov. 11, 1907).

TOM SAWYER (J. Elkus; 1 act, American). *San Francisco, Everett
Junior High School Auditorium, May 22, 1953.

TOM-TOM (S. Graham; 3 acts, American). *New York, National
Broadcasting Company, June 26, 1932 (excerpts; radio perf.); Cleveland, Cleveland Stadium, June 30, 1932 (stage premiere).

Le TONNELIER (N. M. Audinot; 1 act, French, Paris 1761). New York, City Tavern, Oct. 7, 1790.

TONY BEAVER (J. Marais; 1 act, American). *Idyllwild, Cal., Bowman Art Center (Idyllwild School of Music and the Arts), Aug. 1, 1952.

Le TOREADOR (A. Adam; 2 acts, French, Paris 1849). New York, Théâtre Français, Oct. 18, 1866.

TOSCA (G. Puccini; 3 acts, Italian, Rome 1900). New York, Metropolitan Op. H., Feb. 4, 1901.

Die TOTE STADT (E. W. Korngold; 3 acts, German, Hamburg and Cologne 1920). New York, Metropolitan Op. H., Nov. 19, 1921.

Die TOTEN AUGEN (E. d'Albert; 3 acts, German, Dresden 1916). Chicago, Great Northern Th., Nov. 1, 1923.

The Touchstone. See La PIETRA DEL PARAGONE.

The TOWER (M. D. Levy; 1 act, American). *Santa Fe, Opera Th., Aug. 2, 1957.

The TRAITOR MANDOLIN (H. W. Loomis; 1 act, American). *New York, Waldorf-Astoria Hotel, Jan. 11, 1898.

TRANSATLANTIC (G. Antheil; 3 acts, American). *Frankfurt a. M., Opernhaus, May 25, 1930, in German.

The TRANSPOSED HEADS (P. Glanville-Hicks; 6 scenes, American). *Louisville, Ky., Columbia Auditorium (Univ. of Louisville), Apr. 3, 1954.

La TRAVIATA (G. Verdi; 3 acts, Italian, Venice 1853). New York, Academy of Music, Dec. 3, 1856.

The TREASURE (A. D. Geto; American). *Pottersville, N. Y., Schroon Crest, Aug. 22, 1953.

Treasured tokens. See VALERIE.

A TREE ON THE PLAINS (E. Bacon; 2 acts, American). *Spartanburg, S.C., Converse College, May 2, 1942.

A TREE THAT FOUND CHRISTMAS (G. Kleinsinger; American). *New York, Hunter College Auditorium, Dec. 17, 1955 (Little Orchestra Society).

The Trial. See Der PROZESS.

The TRIAL AT ROUEN (N. Dello Joio; 2 acts, American). *New York, National Broadcasting Company, Apr. 8, 1956 (TV perf.).

TRIAL BY JURY (A. Sullivan; 1 act, English, London 1875). New York, Eagle Th., Nov. 15, 1875.

The TRIAL OF LUCULLUS (R. Sessions; 1 act, American). *Berkeley, Cal., Wheeler Auditorium (Univ. of California), Apr. 18, 1947.

Le TRIBUT DE ZAMORA (C. Gounod; 4 acts, French, Paris 1881). New Orleans, French Op. H., Jan. 12, 1888.

Il TRIONFO DELL' ONORE (A. Scarlatti; 3 acts, Italian, Naples 1718). New York, Alma Gluck Th., Nov. 11, 1954, in English, as "The Triumph of honor."

A Trip to the country. See La GITA IN CAMPAGNA.

A Trip to the moon. See Le VOYAGE DANS LA LUNE.

TRIPLE SEC (M. Blitzstein; 1 act, American). *Philadelphia, Bellevue-Stratford Hotel, May 6, 1929.

TRISTAN UND ISOLDE (R. Wagner; 3 acts, German, Munich 1865). New York, Metropolitan Op. H., Dec. 1, 1886.

Trittico. See Il TABARRO; SOUR ANGELICA; GIANNI SCHICCHI.

The Triumph of honor. See Il TRIONFO DELL' ONORE.

The TRIUMPH OF JOAN (N. Dello Joio; 3 acts, American). *Bronxville, N.Y., Bates Hall (Sarah Lawrence College), May 9, 1950.

TROILUS AND CRESSIDA (W. Walton; 3 acts, English, London 1954). San Francisco, War Memorial Op. H., Oct. 7, 1955.

TROMB-AL-CAZAR (J. Offenbach; 1 act, French, Paris 1856). New Orleans, French Op. H., Jan. 1860.

Der TROMPETER VON SAECKINGEN (E. Kaiser; 3 acts, German, Olmütz 1882). New York, Thalia Theater, Jan. 2, 1886 (not Oct. 31, 1885).

Der TROMPETER VON SAECKINGEN (V. E. Nessler; 4 acts, German, Leipzig 1884). New York, Metropolitan Op. H., Nov. 23, 1887.

TROUBLE IN TAHITI (L. Bernstein; 7 scenes, American). *Waltham, Mass., Adolph Ullman Amphitheatre (Brandeis Univ.), June 12, 1952.

The TROUBLED ISLAND (W. G. Still; 3 acts, American). *New York, City Center, Mar. 31, 1949.

Il TROVATORE (G. Verdi; 4 acts, Italian, Rome 1853). New York, Academy of Music, May 2, 1855.

Les TROYENS (H. Berlioz; 2 parts [Part I, "La Prise de Troie;" Part II, "Les Troyens à Carthage"], Carlsruhe 1890, in German; Brussels 1906, in French). New York, Academy of Music, Jan. 13, 1877, in English, as "The Trojans" (Part II; concert form); New York, Seventh Regiment Armory, May 6, 1882, in English, as "The Downfall of Troy" (Part I; concert form); Boston, Boston Op. H., Mar. 27, 1955, in English, as "The Trojans" (abridged version in a prolog and 5 acts; stage perf.).

TRUE BLUE (H. Carey; 1 act, English, London 1755). New York, John Street Th., Apr. 24, 1788.

The TRYST (H. L. Freeman; 1 act, American). *New York, Crescent Th., May 1909.

The TRYSTING PLACE (J. Wolfe; 1 act, American). *Coral Gables, Fl., Box Th. (Univ. of Miami), Nov. 6, 1957.

TURANDOT (G. Puccini; 3 acts, Italian, Milan 1926). New York, Metropolitan Op. H., Nov. 16, 1926.

Il TURCO IN ITALIA (G. Rossini; 2 acts, Italian, Milan 1814). New York, Park Th., Mar. 14, 1826.

The TURN OF THE SCREW (B. Britten; prolog and 2 acts, English, Venice 1954). New York, Theresa Kaufmann Concert Hall (Y.M. and Y.W.H.A.), Mar. 19, 1958 (student cast; New York College of Music); New York, City Center, Mar. 25, 1962 (professional cast).

The TURNPIKE GATE (J. Mazzinghi and W. Reeve; 2 acts, English, London 1799). New York, Park Th., June 8, 1801.

The Twilight heron. See YU-ZURU.

The Twin brothers. See Die ZWILLINGSBRUEDER.

The TWO CADIS (J. Eichberg; 1 act, American). --New York, New French Th., July 12, 1866.

The TWO FIGAROS (text, James Robinson Planché; music compiled from Mozart and Rossini, 2 acts, English, London 1836). New York, National Th., Nov. 16, 1837.

The TWO IMPOSTORS (L. Kondorossy; 1 act, American). *Cleveland, WSRS, Apr. 10, 1955 (radio perf.); Cleveland, Little Th. (Public Auditorium), Oct. 21, 1956 (stage premiere).

The TWO MISERS (C. Dibdin; 2 acts, English, London 1775). New York, John Street Th., July 17, 1786.

TWO TICKETS TO OMAHA (R. Hannay; 1 act, American). *Moorehead, Minn., Old Main Auditorium (Concordia College), July 21, 1960.

Two words. See DEUX MOTS.

- U -

L'ULTIMO DEI MOICANI (P. H. Allen; 3 acts, American). *Florence, Politeama Fiorentino, Feb. 24, 1916, in Italian.

UNCLE TOM'S CABIN (H. Millard; 4 acts, American). *Toronto, Can., Zoological Garden, June 26, 1883.

UNDINE (A. Lortzing; 4 acts, German, Magdeburg 1845). New York, Niblo's Garden, Oct. 9, 1856.

UNDINE (H. Ware; dramatic cantata, American). Baltimore, Peabody Conservatory, May 19, 1923 (stage perf.).

The UNEXPECTED VISITOR (L. Kondorossy; 1 act, American). *Cleveland, Little Th. (Public Auditorium), Oct. 21, 1956.

The UNICORN IN THE GARDEN (R. Smith; 1 act, American).
*Hartford, Conn., Burns School Auditorium, May 2, 1957 (Hartt
College of Music).
The UNICORN, THE GORGON AND THE MANTICORE
(G. C. Menotti; American). *Washington, D.C., Coolidge Auditor-
ium (Library of Congress), Oct. 21, 1956.
The Uninhabited island. See L'ISOLA DISABITATA.
The UNIVERSITY GREYS (A. Kreutz; 2 acts, American).
*University, Miss., Fulton Chapel (Univ. of Mississippi), Mar. 15,
1954.
UTOPIA LIMITED (A. Sullivan; 2 acts, English, London 1893). New
York, Broadway Th., Mar. 26, 1894.
UZ TEVYNE [For the native land] (A. Aleksis; 2 acts,
Lithuanian-American). *Waterbury, Conn., 1919, in Lithuanian.

- V -

V STUDINI (V. Blodek; 1 act, Czech, Prague 1867). New York,
U Hubácku (Downtown National Hall), Apr. 22, 1893.
Le VAL D'ANDORRE (F. Halévy; 3 acts, French, Paris 1848).
New Orleans, Théâtre d'Orléans, Dec. 1849.
VALDO (H. L. Freeman; 1 act, American). *Cleveland, Weisgerber's
Hall, May 1906.
VALERIE, or Treasured tokens (J. R. Fairlamb; 4 acts, Ameri-
can). *Philadelphia, Chestnut Street Th., Dec. 15, 1869.
VANESSA (S. Barber; 3 acts, American). *New York, Metropolitan
Op. H., Jan. 15, 1958.
VANNA (S. Virzi; 2 acts, Italian-American). *New York, Carnegie
Hall, Apr. 9, 1928, in Italian (perf. collapsed after Act I).
Il VASSALO DI SZIGETH (A. Smareglia; 3 acts, Italian, Vienna
1889 in German). New York, Metropolitan Op. H., Dec. 12, 1890,
in German.
La VEGLIA (A. Pedrollo; 1 act, Italian, Milan 1920). New York,
Hotel Pennsylvania, Dec. 20, 1924.
The VEIL (B. Rogers; 1 act, American). *Bloomington, Ind., East
Hall (Indiana Univ.), May 18, 1950.
VELNIAS ISRADEJAS [The Devil inventor] (M. Petrauskas;
3 acts, Lithuanian-American). *Brooklyn N.Y., 1917, in Lithu-
anian (also, South Boston, Mass., Broadway Th., May 20, 1923).
VENDETTA (H. L. Freeman; 3 acts, American). *New York,
Lafayette Th., Nov. 12, 1923.

The VENETIAN GLASS NEPHEW (E. Bonner; 2 acts, American).
*New York, Vanderbilt Th., Feb. 23, 1931.

VENUS AND ADONIS (J. Blow; prolog and 3 acts, masque, English,
London ca. 168-?). Cambridge, Mass., Lowell House, Mar. 11,
1941.

VENUS IN AFRICA (G. Antheil; 3 scenes, American). *Denver,
Little Th. (Univ. of Denver), May 24, 1957.

Les VEPRES SICILIENNES (G. Verdi; 5 acts, French, Paris 1855).
New York, Academy of Music, Nov. 7, 1859, in Italian, as "I
Vespri siciliani."

VERBUM NOBILE (S. Moniuszko; 1 act, Polish, Warsaw 1861).
Philadelphia, Metropolitan Op. H., Feb. 28, 1916.

Das VERLORENE PARADIES (A. Rubinstein; 3 parts, "sacred opera,"
German, Weimar 1855). Cincinnati, Music Hall, June 12, 1879
(Part II; concert form); Boston, Music Hall, May 1, 1883, in English
(complete; concert form).

Die Verkaufte Braut. See PRODANA NEVESTA.

VERMLANDINGARNE (A. Randel; 2 acts, Swedish, Stockholm 1846).
--Chicago, North Side Turner Hall, Nov. 16, 1884.

VERONIQUE (A. Messager; 3 acts, French, Paris 1898). New York,
Broadway Th., Oct. 30, 1905, in English.

Die VERSCHWORENEN, oder Der häusliche Krieg (F.
Schubert; 1 act, German, Vienna 1861). Hoboken, N.J., Feb. 21,
1863 (concert form; Concordia singing society); New York, Terrace
Garden, June 16, 1877 (stage perf.).

VERSIEGELT (L. Blech; 1 act, German, Hamburg 1908). New York,
Metropolitan Op. H., Jan. 20, 1912.

Vertigo. See PEPITO.

VERT-VERT (J. Offenbach; 3 acts, French, Paris 1869). New York,
Stadt Theater, Oct. 31, 1870, in German, as "Kakadu."

I Vespri siciliani. See Les VEPRES SICILIENNES.

La VESTALE (G. Spontini; 3 acts, French, Paris 1807). New Orleans,
Théâtre d'Orleans, Feb. 17, 1828.

VESTAS FEUER (L. van Beethoven; scene of an unfinished opera,
German, 1803). Miami, Miami Beach Auditorium, Dec. 8, 1957
(concert form; Miami Symphony Orchestra).

VESTUVES [The Wedding] (M. Petrauskas and T. Guzutis; 3 acts,
Lithuanian-American). *Boston, Dudley Op. H., June 7, 1919.

The VICAR OF WAKEFIELD (L. Lehmann; 3 acts, English, Manchester, England 1906). Pittsburgh, Carnegie Institute of Technology,
Oct. 15, 1907 (concert form).

La VIDA BREVE   (M. de Falla; 2 acts, Spanish, Nice 1913 in French).
New York, Metropolitan Op. H. , Mar. 6, 1926, in Spanish.

La VIDA DE LA MISION   (C. Venth; 2 acts, American). *San
Antonio, Municipal Auditorium, Oct. 28, 1959, in English.

VIDEOMANIA   (M. Kalmanoff; 1 act, American). *Lincoln, Ill.,
Lincoln College, May 8, 1958.

La VIE PARISIENNE   (J. Offenbach; 5 acts, French, Paris 1866).
New York, Théâtre Français, Mar. 29, 1869.

La VIEJECITA   (M. Fernández Caballero; 1 act, zarzuela, Spanish,
Madrid 1897). New York, Cort Th. , July 14, 1919.

La VIELLE   (J. Fétis; 1 act, French, Paris 1826). --New York, Park
Th. , July 20, 1827 [New Orleans earlier (?)].

Der VIERJAEHRIGE POSTEN   (G. Hinrichs; 1 act, American).
*San Francisco, Grand Op. H. , Apr. 15, 1877, in German.

Le VILLI   (G. Puccini; 2 acts, Italian, Milan 1884). New York,
Metropolitan Op. H. , Dec. 17, 1908.

VINETA   (R. L. Herman; 3 acts, German-American). *Cassel, Hoftheater, June 20, 1891, in German (Breslau, Stadtheater, Dec. 7,
1895, in revised form).

The Vintage. See STERNE'S MARIA.

VIOLANTA   (E. Korngold; 1 act, German, Munich 1916). New York,
Metropolitan Op. H. , Nov. 5, 1927.

The VIOLIN MAKER OF CREMONA   (M. Frey; 1 act, American).
*Pittsburgh, Carnegie Institute of Technology, Mar. 24, 1922.

Le VIOLONEUX   (J. Offenbach; 1 act, French, Paris 1855). --Louis-
ville, Ky., Louisville Th. , July 6, 1860 [earlier elsewhere (?)].

The VIRGIN UNMASK'D   (text, Henry Fielding; 1 act, ballad opera,
English, London 1734). New York, Nassau Street Th. , Apr. 16,
1751.

The VISION OF ARIEL   (L. Saminsky; 1 act, American). Chicago,
Mandel Hall (Univ. of Chicago), May 9, 1954.

Les VISITANDINES   (F. Devienne; 2 acts, French, Paris 1792).
--Philadelphia, Chestnut Street Th. , Sept. 26, 1828 [New Orleans
earlier (?)].

La VIVANDIERE   (B. Godard; 3 acts, French, Paris 1895). New
Orleans, French Op. H. , Dec. 29, 1900.

The VOICE   (L. Kondorossy; 1 act, American). *Cleveland, Severance Chamber Music Hall, May 15, 1954 (concert form); Duxbury,
Mass., Plymouth Rock Center of Music and Drama, Aug. 11, 1954
(stage premiere).

VOICES FOR A MIRROR   (M. Kupferman; 1 act, American). *New
York, Master Institute Th. , June 5, 1957.

La VOIX HUMAINE (F. Poulenc; 1 act, French, Paris 1959). New
York, Grace Rainey Rogers Auditorium (Metropolitan Museum of
Art), Feb. 21, 1960 (preview); New York, Carnegie Hall, Feb. 23,
1960.

VOLPONE (G. Antheil; 3 acts, American). *Los Angeles, Bovard
Auditorium (Univ. of Southern California), Jan. 9, 1953.

The VOLUNTEERS (A. Reinagle; 2 acts, American). *Philadelphia,
New [Chestnut Street] Th., Jan. 21, 1795.

VOODOO (H. L. Freeman; 3 acts, American). *New York, WGBS,
May 20, 1928 (abridged radio perf.); New York, Palm Garden, Sept.
10, 1928 (stage premiere).

Le VOYAGE DANS LA LUNE (J. Offenbach; 4 acts, French, Paris
1875). New York, Booth's Th., Mar. 14, 1877, in English, as "A
Trip to the moon, or A Voyage around the moon" (spectacle by Imre
and Bolossy Kiralfy); San Francisco, Tivoli Op. H., Jan. 2, 1888, in
English, as "A Trip to the moon."

- W -

Der WAFFENSCHMIED (A. Lortzing; 3 acts, German, Vienna 1846).
Milwaukee, Young's Hall, Dec. 7, 1853 (Musik Verein; second perf.
Dec. 13, 1853); New York, Stadt Theater, Feb. 4, 1867 (professional
cast).

The Wags of Windsor. See The REVIEW.

Der WALD (E. Smyth; prolog, 1 act and epilog, German, Berlin 1902).
New York, Metropolitan Op. H., Mar. 11, 1903.

Die Walkuere. See Der RING DES NIBELUNGEN.

La WALLY (A. Catalani; 4 acts, Italian, Milan 1892). New York,
Metropolitan Op. H., Jan. 6, 1909.

WAR AND PEACE (S. Prokofiev; 11 scenes, Russian, Leningrad
1946). New York, National Broadcasting Company, Jan. 13, 1957,
in English (TV perf.).

The WARRIOR (B. Rogers; 1 act, American). *New York, Metropolitan Op. H., Jan. 11, 1947.

The WATERMAN (C. Dibdin; 2 acts, English, London 1774). Philadelphia, Concert-Hall in the Haymarket, Northern Liberties, Apr.
8, 1791.

The Way to Happytown. See Der WEG NACH FREUDEN-
STADT.

The Wedding. See VESTUVES.

The Wedding day. See BRUEDERLEIN FEIN.

The WEDDING KNELL (J. Verrall; 1 act, American). *Seattle,
University Playhouse (Univ. of Washington), Dec. 5, 1952.

The Wedding of Camacho. See Die HOCHZEIT DES
CAMACHO.

The WEDDING RING (C. Dibdin; 2 acts, English, London 1773).
Charleston, S.C., Charleston Th., Mar. 20, 1793.

Der WEG NACH FREUDENSTADT (H. Reutter; 1 act, German,
1947). New York, Provincetown Playhouse, May 10, 1954, in
English, as "The Way to Happytown."

The WELL (L. Mennini; 1 act, American). *Rochester, N.Y.,
Kilbourn Hall (Eastman School of Music), May 8, 1951.

WERTHER (J. Massenet; 4 acts, French, Vienna 1892 in German; Paris
1893 in French). Chicago, Auditorium, Mar. 29, 1894, in French.

WEST SIDE STORY (L. Bernstein; 2 acts, American). *Washington,
D.C., National Th., Aug. 19, 1957 (New York, Winter Garden,
Sept. 26, 1957).

WESTERN CHILD (P. Bezanson; 3 acts, American). *Iowa City,
State Univ. of Iowa, July 28, 1959.

WHAT MEN LIVE BY (B. Martinu; 1 act, English, Hanover 1953 in
German). Interlochen, Mich., National Music Camp, July 31, 1954.

The WHIRLWIND (A. G. Miller; American). *Arlington, Va.,
Washington-Lee Auditorium, Sept. 24, 1953.

The WHISTLER (W. Presser; 2 scenes, American). *Hattiesburg,
Miss., Marsh Fine Arts Building (Mississippi Southern College), Feb.
14, 1959.

The WHITE BIRD (E. T. Carter; 1 act, American). *Chicago,
Studebaker Th., Mar. 6, 1924.

The White sister. See La MONACA BIANCA.

WHITE WINGS (D. Moore; 2 acts, American). *Hartford, Conn.,
Hartt Auditorium (Julius Hartt School of Music), Feb. 9, 1949.

Der WIDERSPAENSTIGEN ZAEHMUNG (H. Goetz; 4 acts,
German, Mannheim 1874). New York, Academy of Music, Jan. 4,
1886, in English; New York, Metropolitan Op. H., Mar. 15, 1916,
in German.

The WIFE OF MARTIN GUERRE (W. Bergsma; 3 acts, American). *New York, Juilliard School of Music, Feb. 15, 1956.

The WIFE OF TWO HUSBANDS (V. Pelissier; 3 acts, American).
*New York, Park Th., Apr. 4, 1804.

The WILD GOOSE CHACE (J. Hewitt; 4 acts, American). *New
York, Park Th., Jan. 24, 1800.

The WILD SWAN (G. Wehner; 3 acts, American). *New York,
Central Park Mall, July 18, 1961.

Der WILDSCHUETZ (A. Lortzing; 3 acts, German, Leipzig 1842).
Brooklyn, N.Y., "Theater-Lokale des Herrn Flossman," Mar. 1856;
New York, Stadt Theater, Mar. 25, 1859.

The WILLIS, or The Night dancers (E. J. Loder; 2 acts, English, London 1846). New York, Olympic Th. , Oct. 6, 1847.

The WILLOW TREE (C. W. Cadman; 1 act, American). *New York, National Broadcasting Company, Oct. 3, 1933 (radio perf.).

The WINGS OF THE DOVE (D. Moore; 2 acts, American). *New York, City Center, Oct. 12, 1961.

WINONA (A. Bimboni; 3 acts, American). *Portland, Ore. , Municipal Auditorium, Nov. 11, 1926.

The WISE AND THE FOOLISH (K. List; 1 act, American). *New York, Theresa Kaufmann Auditorium (Y.M. and Y.W.H.A.), June 2, 1951.

The WISH (G. Antheil; 1 act, American). *Louisville, Ky. , Columbia Auditorium, Apr. 2, 1955.

The WITCH OF SALEM (C. W. Cadman; 2 acts, American). *Chicago, Auditorium, Dec. 8, 1926.

The WIZARDS OF BALIZAR (N. Lockwood; 3 acts, American). Denver, Marjorie Reed Hall (Univ. of Denver), Aug. 1, 1962.

WOZZECK (A. Berg; 3 acts, German, Berlin 1925). Philadelphia, Academy of Music, Mar. 19, 1931.

WULFRIN (R. L. Herman; German-American). *Cassel, Königliches Theater, Oct. 11, 1898, in German.

WUTHERING HEIGHTS (C. Floyd; prolog and 3 acts, American). *Santa Fe, Amphitheatre, July 16, 1958.

- X -

XANTHA (M. La Prade; 2 acts, American). *Golders Green, London, Benmore Hall, Mar. 23, 1917.

XENIA (A. Savine; Serbian, Zurich 1919 in German). New York, Serbian Legation Building, Mar. 21, 1925, in English (excerpts; concert form).

Xerxes. See SERSE.

X-MAL REMBRANDT (E. Zador; 1 act, Hungarian, Budapest 1930). Los Angeles, Royce Hall (Univ. of California), Jan. 16, 1955, in English, as "Forever Rembrandt."

- Y -

The YANKEE PEDLAR (J. Duke; 2 acts, American). *Schroon Lake, N. Y. , Oscar Seagle Memorial Th. , Aug. 17, 1962.

The YEOMEN OF THE GUARD (A. Sullivan; 2 acts, English, London 1888). New York, Casino Th. , Oct. 17, 1888.

YOLANDA OF CYPRUS (C. Loomis; 4 acts, American). *Hamilton, Ont., Canada, Sept. 1929; Chicago, Majestic Th., Oct. 9, 1929 (U. S. premiere).

The YOUNG HUSSAR (M. Kelly; 2 acts, English, London 1807). --Philadelphia, New [Chestnut Street] Th., 1807-08.

YOUTH, LOVE AND FOLLY (M. Kelly; 2 acts, English, London 1805). --Philadelphia, New [Chestnut Street] Th., 1806-07.

YU-ZURU (I. Dan; 1 act, Japanese, Tokyo 1952). New York, Hunter College Playhouse, Jan. 28 (preview Jan. 27), 1960, in Japanese, as "The Twilight heron."

- Z -

ZAIDE (W. A. Mozart; 2 acts, German, 1779). Tanglewood, Lenox, Mass., Theater-Concert Hall (Berkshire Music Center), Aug. 8, 1955, in English.

ZAMPA (L. Hérold; 3 acts, French, Paris 1831). --Boston, Tremont Th., July 26, 1833 [New Orleans earlier (?)].

ZANETTA (D. Auber; 3 acts, French, Paris 1840). New Orleans, Théâtre d'Orléans, Mar. 16, 1841.

ZANETTO (P. Mascagni; 1 act, Italian, Pesaro 1896). New York, Hotel Astoria, Jan. 4, 1898.

Der ZAR LAESST SICH PHOTOGRAPHIREN (K. Weill; 1 act, German, Leipzig 1928). New York, Juilliard School of Music, Oct. 27, 1949, in English, as "The Shah has his picture taken."

Zar und Zimmermann. See CZAR UND ZIMMERMANN.

Die ZAUBERFLOETTE (W. A. Mozart; 2 acts, German, Vienna 1791). New York, Park Th., Apr. 17, 1833, in English (Charles Edward Horn adaptation); Baltimore, late 1853, in German (Baltimore Liederkranz); New York, Stadt Theater, Jan. 23, 1855, in German.

ZAZA (R. Leoncavallo; 4 acts, Italian, Milan 1900). San Francisco, Tivoli Op. H., Nov. 27, 1903.

ZELMIRA (G. Rossini; 2 acts, Italian, Naples 1822). New Orleans, St. Charles Th., Apr. 24, 1836.

ZEMIRE ET AZOR (M. Grétry; 4 acts, French, Fontainebleau 1771). New York, John Street Th., June 1, 1787, in English, as "Selima and Azor;" Charleston, S.C., Théâtre Français, Aug. 6, 1794, in French.

ZENOBIA (L. A. Coerne; 3 acts, American). *Bremen, Stadttheater, Dec. 1, 1905, in German.

ZENOBIA, QUEEN OF PALMYRA (S. G. Pratt; 4 acts, American).
*Chicago, Central Music Hall, June 15, 1882.
Der ZIGEUNERBARON (J. Strauss; 3 acts, German, Vienna 1885).
New York, Casino Th., Feb. 15, 1886, in English, as "The Gypsy
baron;" New York, Thalia Theater, Oct. 5, 1887, in German.
ZIGEUNERLIEBE (F. Lehar; 3 acts, German, Vienna 1909). New
York, Globe Th., Oct. 17, 1911, in English, as "Gypsy love."
ZINGARI (R. Leoncavallo; 2 acts, Italian, London 1912). San Fran-
cisco, Tivoli Op. H., Oct. 30, 1913.
Die ZWILLINGSBRUEDER (F. Schubert; 1 act, German, Vienna
1820). Bethlehem, Pa., Packard Auditorium (Lehigh Univ.), Mar.
9, 1957, in English, as "The Twin brothers."

The asterisk denotes a collaboration.

ADAM, ADOLPHE CHARLES: Le Bijou perdu; Le Brasseur de Preston; Le Châlet; Giralda; Le Postillon de Longjumeau; La Poupée de Nuremburg; Si j'étais roi; Le Sourd; Le Toréador.

ADAM DE LA HALLE: Le Jeu de Robin et Marion.

ADDISON, JOHN: *The Farmer's wife.

ADLER, RICHARD: *Damn Yankees; *The Pajama game.

ADLER, SAMUEL H.: The Outcasts of Poker Flat.

AHLSTROM, DAVID: Charlie's uncle; The Open window; The Three sisters who are not sisters.

ALBERT, EUGENE D': Tiefland; Die Toten Augen.

ALBRIGHT, LOIS: Hopitu.

ALDERMAN, PAULINE: Bombastes furioso.

ALEKSIS, ALEKSANDRAS: Uz tevyne [For the native land].

ALFANO, FRANCO: Madonna imperia; Risurrezione.

ALLEGRA, S.: Ave Maria.

ALLEN, GILBERT: Steal away.

ALLEN, PAUL HASTINGS: Il Filtro; Mamzelle Figaro; Milda; 'O Munasterio; L'Ultimo dei Moicani.

ANDERS, EMILE: King Harald.

ANTHEIL, GEORGE: The Brothers; Transatlantic; Venus in Africa; Volpone; The Wish.

ARENSKY, ANTON STEPANCVICH: The Fountain of Bakhchi-Sarai.

ARGENTO, DOMINICK: The Boor.

ARMSTRONG, WILLIAM DAWSON: The Spectre bridegroom.

ARNE, THOMAS AUGUSTINE: Alfred; Artaxerxes; *Comus; The Guardian out-witted; Love in a village; Neptune and Amphitrite; The Sheep shearing.

ARNOLD, SAMUEL: The Agreeable surprise; Auld Robin Gray; The Battle of Hexham; The Castle of Andalusia; The Children in the wood; The Dead alive; Hunt the slipper; Inkle and Yarico; The Maid of the mill; The Mountaineers; Peeping Tom of Coventry; The Review [The Wags of Windsor]; The Shipwreck; The Son-in-law; The Spanish barber; The Surrender of Calais.

ARNSTEN, IRA B.: The Song of David.

ARRIETA Y CORERS, PASCUAL JUAN EMILIO: Marina.

ARTEMOVSKY, SEMYON STEPANOVICH: Cossacks beyond the Danube.

ATTWOOD, THOMAS: The Adopted child; The Prisoner.

AUBER, DANIEL FRANCOIS ESPRIT: Actéon; L'Ambassadrice; Le Cheval de bronze; Les Diamants de la couronne; Le Dieu et la bayadere; Le Domino noir; L'Enfant prodigue; La Fiancée; Fiorella; Fra Diavolo; Gustave III; Haydée; Le Lac de fées; Lestocq; Le Maçon; La Muette de Portici; La Niege; Les Pantins de Violette; La Part du diable; Le Philtre; La Sirène; Zanetta.

AUBERT, LOUIS FRANCOIS MARIE: Le Forêt bleue.

AUDINOT, NICHOLAS MEDARD: Le Tonnelier.

AUDRAN, EDMOND: La Mascotte; Les Noces d'Olivette; La Poupée.

AVSHALOMOV, AARON: Kuan Yin.

- B -

BACH, JOHANN SEBASTIAN: Mer hahn en neue Oberkeet; Der Streit zwischen Phoebus und Pan.

BACON, ERNST: A Drumlin legend; A Tree on the plains.

BALFE, MICHAEL WILLIAM: The Bohemian Girl; The Daughter of St. Mark; The Devil's in it; The Enchantress; The Maid of Artois; The Puritan's daughter; The Rose of Castile; Satanella; The Siege of Rochelle; The Talisman.

BANCHIERI, ADRIANO: Festino nella sera del giovedi grosse avanti cena.

BARAB, SEYMOUR: Chanticleer; A Game of chance; The Maledroit door; The Rajah's ruby.

BARBER, SAMUEL: A Hand of bridge; Vanessa.

BARBIERI, FRANCISCO ASENJO: Jugar con fuego; El Relámpago; Robinson; *El Sargento Federico; El Barberillo de Lavapiés.

BARILI, ANTONIO: Una Noche in Sevilla.

BARLOW, S. L. M.: Mon ami Pierrot.

BARNETT, JOHN: The Mountain sylph; The Pet of the petticots.

BARON, MAURICE: François Villon.

BARTOK, BELA: A Kékszakállu Herceg Vera [Bluebeard's castle].

BAYLOR, MURRAY: By Gemini.

BEACH, JOHN PARSONS: Pippa's holiday.

BEADELL, ROBERT: The Sweetwater affair.

BECHTEL, FREDERICK: Alfred the great.

BECKETT, WHEELER: The Magic mirror.

BECKLER, STANWORTH: The Outcasts of Poker Flat.

BEESON, JACK: The Sweet bye and bye.

BEETHOVEN, LUDWIG VAN: Fidelio; Vestas Feuer.

BELCHER, MARY WILLIAMS [Mrs. Donald R.]: The Legend of Ronsard and Madelon.

BELLINI, VINCENZO: Beatrice di Tenda; I Capuleti e Montecchi; Norma; Il Pirata; I Puritani; La Sonnambula; La Straniera.

BEMBERG, HENRI: Elaine.

BENEDICT, JULIUS: The Bride of song; The Gipsy's warning; The Lily of Killarney.

BENJAMIN, ARTHUR: The Devil take her.

BENNETT, ROBERT RUSSELL: The Enchanted kiss; Maria Malibran.

BEREZOWSKY, NICOLAI: Babar, the elephant.

BERG, ALBAN: Wozzeck.

BERGE, IRENEE MARIUS: Corsica.

BERGERSEN, BALDWIN: Far harbor.

BERGSMA, WILLIAM: The Wife of Martin Guerre.

BERKELEY, F. H. F.: Rokeby.

BERL, PAUL: Judgment day.

BERLIN, IRVING: Annie get your gun; Call me madam.

BERLIOZ, HECTOR LOUIS: Béatrice et Bénédict; La Damnation de Faust; L'Enfance du Christ; Les Troyens.

BERNSTEIN, LEONARD: Candide; On the town; Trouble in Tahiti; West Side story.

BERTE, HEINRICH: Das Dreimäderlhaus.

BERTON, HENRI MONTAN: Aline, reine de Golconde; François de Foix; Les Maris garçons.

BERTULIS, JUOZAS: Juanimo noutaika [The Humor of youth].

BEVERIDGE, THOMAS: Dido and Aeneas.

BEZANSON, PHILIP: The Golden child; Western child.

BIMBONI, ALBERTO: Il Cancelleto d'oro; In the name of culture; Winona.

BINDER, ABRAHAM WOLFE: A Goat in Chelm.

BIRD, ARTHUR: Daphne.

BISHOP, HENRY ROWLEY: *The Barber of Seville; *Brother and sister; Clari, the maid of Milan; The Fall of Algiers; *The Farmer's wife; Home, sweet home!; Maid of Marian; The Miller and his men; Native land; *Rob Roy MacGregor; The Slave.

BIZET, GEORGES: L'Arlésienne; Carmen; Djamilah; Les Pêcheurs de perles.

BLACHER, BORIS: Abstrakte Oper No. 1; Die Flut; Romeo und Julia.

BLACK, ARNOLD: The Prince and the pauper.

BLAISE, BENOIT: Annette et Lubín.

BLAKESLEE, SAMUEL EARLE: The Legend of Wiwaste.

BLECH, LEO: Versiegelt.

BLITZSTEIN, MARC: The Cradle will rock; The Harpies; I've got the tune; Regina; Triple sec.

BLOCH, ERNEST: Macbeth.

BLOCKX, JAN: De Herbergprinses.

BLODEK, VILEM: V studni.

BLOW, JOHN: Venus and Adonis.

BOCHSA, ROBERT NICHOLAS CHARLES: Judith; La Lettre de change.

BOHRNSTEDT, WAYNE R.: The Necklace.

BOIELDIEU, FRANCOIS ADRIEN: Le Calife de Bagdad; La Dame blanche; La Fête du village voisin; Jean de Paris; Ma tante Aurore; Le Nouveau seigneur du village; Le Petit chaperon rouge.

BOISSELOT, XAVIER: Ne touchez-pas à la reine.

BOITO, ARRIGO: Mefistofele.

BONAWITZ, JOHANN HEINRICH: The Bride of Messina; Ostrolenka.

BONNER, EUGENE: The Venetian glass nephew.

BONONCINI, GIOVANNI: Polifemo.

BONSIGNORE, CAMILLO: I Miserabili.

BORODIN, ALEXANDER PORFIRIEVICH: Prince Igor.

BOUGHTON, RUTLAND: The Immortal hour.

BOYCE, WILLIAM: The Chaplet.

BRADLEY, RUTH: The Barren pines.

BRAHAM, JOHN: * The Cabinet; * The Devil's in it; The English fleet; * Isidore de Merida.

BRAND, MAX: The Gate.

BRANDL, JOHANN: Des Löwen Erwachen.

BRAUN, JOSEPH: Der Kosak und der Freywillige.

BRAY, JOHN: The Indian princess.

BREIL, JOSEPH CARL: The Asra; The Legend; Love laughs at lock-smiths.

BRISTOW, GEORGE FREDERICK: Rip van Winkle.

BRITTEN, BENJAMIN: Albert Herring; Billy Budd; Gloriana; Let's make an opera; A Midsummer night's dream; The Miracle of Saint Nicholas; Noye's fludde; Paul Bunyan; Peter Grimes; Prima donna; A Tale of two cities; The Turn of the screw.

BROEKMAN, DAVID: Barbara Allen; The Toledo war.

BROWN, J. HAROLD: King Solomon.

BRUELL, IGNAZ: Das Goldene Kreuz.

BRUNEAU, ALFRED: L'Attaque du moulin.

BRYAN, CHARLES FAULKNER: Singin' Billy.

BUCCI, MARK: The Boor; The Dress; A Tale for a deaf ear; The Thirteen clocks.

118

BUCHAROFF [Buchhalter], SIMON: A Lover's knot; Sakahra.

BUCK, DUDLEY: Deseret.

BURGE, DAVID: Intervals.

BURNHAM, CARDON V.: Aria da capo; The Nitecap.

BUSONI, FERRUCCIO BENVENUTO: Arlecchino.

BUTLER, O'BRIEN: Muirgheis.

BYRD, WILLIAM CLIFTON: Hold that note; Lyneia; The Scandal
at Mulford Inn.

- C -

CADMAN, CHARLES WAKEFIELD: The Garden of mystery;
Shanewis; The Sunset trail; The Willow tree; The Witch of Salem.

CAGNONI, ANTONIO: Don Bucefalo.

CALDWELL, MARY ELIZABETH: Pepito's golden flower.

CAMPBELL, MARION: Osceola.

CANDAILLE, PIERRE JOSEPH: Pizarre.

CANNINGS, THOMAS: Beyond belief.

CARAFA DE COLOBRANO, MICHELE ENRICO: Le Solitaire.

CARDILLO, SALVATORE NAPOLEONE: Romilda.

CAREY, HENRY: The Contrivances; Damon and Phillida; The Honest
Yorkshire-man; True blue.

CARISSIMI, GIACOMO: Giona.

CARR, BENJAMIN: The American in London; The Archers; Bourville
Castle;

CARTER, ERNEST TROW: The Blonde donna; The White bird.

CARTER, THOMAS: The Fair American; The Rival candidates.

CARUSO (?), L.: Monsieur de chiffone.

CASTIL-BLAZE, FRANCOIS HENRI JOSEPH: Les Folies
amourauses.

CATALANI, ALFREDO: Loreley; La Wally.

CELLIER, ALFRED: The Spectre knight.

CHABRIER, ALEXIS EMANUEL: Briséïs; Un Education manquée;
L'Etoile.

CHADWICK, GEORGE WHITEFIELD: Judith; Love's sacrifice.

CHAMPEIN, STANISLAS: Les Dettes; La Mélomanie.

CHANLER, THEODORE WARD: The Pot of fat.

CHAPI, RUPERTO: La Calandria; El Puñao de rosas; El Rey que rabió;
La Tempestad.

CHARPENTIER, GUSTAVE: Julien; Louise.

CHAVEZ, CARLOS: Panfilo and Laurette.

CHERUBINI, MARIE LUIGI ZENOBIO CARLO SALVATORE:
Les Deux journées; L'Hôtellerie portugaise; Medée.

CHESLOCK, LOUIS: The Jewel merchants.

CHISHOLM, ERIK: Black roses; Dark sonnet; Simoon.

CHUDACOFF, EDWARD: The Circus.

CHUECA, FEDERICO: *La Gran via.

CIEUTAT, HENRI MAURICE: Pierrot luni.

CILEA, FRANCESCO: Adriana Lecouvreur; L'Arlesiana.

CIMAROSA, DOMENICO: L'Italiana in Londra; Il Matrimonio segreto.

CLAFLIN, AVERY: La Grande Bretèche; Hester Prynne.

CLAPISSON, ANTOINE LOUIS: La Perruche.

CLARKE, HENRY LELAND: The Loafer and the loaf.

CLEMENS, JOHN: Justina.

COATES, ALBERT: Gainsborough's duchess.

COCKSHOTT, GERALD: Apollo and Persephone; A Fawn in the forest.

COERNE, LOUIS ADOLPHE: Zenobia.

COHN, JAMES: The Fall of the city.

COLLINS, ANTHONY: Catherine Parr.

CONDELL, HENRY: *The Farmer's wife.

CONVERSE, FREDERICK SHEPHERD: The Pipe of desire; The Sacrifice.

COPLAND, AARON: The Second hurricane; The Tender land.

COPPOLA, PIER ANTONIO: Nina pazza per amore.

CORNELIUS, PETER: Der Barbier von Bagdad.

CUI, CESAR ANTONOVICH: Puss in boots.

CURTI, FRANZ: Lili-Tsee.

- D -

DALAYRAC, NICOLAS: L'Amant statue; Azémia; Camille; Deux mots; Les Deux petits Savoyards; Gulistan; Gulnare; Une Heure de mariage; La Jeune prude; Maison à vendre; Nina; Raoul, sire de Créqui; Renaud d'Ast.

DALLA PICCOLA, LUIGI: Job; Il Prigioniero.

DAMROSCH, WALTER JOHANNES: Cyrano; The Man without a country; The Opera cloak; The Scarlet letter.

DAN, IKUMA: Yu-Zuru.

D'ANTALFFY, DEZSO: Onteora's bride.

DARGOMYZHSKY, ALEXANDER SERGEIEVICH: Rusalka.

DAVIES, JOHN: The Forest rose.

DAVIS, ALLAN: The Ordeal of Osbert; Otherwise, Engaged; The Sailing of the Nancy Bell.

DAVIS, KATHERINE: The Disappointed impresario.

DAVY, JOHN: *The Cabinet; *The Farmer's wife; Rob Roy Mac Gregor; Spanish dollars.

DE BANFIELD, RAFFAELO: Lord Byron's love letter.

DEBUSSY, ACHILLE CLAUDE: L'Enfant prodigue; Le Martyre de Saint Sébastien; Pélleas et Melisande.

DE FALLA, MANUEL: El Retablo de Maese Pedro; La Vida breve.

DE KOVEN, REGINALD: The Canterbury pilgrims; Rip van Winkle; Robin Hood.

DE LEONE, FRANCESCO B.: Alglala; Capriccio di miliardario.

DELIBES, LEO: La Fille du meunier; Lakmé.

DELLA MARIA, PIERRE ANTOINE DOMINIQUE: Le Prisonnier.

DELLI PONTI, R.: *Haschisch.

DELLO JOIO, NORMAN: Blood moon; The Ruby; The Trial at Rouen; The Triumph of Joan.

DEVIENNE, FRANCOIS: Les Visitandines.

DEZEDE, NICOLAS: Alexis et Justine.

DIAZ, EUGENE: Benvenuto.

DIBDIN, CHARLES: Lionel and Clarissa; The Padlock; Poor Vulcan; The Quaker; The Recruiting serjeant; The Romp; The Two misers; The Waterman; The Wedding ring.

DI GIOVANNI, ROCCO: Medea.

DI JULIO, MAX: Baby Doe.

DITTERSDORF, KARL DITTERS VON: Doctor und Apotheker.

DOELLNER, ROBERT: Escape from liberty.

DOHNANYI, ERNST VON: Tante Simone.

DONIZETTI, GAETANO: Anna Bolena; Belisario; Betly; Il Campanello di notte; Don Pasquale; Don Sebastien; Il Duca d'Alba; L'Elisir d'amore; La Favorite; La Fille du régiment; Il Furioso nell' isola di San Domingo; Gemma di Vergy; Linda di Chamounix; Lucia di Lammermoor; Lucrezia Borgia; Maria di Rohan; Marino Faliero; Les Martyrs (Il Poliuto); Parisiana; Rita; Roberto Devereaux.

DORAN, MATT: The Committee.

DRAKE, EARL R.: The Blind girl of Castel-Cuille.

DUBENSKY, ARCADY: A Romance with a double bass.

DUFFY, JOHN: The Eve of Adam.

DUKAS, PAUL: Ariane et Barbe-Bleu.

DUKE, JOHN: Captain Lovelock; The Sire de Maledroit; The Yankee pedlar.

DUNI, EGIDIO ROMOALDO: Les Deux chasseurs et la laitiere.

DUSSEK, JOHANN LADISLAUS: *The Captive of Spilberg.

DUVAL, ALEXANDRE: L'Oncle-valet.

DVORAK, ANTONIN: Rusalka.

DVORKIN, JUDITH: Crescent eyebrow.
DZERZHINSHY, IVAN IVANOVICH: The Quiet Don.

- E -

EAMES, HENRY PURMORT: The Sacred tree of the Omaha.
EDELMAN, JOHANN FRIEDRICH: Ariane dans l'île de Naxos.
EDWARDS, JULIAN: King René's daughter; The Patriot.
EGGERS, ANTON C.: Nina.
EGK, WERNER: Der Revisor.
EICHBERG, JULIUS: The Doctor of Alcantara; A Night in Rome; The
     Rose of Tyrol; The Two cadis.
EINEM, GOTTFRIED VON: Der Prozess.
ELKUS, JONATHAN: The Outcast of Poker Flat; Tom Sawyer.
ELLSTEIN, ABRAHAM: The Golem; The Thief and the hangman.
ELMORE, ROBERT: It began at breakfast.
ENGEL, LEHMAN: Brother Joe; The Malady of love; Pierrot of the
     minute; The Soldier.
ENNA, AUGUST: Pigen med svolstikkerne.
ENNA, EMIL: The Dawn of the west.
EPPERT, CARL E.: Kaintuckee.
ERISMAN, HANS: Don Pedro.
ERLANGER, CAMILLE: Aphrodite.
ERLANGER, FREDERIC d': Noël.
ERNEST II, Duke of Saxe-Coburg-Gotha: Diana von Solange.
ESTELLES, RAMON: *La Marcha de Cadiz.

- F -

FAIRLAMB, JAMES REMINGTON: Valerie [Treasured tokens].
FALL, LEO: Brüderlein fein.
FARBERMAN, HAROLD: Medea.
FERNANDEZ CABALLERO, Manuel: Los Africanistas; La Gallina
     ciega; El Lucero del alba; La Viejecita.
FERRARI, S. A. de: Pipelè.
FETIS, FRANCOIS JOSEPH: La Vieille.
FEVRIER, HENRI: Gismonda; Monna Vanna.
FINE, VIVIAN: A Guide to the life expectancy of a rose.
FINK, MYRON: The Boor; Jeremiah.
FIORAVANTI, VINCENZO: Il Ritorno di Pulcinella.
FIORE, ROLAND MICHAEL: Linda.
FLAGELLO, NICHOLAS: The Sisters.

FLANAGAN, WILLIAM: Bartleby.

FLICK-STEGER, CHARLES L.: Dorian Gray; Leon und Edrita.

FLORIDIA-NAPOLINO, PIETRO: Paoletta.

FLOTOW, FRIEDRICH, Freiherr von: Alessandro Stradella; Martha; L'Ombre.

FLOYD, CARLISLE: Fugitives; The Passion of Jonathan Wade; Slow dusk; Susannah; Wuthering Heights.

FORE, BURDETTE: Aria da capo.

FORREST, GEORGE: *Kismet; *Song of Norway.

FORREST, HAMILTON: Camille; Daelia; Don Fortunio, A Matinee idyll.

FOSS, LUKAS: Griffelkin; Introductions and goodbyes; The Jumping frog of Calaveras County.

FRAGALE, FRANK D.: Dr. Jekyll and Mr. Hyde.

FRANCAIX, JEAN: Le Diable boiteux.

FRANCHETTI, ALBERTO: Asrael; Cristoforo Colombo; Germania.

FRANCHETTI, ALDO: Namiko-San.

FRANCHETTI, ARNOLD: The Anachronisn; The Game of cards; The Lion; The Maypole; Prelude and fugue.

FREDERICK II (the Great): Il Re pastore.

FREED, ISADORE: The Princess and the vagabond.

FREEMAN, HARRY LAWRENCE: The Martyr; The Tryst; Valdo, Vendetta; Voodoo.

FREER, ELEANOR EVERST: The Brownings go to Italy; A Christmas tale; Frithiof; The Legend of Spain; The Legend of the piper; Massimilliano.

FREY, MATTHEW: The Violin maker of Cremona.

FRIDZERI, ALESSANDRO: Les Souliers mors-dorés.

FRIML, RUDOLF: The Firefly; Katinka; *Rose-Marie.

FRY, WILLIAM HENRY: Leonora; Notre Dame de Paris.

FUX, JOHANN JOSEPH: Costanza e Fortezza.

- G -

GABURO, KENNETH: The Snow queen.

GALUPPI, BALDASSARE: Il Filosofo di campagna.

GANNE, LOUIS GASTON: Hans, le jouer de flûte.

GARCIA, MANUEL DEL POPOLO VINCENTE: L'Amante astuto; La Figlia dell' aria.

GARLAND, CHARLES: If men played cards as women do.

GARLAND, KATHRYN: Ruth

GAVEAUX, PIERRE: L'Amour filial; Le Bouffe et le tailleur; Le Diable en vacances; Le Petit matelot.

123

GAZTAMBIDE, JOAQUIN: El Juramento; * El Sargento Federico.

GERMAN, EDWARD: Merrie England; Tom Jones.

GERSHWIN, GEORGE: 135th Street; Of thee I sing; Oh, Kay!; Porgy and Bess; * Song of the flame.

GESENSWAY, LOUIS: Buffo and his talking dog.

GETO, ALFRED D.: The Treasure.

GIANNINI, VITTORIO: Beauty and the beast; Blennerhasset; The Harvest; Lucedia; Rehearsal call; The Scarlet letter; The Taming of the shrew.

GIBBONS, CHRISTOPHER: * Cupid and death.

GIDE, CASIMIR: * La Tentation.

GIGLIO, CLEMENTE: La Monaca bianca.

GILLIS, DON: Pep rally.

GIORDANO, UMBERTO: Andrea Chenier; La Cena delle beffe; Fedora; Madame Sans-Gêne; Mese Mariano; Siberia.

GLAESER, F.: Des Adlers Horst.

GLANVILLE-HICKS, PEGGY: The Glittering gate; Nausicaa; The Transposed heads.

GLEASON, FREDERICK GRANT: Otho Visconti.

GLINKA, MIKHAIL IVANOVICH: A Life for the czar; Russlan and Ludmila.

GLUCK, CHRISTOPH WILLIBALD von: Alceste; Armide; Le Cadi dupé; Hippolyte et Aricie; Iphigénie en Aulide; Iphigénie en Tauride; L'Ivrogne corrigé; Die Maienkonigin; Orfeo ed Euridice; La Rencontre imprévue.

GNECCHI, VITTORIO: Casandra.

GODARD, BENJAMIN: La Vivandière.

GOETZ, HEINRICH: Der Widerspänstigen Zahmung.

GOLDMARK, CARL: Das Heimchen am Herd; Die Königin von Saba; Merlin.

GOMES, ANTONIO CARLOS: Il Guarany.

GOODMAN, ALFRED GRANT: The Audition.

GOODMAN, J. F.: The Pizza pusher.

GOOSSENS, EUGENE: Judith.

GOTTLIEB, JACOB: Sonata allegro.

GOUNOD, CHARLES FRANCOIS: La Colombe; Faust; Le Médecin malgré lui; Mireille; Philémon et Baucis; La Reine de Saba; Roméo et Juliette; Le Tribut de Zamora.

GRAHAM, SHIRLEY: Tom-tom.

GRANADOS Y CAMPINA, ENRIQUE: Goyescas.

GREGORI, ELSE: * Haschisch.

GRETCHANINOV, ALEXANDER TIKHONOVICH: Dobrinya Nikitich.

GRETRY, ANDRE ERNEST MODESTE: La Caravane du Caire; Les
Deux avares; L'Epreuve villageoise; Les Evenements imprévues; La
Fausse magie; Les Fausses apparences; Guillaume Tell; Le Jugement
de Midas; Richard Coeur-de-Lion; La Rosière de Salency; Silvain; Le
Tableau parlant; Zemire et Azor.

GRIEG, EDVARD HAGERUP: Olav Trygvason; Peer Gynt.

GRISAR, ALBERT: Les Amours du diable; Diamond cut diamond;
Gilles Ravisseur.

GROSS, ROBERT: The Bald soprano.

GROTH, HOWARD: Petruchio.

GRUENBERG, LOUIS: The Emperor Jones; Green mansions; Jack and
the beanstalk.

GUERRERO, JACINTO: Los Gavilanes.

GUERRIERI, STEFANO: Evandro.

GUSTAFSON, DWIGHT: The Hunted; The Jailer.

GUZUTIS, TOMAS: * Vestuves [The Wedding].

- H -

HADLEY, HENRY KIMBALL: Azora; Bianca; Cleopatra's night; A
Night in old Paris; Safié.

HAGEMAN, RICHARD: Caponsacchi.

HAGER, GEORGE: Pan.

HALEVY, JACQUES FRANCOIS FROMENTAL ELIE: Charles
VI; L'Eclair; La Fée aux roses; La Juive; La Reine de Chypre; * La
Tentation; La Val d'Andorre.

HAMM, CHARLES EDWARD: The Box; The Cask of Amontillado;
The Monkey's paw; The Salesgirl; A Scent of sarsaparilla; The
Secret life of Walter Mitty.

HANDEL, GEORGE FREDERICK: Acis and Galatea; Alcina;
Belshazzar; Deidamia; Ezio; Giulio Cesare; Messiah; Il Pastor fido;
Rodelinda; Serse; Theodora.

HANNAY, ROGER: Two tickets to Omaha.

HANSON, HOWARD: Merry Mount.

HANSON, WILLIAM FREDERICK: The Bleeding heart of Timpanogas; Täm-Män-Näcup.

HARLING, WILLIAM FRANKE: Alda; Deep river; A Light from St.
Agnes.

HARRISON, LOU: Rapunzel.

HAUBIEL, CHARLES: Sunday costs five pesos.

HAUFRECHT, HERBERT: Boney Quillen.

HAWKINS, MICAH: The Sawmill.

HAYDN, FRANZ JOSEF: La Canterina; L'Isola disbitata; Il Mondo della luna; Orlando paladino; Lo Speziale.

HECKSCHER, CELESTE DE LONGPRE: The Rose of destiny.

HEINRICH, ANTHONY PHILIP: The Child of the mountain.

HELM, EVERETT BURTON: Adam and Eve; Die Belagerung von Tottenburg.

HERBERT, VICTOR: Babes in Toyland; The Fortune teller; Madeleine; Mlle Modiste; Natoma; Naughty Marietta; The Red Mill; The Serenade; Sweethearts.

HERMAN, REINHOLD LUDWIG: Lanzelot, Spielmannsglück, Sundari, Vineta; Wulfrim.

HEROLD, LOUIS JOSEPH FERDINAND: La Clochette; Marie; Le Pré aux clercs; Zampa.

HERRMANN, BERNARD: A Christmas carol.

HEWITT, JAMES: The Cottagers; The Mysterious marriage; The Patriot; Robin Hood; The Spanish castle; Tammany; The Wild chace.

HINDEMITH, PAUL: Hin und zurück; Mathis der Maler; Neues vom Tage; Sancta Susanna.

HINRICHS, GUSTAV: Onti-Ora; Der Vierjährige Posten.

HIVELY, WELLS: Junípero serra.

HOCHMAN, ARTHUR: Fiammetta.

HOFF, BERNARD: *Moses.

HOIBY, LEE: Beatrice; The Scarf.

HOLLINGSWORTH, STANLEY: La Grande Bretèche; The Mother.

HOLST, GUSTAV THEODORE: At the Boar's Head; The Perfect fool.

HOLTON, BOB: A Real strange one.

HONEGGER, ARTHUR: Jeanne d'Arc au bûcher; Judith; Nicholas de Flue.

HONIGMAN, SAUL: The Ticket.

HOOK, JAMES: The Double disguise; The Soldier's return.

HOPKINS, JEROME: Samuel.

HORN, CHARLES EDWARD: Ahmed al Kamel; The Bee-hive; The Death fetch; *The Devil's bridge; Dido; The Maid of Saxony; Nadir and Zuleika; *The Pirates (Isidore de Merida); The Quartette.

HOSCHNA, CARL L.: Madame Sherry.

HOVHANESS, ALAN: Blue flame.

HOUSELEY, HENRY: Narcissus and Echo.

HOWLAND, WILLIAM LEGRAND: Nita; Sarrona.

HUBERT, JEAN: Pierrot qui pleure et Pierrot qui rit.

HUGO, JOHN ADAM: The Temple dancer.

HUMEL, GERALD: The Proposal.

HUMPERDINCK, ENGELBRECHT: Hänsel und Gretel; Die Königs-
kinder; Das Mirakel.
HUMPHREY, HENRY SIGURD: Mayerling.

- I -

IBERT, JACQUES: Angelique; Le Roi d'Yvetot.
ISOUARD, NICOLO: Le Billet de loterie; Cendrillon; Jeannot et Colin;
Joconde; Lully et Quinault; Les Rendez-vous bourgeois.

- J -

JACOBI, FREDERICK: The Prodigal son.
JACOBI, VICTOR: * Apple blossoms; Sybil.
JAKOBOWSKI, E.: Erminie.
JANACEK, LEOS: Jenufa; Katya Kabanova.
JOHNSON, LOCKREM: A Letter to Emily.
JOHNSON, MARY: The Thirteen clocks.
JONES, GEORGE THADDEUS: The Cage.
JONES, JOHN: The Enchanted horse.
JONES, SIDNEY: The Geisha.
JORDAN, JULES: Rip van Winkle.

- K -

KAGEN, SERGIUS: Hamlet.
KAHN, EMIL: The Ribbon.
KAISER, EMIL: Der Trompeter von Säckingen.
KALMANOFF, MARTIN: Brandy is my true love's name; The Empty
bottle; Fit for a king; Noah and the stowaway; Opera, opera; A Quiet
game of cribble; Videomania.
KANITZ, ERNEST: Room 12; Royal auction.
KASSERN, TADEUSZ ZYGFRIED: Sun-up.
KASTLE, LEONARD: Deseret; The Swing.
KAUFFMANN, LEO JUSTINUS: Das Perlenhemd.
KAUFFMANN, WALTER: A Parfait for Irene; The Scarlet letter.
KAY, ULYSSES: The Juggler of Our Lady.
KAYDEN, MILDRED: Mardi Gras.
KECHLEY, GERALD: The Beckoning fair one; The Golden lion.
KELLY, MICHAEL: * The Captive of Spilberg; Cinderella; The Gay
deceivers (see Les Evenements imprévues); Of age to-morrow; * The
Peasant boy; Youth, love and folly.

KERKER, GUSTAV ADOLPH: The Belle of New York.

KERN JEROME: Lamplight; Music in the air; Oh, lady! lady!; Roberta; Show boat.

KIENZL, WILHELM: Der Evangelimann; Der Kuhreigen.

KILPATRICK, JACK FREDERICK: The Blessed wilderness.

KIRKPATRICK, HOWARD: Olaf.

KLEIN, MANUEL: Bow Sing.

KLEINSINGER, GEORGE: archy and mehitabel; A Tree that found Christmas.

KNOWLTON, E. BRUCE: The Monk of Toledo.

KODALY, ZOLTAN: Harry Janos; Székely fanó [The Spinnery].

KONDOROSSY, LESLIE: The Midnight duel; Mystic fortress; A Night in the Puszta; The Pumpkin; The String quartet; The Two imposters; The Unexpected visitor; The Voice.

KONSKI, ANTOINE de: Le Sultan de Zanzibar.

KORNGOLD, ERICH WOLFGANG: Der Ring des Polykrates; Die Tote Stadt; Violanta.

KOUTZEN, BORIS: The Fatal oath.

KOVAROVIC, KAREL: Psohlavci [Dog's heads].

KRANE, SHERMAN: The Giant's garden.

KREISLER, FRITZ: * Apple blossoms.

KRENEK, ERNST: The Bell tower; Dark waters; Jonny spielt auf.

KREUTZ, ARTHUR: Acres of sky; Sourwood Mountain; The University greys.

KREUTZER, KONRADIN: Das Nachtlager von Granada.

KREUTZER, RODOLPHE: Paul et Virginie.

KROLL, LOUIS: La Bella; Mme. Butterfly recovers.

KUBIK, GAIL: Boston baked beans; A Mirror in the sky.

KUPFERMAN, MEYER: The Curious hen; Draagènfoot girl; In a garden; Voices for a mirror.

KURKA, ROBERT: The Good soldier Schweik.

- L -

LACY, MICHAEL ROPHINO: The Israelites in Egypt.

LADERMAN, EZRA: Goodbye to the clown; The Hunting of the snark; Jacob and the Indians; Sarah.

LA GRASSA, L.: Anne of Austria.

LALO, EDOUARDO: Le Roi d'Ys.

LA MONTAINE, JOHN: Novellis, novellis.

LANDAU, SIEGFRIED: The Sons of Aaron.

LAPARRA, RAOUL: La Habanera.

LAPHAM, CLAUDE: Sakura.

LA PRADE, ERNEST: Xantha.

LARA, ISIDORE de : Messaline.

LATTUADA, FELICE: Le Preziose ridicole.

LAUFER, BEATRICE: 'Ile.

LAWES, HENRY: Comus.

LAWRENCE, CHARLES W.: Atsumori.

LAZZARI, SYLVIO: Le Sauteriot.

LEBRUN, LOUIS SEBASTIEN: Le Rossignol.

LECOCQ, CHARLES: La Fille de Madame Angot; Giroflé-Girofla; Les Prés Saint-Gervais.

LEE, DAI-KEONG: The Poet's dilemma; Speakeasy.

LEGINSKA, ETHEL: Gale; The Rose and the ring.

LEHAR, FRANZ: Die Lustige Witwe; Zigeunerliebe.

LEHMAN, LIZA: The Vicar of Wakefield.

LEHNER, DERRICK NORMAN: The Harvest; The Necklace of the sun.

LEONCAVALLO, RUGGIERO: La Bohème; Edipo re; Pagliacci; Zaza; Zingari.

LEONI, FRANCO: L'Oracolo.

LEPS, WASSILI: Andon; Hoshi-San.

LEROUX, XAVIER: Le Chemineau; La Reine Fiammette.

LESSNER, GEORGE: The Nightingale and the rose.

LESTER, THOMAS WILLIAM: Manabozo.

LETOVSKY, STANISLAV: Frau Anne, die Dame am Putztisch.

LEVISTER, ALONZO: Blues in the subway.

LEVY, MARVIN DAVID: Escurial; Sotoba komachi; The Tower.

LIEBERMANN, ROLF: The School for wives.

LIMNANDER, ARMAND: Les Monténégrins.

LINDEN, EINAR: Le Jardinier.

LINDSEY, EDWIN S.: Elizabeth and Leicester.

LINLEY, THOMAS, sr., and T. Linley, jr.: The Duenna; The Gentle shepherd.

LISSENKO, NIKOLAI VITALIEVICH: Taras Bulba.

LIST, KURT: The Wise and the foolish.

LISZT, FRANZ: Die Legende von der heiligen Elisabeth.

LLEO, V.: Ruido de campanas.

LOCKE, MATTHEW: *Cupid and death.

LOCKWOOD, NORMAND: Early dawn; The Scarecrow; The Wizards of Balizar.

LODER, EDWARD JAMES: The Andalusian; The Willis.

LODER, GEORGE: *Comus.

LOESSER, FRANK: Guys and dolls; The Most happy fella.

LOEWE, FREDERICK: Brigadoon; My fair lady.

LOMBARD, LOUIS: Errisinola.

LOOMIS, CLARENCE: The Fall of the house of Usher; A Night in
    Avignon; Revival; Yolanda of Cyprus.

LOOMIS, HARVEY WORTHINGTON: The Traitor mandolin.

LORTZING, ALBERT: Die Beiden Schützen; Czar und Zimmermann;
    Der Pole und sein Kind; Undine; Der Waffenschmied; Der Wildschütz.

LOVINGOOD, PENMAN: Memelek.

LOW, JAMES: Moby Dick.

LUALDI, ADRIANO: Le Furie de Arlecchino.

LUDERS, GUSTAVE: The Prince of Pilsen.

LUENING, OTTO: Evangeline.

LULLY, JEAN BAPTISTE: Amadis; Armide.

LYFORD, RALPH: Castle Agrazant.

- M -

MC CLAIN, FLOYD: The Princess and the frog; The Snack shop.

MACFARREN, GEORGE ALEXANDER: Jessy Lea; The Soldier's
    legacy.

MC KEE, JEANELLEN: Collector's piece.

MAEDER, JAMES GASPARD: The Peri.

MAGANINI, QUINTO: Tennessee partner.

MAGNUSON, KARL: Adam and Eve and the devil.

MAILLART, AIME: Les Dragons de Villars; Gastibelza.

MAILMAN, MARTIN: The Hunted.

MALIPIERO, GIAN FRANCESCO: Il Finto Arlecchino; Sette
    canzoni.

MANCINELLI, LUIGI: Ero e Leandro.

MANNING, EDWARD: Rip van Winkle.

MARAIS, JOSEF: African heartbeat; Tony Beaver.

MARCHETTI, FILIPPO: Ruy Blas.

MARETZEK, MAX: Sleepy Hollow.

MARINUZZI, GINO: Jacquerie.

MARSCHNER, HEINRICH: Der Holzdieb; Der Templer und die Jüdin.

MARSH, LUCILLE CREWS: The Concert.

MARTIN, FRANK: Der Sturm.

MARTINELLI, RODOLFO: Alone I stand.

MARTINU, BOHUSLAV: Comedy on the bridge; The Marriage.

MASCAGNI, PIETRO: Amica; L'Amico Fritz; Cavalleria rusticana;
    Iris; Isabeau; Lodoletta; Zanetto.

MASON, WILTON: Kingdom come.

MASSE, VICTOR FELIX MARIE: Galatée; Les Noces de Jeannette; Paul et Virginie.

MASSENET, JULES: Cendrillon; Le Cid; Cléopâtre; Don Quichotte; Esclarmonde; Grisélides; Hérodiade; Le Jongleur de Notre-Dame; Manon; La Navarraise; Le Portrait de Manon; Le Roi de Lahore; Sapho; Thais; Werther.

MAURAGE, AUGUSTE: Les Noces d'or.

MAXFIELD, RICHARD: Stacked deck.

MAYER, CARL: The Conspiracy of Pontiac.

MAYER, ROBERT: The Porter at the door.

MAYR, JOHANN SIMON: Che originali.

MAZZINGHI, JOSEPH: * The Turnpike gate.

MEHUL, ETIENNE NICOLAS: Bion; Une Folie; L'Irato; Joseph; Stratonice.

MELANI, JACOPO: La Tancia.

MENDELSSOHN-BARTHOLDY, FELIX: Antigone; Athalia; Elijah; Die Heimkehr aus der Fremde; Die Hochzeit des Camacho; A Midsummer night's dream; Paulus [St. Paul].

MENNINI, LOUIS: The Rope; The Well.

MENOTTI, GIAN CARLO: Amahl and the night visitors; Amelia al ballo; The Consul; The Island god; Maria Golovin; The Medium; The Old maid and the thief; The Saint of Bleecker Street; The Telephone; The Unicorn, the gordon and the manticore.

MERCADANTE, GIUSEPPE SAVERIO: Il Bravo; Donna Caritea; Elisa e Claudio; Il Giuramento.

MERMET, AUGUSTE: Roland à Roncevaux.

MESSAGER, ANDRE: La Basoche; Madame Chrysanthème; Monsieur Beaucaire; Passionnément; Veronique.

MEYERBEER, GIACOMO: L'Africaine; L'Etoile du nord; Les Huguenots; Marguerite d'Anjou; Le Pardon de Ploermel (Dinorah); Le Prophète; Robert le diable.

MEYEROWITZ, JAN: The Barrier; Eastward in Eden; Esther; Godfather Death; The Meeting; Port town; Simoon.

MICELI, GIUSEPPE: Alma latina.

MIDDLETON, ROBERTL The Nightingale is guilty.

MILANO, ROBERT L.: The Hired hand.

MILDENBERG, ALBERT: Raffaelo.

MILHAUD, DARIUS: L'Abandon d'Ariane; Christophe Colomb; David; L'Enlevement d'Europe; Fiesta; Les Malheurs d'Orphee; Médée; Le Pauvre matelot.

MILLARD, HARRISON: Deborah; Uncle Tom's cabin.

MILLER, ALMA GRAYCE: The Whirlwind.

MILLER, FRANK: Thespis.

MILLOECKER, KARL: Der Bettelstudent; Der Feldprediger.
MOHAUPT, RICHARD: Double trouble.
MOLLENHAUER, EMIL: The Corsican bride.
MONIUSZKO, STANISLAW: Flis; Halka; Hrabina; Straszny dwór;
Verbum nobile.
MONSIGNY, PIERRE ALEXANDRE: La Belle Arsène; Le Deserteur;
On ne s'avise jamais de tout.
MONTEMEZZI, ITALO: L'Amore dei tre rei; Giovanni Gallurese;
L'Incantesimo; La Nave; La Notte di Zoraima.
MONTEVERDI, CLAUDIO: Il Ballo delle ingrate; Il Combattimento
di Tancredi e Clorinda; L'Incoronazione di Poppea; Orfeo; Il Ritorno
d'Ulisse in patria; Tirsi e Clori.
MONTFORT, A.: Polichinelle.
MOORE, DOUGLAS: The Ballad of Baby Doe; The Devil and Daniel
Webster; The Emperor's new clothes; Gallantry; Giants in the earth;
The Headless horseman; White wings; The Wings of the dove.
MOORE, HOMER: Louis XIV; The New world.
MOORE, MARY CARR: David Rizzio; The Flaming arrow; Narcissa;
The Oracle; Los Rubios.
MOOREHEAD, JOHN: * The Cabinet.
MOPPER, IRVING: The Door.
MORET, ERNEST: Lorenzaccio.
MORRIS, HAYWARD: In paradise.
MOSES, ABRAM: Melody in "I."
MOSS, LAWRENCE: The Brute.
MOSZKOWSKI, MORITZ: Boabdil.
MOUSSORGSKY, MODEST: Boris Godounov; The Fair at Sorochinsk;
Khovantchina.
MOZART, WOLFGANG AMADEUS: Bastien und Bastienne; La
Clemenza di Tito; Cosi fan tutte; Don Giovanni; Die Entführung aus
dem Serail; La Finta giardiniera; La Finta semplice; Idomeneo; Le
Nozze di Figaro; Thamos; Zaide; Die Zauberflöte.
MUELLER, WENZEL: Die Schwestern von Prag; Die Teufelmühle am
Wienerberg.
MULDOON, GEORGE: Illusion for three.

- N -

NABOKOV, NICOLAS: The Holy devil.
NAPRAVNIK, EUARD: Dubrovsky.
NELSON, RON: The Birthday of the infanta.
NESSLER, VICTOR ERNST: Der Rattenfänger von Hameln; Der Trom-
peter von Säckingen.

NEUENDORFF, ADOLPH: Don Quixote; Der Minstrel.
NEVIN, ARTHUR FINLEY: A Daughter of the forest; Poia.
NEWBERN, KENNETH: The Armor of life.
NICOLAI, OTTO: Die Lustigen Weiber von Windsor.
NIETO, M.: El Gorro frigio.
NORDOFF, PAUL: The Masterpiece.
NORDEN, NORRIS LINDSAY: Nebrahma.
NOUGES, JEAN: Quo vadis?
NOWAK, LIONEL AUGUSTUS: The Clarkstown witch; Katydids.
NOYES-GREENE, EDITH: Osseo.

- O -

OFFENBACH, JACQUES: Les 66!; Barbe-Bleu; Les Bavards; La Belle
Hélène; Belle Lurette; La Boulangere a des ecus; Les Braconniers; Les
Brigands; La Chanson de Fortunio; La Chatte métamorphosée en
femme; Les Contes d'Hoffmann; La Créole; Une Demoiselle en loterie;
Les Deux aveugles; Dick Wittington and his cat; Geneviève de
Brabant; Les Géorgiennes; Le Grande duchesse de Gérolstein; L'Ile de
Tulipatan; Jacqueline; Jeanne qui pleure et Jean qui rit; La Joli par-
fumeuse; Lischen et Fritzchen; Madame Favart; Madame l'archiduc;
Un Mari a la porte; Le Mariage aux lanternes; Monsieur Choufleuri;
Une Nuit blanche; Orphee aux Enfers; Pépito; La Périchole; Périnette;
Pomme d'api; Le Pont des soupirs; La Princesse de Trébizonde; Robin-
son Crusoé; Le Roi Carotte; La Rose de Saint-Flour; Le Soldat magicien
[La Fifre enchanté]; Trom-al-cazar; Vert-vert; La Vie parisienne; Le
Violoneux; Le Voyage dans la lune.
O'KEEFEE, JOHN: The Highland reel.
OREFICE, GIACOMO: Chopin.
ORFF, CARL: Carmina burana; Die Kluge; Der Mond.
OVERTON, HALL: The Enchanted pear tree.
OZIER, JULIUS: The Bride of Bagdad.

- P -

PACINI, GIOVANNI: Gli Arabi nelle Gallie; Medea; Saffo.
PADEREWSKI, IGNAZ JAN: Manru.
PAER, FERDINANDO: I Fuorusciti di Firenza; Le Maître de chapelle.
PAINE, JOHN KNOWLES: Azara.
PAISIELLO, GIOVANNI: Il Barbiere di Siviglia; Il Rè Teodoro in
Venezia; La Serva padrona.
PALADILHE, EMILE: Le Passant.
PARELLI, ATTILIO: I Dispettosi amanti.

PARELLI, NATALE: Belshazzar; Clarissa Harlowe.

PARK, STEPHEN F.: Sally back and forth.

PARKER, HORATIO WILLIAM: Fairyland; Mona.

PARMENTIER, FRANCIS GORDON: The Little prince.

PASCAL, CLAUDE: La Farce du contrebandier.

PATTERSON, FRANK[LIN] PEALE: Beggar's love; The Echo.

PATTON, WILLARD: Pocahontas.

PEDROLLO, ARRIGO: La Veglia.

PELISSIER, VICTOR: The Danaides; Edwin and Angelina; The Good neighbor; The Launch; Sterne's Maria [The Vintage]; The Wife of two husbands.

PEMBERTON, CHARLES E.: The Painter of dreams.

PEPUSCH, JOHN CHRISTOPHER: The Beggar's opera; Polly.

PERAGALLO, MARIO: La Gita in campagna.

PERGOLESI, GIOVANNI BATISTA: La Contadina astute; Il Flaminio; Lo Frate 'nnamorato; Il Geloso schernito; Il Maestro di musica; La Serva padrona.

PERI, ACHILLE: Giuditta.

PERI, JACOPO: Euridice.

PERRY, JULIA: The Cask of Amontillado.

PETER, DARRELL: The Parrot.

PETIT, PIERRE: Le Jeu de l'amour et du hassard.

PETRASSI, GOFFREDO: Morte dell' aria.

PETRAUSKAS, MIKAS: Egle, Zalciu karaliene [Egle, Queen of the Snakes]; Velnias isradejas [The Devil inventor]; *Vestuves [The Wedding].

PETRELLA, ERRICO: Il Carnevale di Venezia; Ione.

PHILIDOR, FRANCOIS: Le Maréchal ferrant.

PHILLIPS, BURRELL: Don't we all.

PICCINNI, ALEXANDRE: La maison en loterie.

PIERNE, GABRIEL: Les Enfants de Bethléem; Sophie Arnould.

PIKET, FREDERICK: Isaac Levi; Satan's trap.

PILATI, A.: Jean le sot.

PIRANI, EUGENIO: Black blood; Das Hexenlied.

PIZZETTI, ILDEBRANDO: Assassinio nella cattedrale; Fra Gherardo.

PIZZI, EMILIO: Gabriella.

PLANQUETTE, ROBERT: Les Cloches de Corneville.

POISE, FERDINAND: Le Surprise d'amour.

PONCHIELLI, AMILCARE: La Gioconda.

PORTER, COLE: Kiss me Kate; Panama Hattie.

POULENC, FRANCIS: Dialogues des Carmelites; Les Mamelles de Tiresias; La Voix humaine.

POUND, EZRA LOOMIS: The Testament of François Villon.

PRATT, SILAS GAMALIEL: Lucille; Zenobia.

PREVOST, EUGENE PROSPER: Blanche et René; Cosimo; La Esmeralda.

PROKOFIEV, SERGEI SERGEIVICH: Bethrothal at a monastery; The Gambler; The Love of three oranges; War and peace.

PRUNTY, WILLIAM: The Lotus tree.

PUCCINI, GIACOMO: La Bohème; Edgar; La Fanciulla del West; Gianni Schicchi; Madama Butterfly; Manon Lescaut; La Rondine; Sour Angelica; Il Tabarro; Tosca; Turandot; Le Villi.

PURCELL, HENRY: Dido and Aeneas; Dioclesian; Don Quixote; The Fairy queen; King Arthur.

- Q -

QUISLANT: * Doloretes.

- R -

RABAUD, HENRI: Mârouf.

RACHMANINOV, SERGEI VASILIEVICH: Aleko; The Miser knight.

RAIMUND, FERDINAND: Der Alpenkönig und der Menschenfeind.

RAMEAU, JEAN PHILIPPE: Castor et Pollux; Les Indes galantes; Pygmalion.

RANDEL, ANDREAS: Vermlandingarne.

RAPHING, SAM: Dr. Heidegger's experiment.

RAVEL, MAURICE: L'Enfant et les sortileges; L'Heure espagnole.

REDDING, JOSEPH DEIGHN: Fay-Yen-Fah.

REED, H. OWEN: Earth-trapped; Michigan dream.

REEVE, WILLIAM: * Brother and sister; * The Farmer's wife; * Oscar and Malvina; The Purse; The Sicilian romance; * The Turnpike gate.

REINAGLE, ALEXANDER: Auld Robin Gray; The Savoyard; Slaves in Algiers; The Volunteers.

REINECKE, CARL: Ein Abenteuer Handels.

REISER, ALOIS: Gobi.

RESPIGHI, OTTORINO: La Bella addormentata nel bosco; La Campana sommersa; La Fiamma.

REUTTER, HERMANN: Der Weg nach Freudenstadt.

REYER, ERNEST: Salammbo; Sigurd.

REZNICEK, EMIL NIKOLAUS: Spiel oder ernst?

RICCI, LUIGI: Chiara di Rosembergh; Crispino e la comare (with Federico Ricci).

RICCITELLI, PRIMO: I Compagnacci.

RIEMANN, FERDINAND: Die Brilleninsel.

RIETI, VITTORIO: Don Perlimplin; The Pet shop.

RIMSKY-KORSAKOV, NIKOLAI ANDREIEVICH: Le Coq d'or;
The Czar's Bride; The Legend of the invisible city of Kitezh and the
maiden Fevronia; The Maid of Pskov; Mozart and Salieri; Sadko;
Snegourotchka; The Tale of the Tsar Saltan [The Bumble Bee Prince].

ROBB, JOHN D.: Little Joe.

ROCCA, LODOVICO: Il Dibuc.

RODGERS, RICHARD: Carousel; Flower drum song; The King and I;
Oklahoma!; Pal Joey; South Pacific.

ROGERS, BERNARD: The Marriage of Aude; The Nightingale; The
Veil; The Warrior.

ROIG, G.: La Mulata.

ROMBERG, SIGMUND: The Desert song; Blossom time; Maytime; My
Maryland; The New moon; Nina Rosa; The Student prince.

ROME, HAROLD: Fanny.

ROOKE, WILLIAM MICHAEL: Amilie.

ROPARTZ, JOSEPH GUT MARIE: Le Diable couturier.

ROREM, NED: A Childhood miracle.

ROSENTHAL, MANUEL: La Poule noire.

ROSS, JERRY: *Damn Yankees; *The Pajama game.

ROSSINI, GIOACCHINO ANTONIO: Il Barbiere di Siviglia; La
Cambiale di matrimonio; La Cenerentola; Le Comte Ory; Eduardo e
Cristina; La Gazza ladra; Guillaume Tell; L'Inganno felice; L'Italiana
in Algeri; Ivanhoé; Mosè in Egitto; L'Occasione fal il ladro; Otello; La
Pietra del paragone; Le Siège de Corinthe [L'Assedio di Corinto]; Il
Signor Bruschino; Tancredi; Il Turco in Italia; Zelmira.

ROUSSEAU, JEAN JACQUES: Le Devin du village; Pygmalion.

ROUSSEL, ALBERT: La Testament de la tante Caroline.

ROY, KLAUS GEORGE: Sterlingman.

RUBINO, PASQUALE: Il Filo d'Arianna.

RUBINSTEIN, ANTON: The Demon; Die Maccabäer; Moses; Nero;
Der Thurm zu Babel; Das Verlorene Paradies.

RUBINSTEIN, BERYL: The Sleeping beauty.

RUGER, MORRIS HUTCHINS: The Fall of the house of Usher;
Gettysburg.

- S -

SABLE, DANIEL: The Informer.

SAINT-SAENS, CAMILLE: Dejanire; Phryné; Samson et Dalila.

SAKELLARIDIS, THEODORE: Perouze.

SALVAYRE, GASTON: Richard III.

SALVIONI, CARLO: La Casa da vendere; Coriolanus before Rome.

SAMINSKY, LAZARE: Gagliarda of a merry plague; The Vision of Ariel.

SAUGET, HENRI: Le Contrebasse.

SAVINE, ALEXANDER: The Girl from Sanjak; Xenia.

SCARLATTI, ALESSANDRO: Il Trionfo dell' onore.

SCARMOLIN, A. LOUIS: The Interrupted serenade.

SCHAD, WALTER CHARLES: Plango.

SCHARWENKA, XAVER: Mataswintha.

SCHENK, JOHANN: Der Dorfbarbier.

SCHILLINGS, MAX von: Mona Lisa.

SCHOENBERG, ARNOLD: Erwartung; Die Glückliche Hand; Pierrot lunaire.

SCHUBERT, FRANZ PETER: Rosamunda von Cypern; Die Verschworenen [Der häusliche Krieg]; Die Zwillingsbrüder.

SCHUMAN, WILLIAM: The Mighty Casey.

SCHUMANN, WALTER: John Brown's body.

SCHWARTZ, PAUL: The Experiment.

SENEZ, CAMILLE de: Horus.

SERRANO, JOSE: La Mala sombra.

SERULNIKOFF, JACK: This evening.

SESSIONS, ROGER: The Trial of Lucullus.

SEYFRIED, IGNAZ XAVER: Die Ochsenmenuette.

SEYMOUR, JOHN LAURENCE: In the pasha's garden.

SHAW, MARTIN: Mr. Pepys.

SHELDON, ROBERT: A Fifth for bridge.

SHIELD, WILLIAM: Aboard and at home; The Farmer; The Flitch of bacon; Fountainebleau; Hartford-Bridge; The Lock and key; Love in a camp; Marian; The Midnight wanderers; The Noble peasant; * Oscar and Malvina; The Poor soldier; The Rival soldiers; Robin Hood; Rosina.

SHIMIZU, OSAMU: The Mask maker.

SHOSTAKOVICH, DMITRI DMITRIEVICH: Lady Macbeth of Mzensk.

SIEGMEISTER, ELIE: Miranda and the dark young man; My darling Corie; Sing out, sweet land!

SKILTON, CHARLES SANFORD: The Sun bride.

SLATES, PHILIP M.: The Bargain; The Candle.

SMAREGLIA, ANTONIO: Il Vassalo di Szigeth.

SMETANA, BEDRICH: Dalibor; Dve vdovy [The Two widows]; Hubicka [The Kiss]; Prodaná nevesta [The Bartered bride].

SMITH, JULIA: Cockcrow; Cynthia Parker; The Gooseherd and the goblin; The Stranger of Manzano.

SMITH, RUSSELL: The Unicorn in the garden.

SMYTH, ETHEL: Der Wald.

SNELL, GORDON: Gentlemen's island.

SOBOLEWSKI, EDWARD: Mohega.

SODERO, CESARE: Ombre russe.

SOLIE, JEAN PIERRE: La Diable à quatre.

SOKOLOFF, NOEL: The Franklin's tale.

SOLOMON, EDWARD: Bille Taylor.

SOUTHARD, LUCIEN H.: Omano.

SOUTULLO OTERO, REVERIANO: *La Leyenda del beso.

SPINELLI, NICCOLA: A basso porto.

SPOHR, LUDWIG: Jessonda.

SPONTINI, GASPARO: Fernand Cortez; La Vestale.

STAMFORD, CHARLES VILLIERS: Shamus O'Brien.

STARER, ROBERT: The Intruder.

STEARNS, THEODORE P.: Snowbird.

STEIBELT, DANIEL: Roméo et Juliette.

STEVENS, NOEL SCOTT: The Enchanted canary.

STEWART, HUMPHREY JOHN: The Hound of Heaven.

STILL, WILLIAM GRANT: The Troubled island.

STOESSEL, ALBERT: Garrick.

STORACE, STEPHEN: The Cherokee; The Doctor and the apothecary; The Haunted tower; Lodoiska; My grandmother; No song, no supper; *The Pirates; The Prize; The Siege of Belgrade; The Three and the deuce!

STOTHART, HERBERT: *Rose-Marie; *Song of the flame.

STRAKOSCH, MORITZ: Giovanna prima di Napoli.

STRAMIELLO, ERNEST: Maggio fiorentino.

STRASSBURG, ROBERT: Chelm.

STRAUS, OSKAR: Der Tapfere Soldat [The Chocolate soldier].

STRAUSS, JOHN L.: The Accused.

STRAUSS, JOHANN: Der Carneval in Rom; Die Fledermaus; Der Lustige Krieg; Prinz Methusalem; Das Spitzentuch der Königin; Der Zigeunerbaron.

STRAUSS, RICHARD: Die Aegyptische Helena; Arabella; Ariadne auf Naxos; Capriccio; Daphne; Elektra; Feuersnot; Die Frau ohne Schatten; Der Rosenkavalier; Salome; Die Schweigsame Frau.

STRAVINSKY, IGOR: L'Histoire du soldat; Mavra; Noah and the flood; Oedipus rex; Perséphone; The Rake's progress; Renard; Le Rossignol.

STRIGGIO, ALESSANDRO: Il Cicalamento delle donne al bucato e la caccia.

STROCK, OSKAR: *Moses.

STRUBE, GUSTAV: Ramona.

STUART, LESLIE [pseud. of Thomas A. Barrett]: Florodora.

STYNE, JULE: Gentlemen prefer blondes.

SULLIVAN, ARTHUR: The Contrabandista; Cox and Box; The Emerald
   isle; The Gondoliers; The Grand duke; H. M. S. Pinafore; Iolanthe;
   The Mikado; Patience; The Pirates of Penzance; Princess Ida; The Rose
   of Persia; Ruddigore; The Sorcerer; Trial by jury; Utopia limited; The
   Yeomen of the guard.

SULLY, FRANCIS T.: Fortunio and his seven gifted sons.

SUPPE, FRANZ von: Boccaccio; Donna Juanita; Fatinitza; Flotte
   Bursche; Leichte Kavallerie; Die Schöne Galatea.

- T -

TALMA, LOUISE: The Alcestiad.

TAMKIN, DAVID: The Dybbuk.

TAYLOR, DEEMS: The Dragon; The King's henchman; Peter Ibbetson;
   Ramuntcho.

TAYLOR, RAYNOR: Buxom Joan; Capocchio and Dorinna; The Gray
   mare's the best horse; May day; The Old woman of eighty-three.

TCHAIKOVSKY, PIOTR ILYICH: Cherevichky; Eugene Oegin;
   Iolanthe; Mazeppa; Pique dame; Snegourotchka.

TCHEREPNIN, ALEXANDER NIKOLAIEVICH: La Fée et la
   cultivateur; Ol-Ol.

TELEMANN, GEORG PHILIPP: Pimpinone.

THOMAS, AMBROISE: Le Caïd; La Double echelle; Hamlet; Mignon;
   Le Songe d'une nuit d'été.

THOMAS, ARTHUR GORING: Esmeralda.

THOMAS, GERTRUDE AULD: Hazila.

THOMPSON, RANDALL: Solomon and Balkis.

THOMSON, VIRGIL: Four saints in three acts; The Mother of us all.

THRANE, VALDEMAR: Fjeldeventyret.

THUILEE, LUDWIG: Lobetanz.

TIETJENS, PAUL: The Tents of the Arabs.

TIRINDELLI, PIER ADOLFO: Blanc et noir.

TOCH, ERNST: Egon und Emilie; Die Prinzessin auf der Erbse.

TONNING, GERARD: Blue Wing; Leif Erikson.

TORROBA, FEDERICO MORENO: La Chulapona; Luisa Fernanda.

TRAETTA, FILIPPO [Philip]: Harlequin's triumph in war and
   peace.

TROGAN, ROLAND: The Hat man.

VACCAI, NICCOLO: Giulietta e Romeo.

VALVERDE, JOAQUIN: La Gran via; * La Marcha de Cadiz.

VALVERDE, JOAQUIN, JR.: El Estuche de monerias; El Pobre valbuena.

VAN BUSKIRK, CARL: The Land between the rivers.

VAN ETTEN, JANE [Mrs. Alfred Burritt Andrews]: Guido Ferranti.

VAN GROVE, ISAAC: The Music robber; The Other wise man.

VAUGHAN WILLIAMS, RALPH: Hugh the drover; The Poisoned kiss; Riders to the sea; The Shepherds of the Delectable Mountains; Sir John in love.

VECCHI, ORAZIO: L'Amfiparnasso.

VENTH, CARL: Pan in America; The Rebel; La Vida de la mision.

VERDI, GIUSEPPE: Aida; Aroldo; Attila; Un Ballo in maschera; Don Carlos; I Due Foscari; Ernani; Falstaff; La Forza del destino; Un Giorno di regno; Jérusalem; I Lombardi; Luisa Miller; Macbeth; I Masnadieri; Nabucodonosor; Otello; Rigoletto; Simone Boccanegra; La Traviata; Il Trovatore; Les Vepres siciliennes.

VERNON, ASHLEY [pseud. of Kurt Manschinger]: The Barber of New York; Cupid and Psyche; Grand slam.

VERRALL, JOHN: The Cowherd and the sky maiden; Three blind mice; The Wedding knell.

VERT Y CARBONELL, JUAN: * La Leyenda del beso.

VERSTOVSKY, ALEKSEI NIKOLAIEVICH: Ascold's tomb.

VILLA-LOBOS, HEITOR: Magdalena.

VIRZI, SALVATORE: Il Cancelleto d'oro; The Princess and the spindle; Sulamita; Vanna.

VITALIS, GEORGE: Golfo.

VITTADINI, FRANCO: Anima allegra.

VIVES, AMADEO: Bohemios; * Doloretes; Maruxa.

- W -

WAD, EMMANUEL: Swing low.

WAGANAAR, BERNARD: Pieces of eight.

WAGHALTER, IGNAZ: Mandragola.

WAGNER, RICHARD: Der Fliengende Holländer; Lohengrin; Die Meistersinger von Nürnberg; Parsifal; Rienzi; Der Ring des Nibelungen (Das Rheingold; Die Walkure; Siegfried; Götterdammerung); Tannhäuser; Tristan und Isolde.

WALD, MAX: A Provincial episode.

WALLACE, WILLIAM VINCENT: The Desert flower; Lurline; Maritana.

WALTON, WILLIAM: Troilus and Cressida.

WARD, ROBERT: The Crucible; He who gets slapped.

WARE, HARRIET: Undine.

WEBER, BERTHA: The Mysterious characters of Mr. Fu.

WEBER, CARL MARIA von: Abu Hassän; Euryanthe; Der Freischütz; Oberon; Preciosa.

WECKERLIN, JEAN BAPTISTE THEODORE: La Laitiere de Trianon; Les Revenants bretons.

WEHNER, GEORGE: The Amiable beast; Frisco Mame; The Mark of kings; So sings the bell; Star in the night; The Wild swan.

WEIGEL, EUGENE: The Mountain child.

WEIGL, JOSEPH: Die Schweizerfamilie.

WEILL, KURT: Down in the valley; Die Dreigroschenoper; The Eternal road; Der Ja-Sager; Knickerbocker holiday; Lady in the dark; One touch of Venus; Street scene; Der Zar lässt sich photographieren.

WEINBERG, JACOB: Hechalutz [The Pioneers].

WEINBERGER, JAROMIR: Svanda dudák [Schwanda].

WEINER, LAZAR: The Golem.

WEIS, KAREL: Der Polnische Jude.

WEISGALL, HUGO: Purgatory; Six characters in search of an author; The Stronger; The Tenor.

WELSH, THOMAS: * The Farmer's wife.

WESTERGAARD, PETER: Charivari.

WETZLER, HANS HERMANN: Die Baskische Venus.

WHITE, CHARLES CAMERON: Ouanga.

WHITE, JOHN D.: The Legend of Sleepy Hollow.

WHITON, PETER: The Bottle imp.

WICKHAM, FLORENCE: Rosalind.

WILDER, ALEC: Cumberland fair; The Impossible forest; Kittiwake Island; The Lond way; The Lowland sea; Miss Chicken Little; Sunday excursion.

WILLIAMS, GUY BEVIER: The Master thief.

WILLIAMS, RONALD RAY: The Introduction; Oleander red.

WINSLOW, RICHARD: Sweeny agonistes.

WINTER, PETER von: * The Peasant boy.

WOLF, HUGO: Der Corregidor.

WOLF-FERRARRI, ERMANNO: L'Amore medico; Le Donne curiose; I Giojelli delle Madonna; I Quattro rusteghi.

WOLFE, JACQUES: Mississippi legend; The Trysting place.

WOLFF, ALBERT: L'Oiseau bleu.

WOOD, JOSEPH: The Mother.
WOODWARD, SAMUEL [playwright]: The Deed of gift.
WOOLLEN, RUSSELL: The Decorator.
WRIGHT, ROBERT: *Kismet; *Song of Norway.
WYKES, ROBERT: The Prankster.

- Y -

YOUMANS, VINCENT: No, no, Nanette.

- Z -

ZADOR, EUGEN: Christopher Columbus; X-mal Rembrandt.
ZAJC, IVAN: Nikola Subić Zrinski.
ZANDONAI, RICCARDO: Conchita; Francesca da Rimini.
ZEISL, ERIC: Leonce und Lena.
ZIMBALIST, EFREM: Honeydew; Landara.
ZINGARELLI, NICOLA ANTONIO: Giulietta e Romeo.
ZOELLNER, HEINRICH: Bei Sedan; Matteo Falcone.
ZUMPE, HEINRICH: Farinelli.